The Insider's Automatic Options Strategy

How To Win On Better Than 9 Out Of 10 Trades With Extremely Low Risk

JON SCHILLER

ISBN 0-930233-49-2

Published by Windsor Books
P.O. Box 280
Brightwaters, N.Y. 11718

Manufactured in the United States of America

ISBN 0-930233-49-2

CAVEAT: It should be noted that all commodity trades, patterns, charts, systems, etc., discussed in this book are for illustrative purposes only and are not to be construed as specific advisory recommendations. Further note that no method of trading or investing is foolproof or without difficulty, and past performance is no guarantee of future performance. All ideas and material presented are entirely those of the author and do not necessarily reflect those of the publisher or bookseller.

This up-to-date book explains in easy to understand terms how sophisticated traders can make money *each month* safely (with small risk) and make capital grow by trading in the *Options Markets.*

The book describes six categories of Options Markets: (1) Stock Index Options; (2) Common Stock Options; (3) Foreign Currency Options; (4) Precious Metal (Gold & Silver) Options; (5) Commodity Futures Options and (6) Treasury Issue Options.

The book is broken into five sections, with a total of 10 chapters. Section 1 defines the terms used in option trading and presents several examples of option trading strategies. Section 2 describes the six option markets in detail. Section 3 presents the statistics and modeling of option strategies. Section 4 describes a BASIC computer program and PC spread sheets as tools for option trading.

Several protective trading strategies are discussed but the author recommends primarily the use of the *short spread* as the best compromise of return versus risk. For those who wish to take essentially *no risk,* the book describes the *protected straddle* which sacrifices return for a small, limited exposure to loss.

The underlying statistics of the option markets are discussed with emphasis on how to use statistics to reduce trading risk. The concept of *standard deviation,* is used to limit the risk of loss. For example, a spread with *strike prices* separated by $\pm 2\sigma$ assures a 90% probability of making a profit at the beginning of the option month.

The book shows the reader the *nuts and bolts* of establishing option short spreads, including the necessary details of practical option trading. The book even explains how to place the order for a safe option position with your broker.

The final section describes a computer program the author has written for option trading. This section describes the main menu for selecting what to do. The computer program, called OPTEVAL, allows the user to (1) Evaluate new short spread positions, (2) Evaluate existing short spread positions and (3) Automatically generate tables of index option market values using a mathematical model called OPVAM developed in Chapter 8 of the book.

For those readers who wish to use the computer software or the PC spread sheets sprinkled throughout the book, the software listing in BASIC and the spread sheet equation listings are provided as appendices.

* * *

Jon Schiller is a computer scientist with a BS from Caltech and a PhD from the University of Southern California where he served for several years as an Adjunct Professor directing research in personal computer software and hardware. The author has more than 25 years experience in stock and futures trading. He managed a small company pension fund for almost 10 years. He has developed software to facilitate option trading using a low risk strategy that avoided disaster during the October stock market collapses of 1987 and 1989.

He is currently active in option trading on his own account using the strategies and techniques described in the book - with notable financial success. He continues to develop personal computer software and spread sheets to make his option trading easier and more profitable.

TABLE OF CONTENTS

APPENDIX

Glossary

In order to understand options trading it is necessary to understand the specialized vocabulary of options. I suggest you refer back to this glossary when you encounter a word or phrase in the book that is not clear or that I failed to explain adequately. Some of the terms used in this glossary were adapted from the American Stock Exchange, Inc., booklet entitled *Call Options*. Others were adapted from the booklet entitled *Characteristics and Risks of Standardized Options*, a report which explains the rules of the seven organizations that control American option trading:

- American Stock Exchange, Inc. ....AMEX
- Chicago Board Options Exchange, Inc. ....CBOE
- National Association of Securities Dealers, Inc. ....NASD
- New York Stock Exchange, Inc. ....NYSE
- Pacific Stock Exchange, Inc. ....PaSE
- Philadelphia Stock Exchange, Inc. ....PhSE
- The Options Clearing Corporation ....OCC

WHAT IS AN OPTION?

An **option** is a legal contract that gives the holder the right to buy or sell a specified number or amount of the underlying financial instrument or security (stock, stock index, currency, precious metal, treasury issue) at a fixed price called the strike price (or exercise price) within a specified time period ending with the expiration time.

American options can be exercised at any time before they expire.

European options can be exercised only during a specified period immediately before expiration.

i

GLOSSARY OF OPTION TRADING

At-The-Money. A situation in which the strike price is equal to the market price of the underlying financial instrument.

Call. An option contract that entitles the holder to buy a number of shares or amount of the underlying financial instrument at a stated price on or before a fixed expiration date.

Class Of Options. Options contracts of the same type (call or put) covering the same underlying financial instrument.

Closing Purchase. A transaction in which a seller (writer) liquidates his/her position by purchasing an option having the same terms as the option he/she previously sold (wrote).

Closing Sale. A transaction in which a purchaser liquidates his/her position by selling an option having the same terms as the option he/she previously purchased.

Combination. The purchase or sale of an equivalent number of puts and calls on a given underlying financial instrument which have different exercise prices and/or expiration dates.

Contract. A call or put issued by The Options Clearing Corporation.

Covered Option. An option in which the seller (or writer) owns the underlying financial instrument, as opposed to uncovered (sometimes called naked), where the option is written against cash or other margin.

Early Assignment (also called **Exercise Notice**). An arbitrary action by the options board closing out an in-the-money option position requiring immediate settlement. Index options are settled in cash. Other options are settled by buying or selling the underlying financial instrument.

Exercise. To buy or sell an option.

Exercise Limits. Limits on the number of option contracts relating to an underlying financial instrument which may be exercised within 5 consecutive business days by any investor (or investors acting together).

Exercise Price or **Strike Price.** The price per share at which the holder of an option may buy (call) or sell (put) the underlying financial instrument upon exercise.

Expiration Date or **Maturity Date.** The last day on which the option may be exercised. Most options expire on the third Friday of the option month.

Financial Instrument. The basis for options. It can be a stock index, a stock, currency, precious metal (gold or silver), treasury issue (bond or note), or commodity futures.

Hope Value (same as premium). The hope that the price will change the premium value into intrinsic value.

In-The-Money. A situation in which the strike price is below the market price of the underlying financial instrument for a call, or the strike price is above the market price of the underlying financial instrument for a put.

Intrinsic Value. The excess of the market value of the underlying financial instrument over the strike price of the option for a call. The excess of the strike price of the option over the market value of the underlying financial instrument for a put.

Long Position. A trader has a long position if he/she has bought puts or bought calls. A **net** long position is when he/she has bought more puts or calls than he/she has sold.

Open Interest. The number of outstanding contracts in a given market class.

Opening Purchase. A transaction in which an investor becomes the holder of an option.

Opening Sale. A transaction in which an investor becomes the seller (writer) of an option.

Option. A legal contract which gives the holder the right to buy or sell a specified number or amount of the underlying financial instrument at a fixed price within a specified time period ending with the expiration date.

The Options Clearing Corporation (OCC). The issuer of all options contracts traded on the American Stock Exchange.

Time Value. Same as premium value.

Uncovered Position. See covered position.

Underlying Financial Instrument. The basis for the option. It can be a stock index, a common stock, a currency (£, DM, ¥, etc.), a precious metal (gold or silver), a treasury issue (bond or note), or commodity futures (soybeans, sugar, etc.).

Underlying Security. Same as underlying financial instrument.

Underlying Stock. The stock subject to being purchased or sold upon exercise of the option.

Writer. The seller of an option contract.

Out-Of-The-Money. A situation in which the strike price is above the market price of the underlying financial instrument for a call, or the strike price is below the market price of the underlying financial instrument for a put.

Position Limits. Limits set upon the number of option contracts on the same side of the market relating to an underlying financial instrument that any investor (or investors acting together) may control.

Premium. The amount that the price of a put or call is above the intrinsic value. This is determined through the market process. If the option is out-of-the-money, *all* the price is premium. An option in-the-money can have both an intrinsic and premium component. At expiration all premium prices become zero.

Put. An option contract that entitles the holder to sell a number of shares or amount of the underlying financial instrument at a stated price on or before a fixed expiration date.

Series. Options of the same class having the same exercise price and expiration time.

Short Position. A trader has a short position if he has sold puts or sold calls. A **net** short position is when he has sold more puts or calls than he has bought.

Short Spread or Strangle. A position in which the trader has sold both put and call options with strike prices on either side of the market value of the same underlying instrument.

Spread. Being long one or more options of a given call and concurrently maintaining a short position of one or more options of a different exercise price and expiration time, covering the same underlying financial instrument.

Spread Width. The difference between the strike prices of the puts and calls making up the spread position.

Straddle. The purchase or sale of an equivalent number of puts and calls on a given underlying financial instrument with the same exercise price and expiration date.

PART 1

CONCEPTS FOR OPTION TRADING

Chapter 1

A Strategy To Make Money Month After Month

So the question is: *Can we make money safely in spite of the extreme volatility that occurs in the stock market?* The answer is **yes** and this book tells how to do it.

The strategy used to make money safely in the financial markets is called *Option Short Spreads.* This strategy involves the selling of *call* options and *put* options (see Glossary) for the current month such that the option position will make money so long as the market does not go above an *upper* limit nor below a *lower* limit during the month. In other words, as long as the market fluctuates between the *spread* of the upper and lower limits, your *Option Short Spread* position will make money. Obviously, the wider the *spread* between the limits, the lower the risk and vice versa. On the other hand, the narrower the spread, the more money the Option Short Spread will make. In other words, there is a classical trade-off between risk and the amount of money to be made. The higher the risk, the greater the monetary return, and vice versa.

Golden Rule Number 1 of this strategy, which was reinforced by *Black Monday* — October 19, 1987 — is that **you never takes a position for a longer time period than the current option month,** which ends on the third Friday of each month. It was very fortunate for those trading in October option short spreads that the October options closed on the Friday *before Black Monday.* In other words, traders using the strategy described in this book were not in the market on *Black Monday.* Their positions had closed out automatically the previous Friday.

Golden Rule Number 2 is never change your position the day after a huge drop (or rise) — let the market adjust before you take protective action. Patience, NOT panic, can save you from disastrous losses when a market collapse or rise occurs a short time before option expiration (October 1989 and May 1990).

We shall examine techniques for selecting an Option Short Spread. The spread limits should have a sufficiently low risk, so you will be at ease with the investment. Also, the timing is such that the risk extends over a limited time period — usually four or five weeks — during the current option month. The risk decreases as the option month passes — unless there is some unusually violent disruption of the market.

We will see how to take corrective action in case a sudden market change threatens your short spread. American options allow changes at any time during the option period, but European options only permit changes during a short window before expiration. For this reason, I use only American options. For safety reasons, you should do likewise.

WHAT ARE OPTIONS?

An option is a financial instrument that gives the buyer the opportunity to realize a profit if the market for the underlying security changes in the favorable direction. At the present time there are options available for many financial instruments including stock indexes, common stocks, foreign currencies, treasury bonds and notes, precious metals, and commodity futures. I will describe option trading in each of these six types of options — I'll also show you which are best to use and explain why they're best.

There are four possible option positions: *Long* or *Short* positions for *Puts* and *Calls*. The buyer (long) of a put option makes money if the market goes down. Conversely, the seller (short) of a put option makes money if the market goes up. The buyer (long) of a call option makes money if the market goes up. Conversely, the seller (short) of a call option makes money if the market goes down. Just remember: put down and call up! Shown schematically:

Market Value ↑ = Call option ↑, Put option ↓
Market Value ↓ = Call option ↓, Put option ↑

In other words, when the market value goes up, call option prices go up while put option prices go down, and vice versa.

An option has associated with it a certain market value called a *strike price*. A *call* option has an intrinsic value on the expiration date if the market price is greater than the strike price. The *call intrinsic value equals the market price minus the strike price*. A *put* option has an intrinsic value on the expiration date if the market price is less than the strike price. The *put* intrinsic value equals the strike price minus the market price.

An option is valid for a set time period. On a given date an option expires — on that date an automatic settlement takes place and any intrinsic value is paid to the option

5

buyer — the option seller has to pay out any intrinsic value. The intrinsic value may be zero on the expiration date, in which case the option buyer loses all the premium he paid for the option. Conversely, the seller gets to keep all he sold it for — the full premium. The intrinsic value may be less than the premium paid to the option buyer or the credit received by the option seller. In this case the buyer loses a fraction of the money he paid in the first place — and the seller has to give back part of the money he received.

The value, or market price, of an option has two components: the *intrinsic* value plus the *premium* value. If an option has *intrinsic* value, it is said to be ***in-the-money***. The premium is the amount above the intrinsic value that the market forces determine. The buyer of the option pays the intrinsic value (if any) plus the premium. The seller receives the same amount. If there is no *intrinsic* value, the option is said to be ***out-of-the-money***. A buyer wants the option to finish in-the-money. A seller wants the option to finish out-of-the-money.

Common Stock Options

Please refer to Table 1.1, which gives the Stock Option values for the common stock UAL. UAL is currently one of the best common stock options to use because of its wide range of strike prices. Other suitable stock options will be given in Chapter 5. Most common stock options have such limited strike prices offered that they are not useful vehicles for short spread option trading. You must search the tables for stock options with a wide range of strike prices. Tables like 1.1 for the various stock option exchanges are available daily in the Wall Street Journal, Investor's Daily or in the financial section of many newspapers. Note that the market price of the June UAL call option with strike price 150 (JUNE C150) is 7 1⁄8. The intrinsic value of JUNE C150 is the UAL market value, 151 1⁄2 less the strike price of 150, or intrinsic value = 1 1⁄2. Therefore the premium = market price 7 1⁄8, less intrinsic value 1 1⁄2, or 5 5⁄8. On the other hand, the market price for the June call option with strike price 155 is 4 3⁄4. Since the strike price is greater than the market value of the UAL stock (151 1⁄2) then the intrinsic value is zero and the premium equals the market value, or 4 3⁄4. During the life of the option, it may have both intrinsic and premium value. However, at the time of expiration, the option will only have intrinsic value. In other words, at expiration time, the option premium goes to zero and it is worthless if the option is out-of-the-money. A put option is worthless at expiration if the market value of the underlying financial instrument is greater than the strike price. A call option is worthless at expiration if the market value is less than the strike price.

TABLE 1.1 STOCK OPTION TABLE FOR UAL STOCK: Buy Call Option
Tuesday May 29, 1990 — 3 PM New York Time

STRIKE PRICE	CALLS			PUTS		
	JUNE	JUL	AUG	JUN	JUL	AUG
115	s	s	r	s	s	2 3/8
120	s	s	38	s	s	3 1/2
125	s	s	r	s	s	4 3/4
130	r	s	r	1 1/4	s	r
135	19 1/8	s	26 1/2	1 1/2	s	7
140	r	s	r	2 3/8	s	8 1/2
145	12 3/8	r	r	3 1/2	r	9 7/8
150	7 1/8	r	15 1/2	4 3/4	r	11 1/4
151 1/2 = MARKET VALUE AT 3 PM OF UAL STOCK						
155	4 3/4	r	12	7	r	13 1/4
160	2 1/2	r	9 1/4	9 1/2	r	r
165	1 3/8	s	7	r	s	17 1/4
170	s	s	4 3/4	s	s	r
175	s	s	3 1/4	s	s	r

s = option doesn't exist   r = option not traded that day

The basic trading strategy recommended in this book is the use of short spreads. It involves selling an equal number of put and call options for the current option month, with the put strike price below the market and the call strike price above the market. The distance between the put and call strike prices is the spread width. The wider the spread the lower the risk and the lower the initial profit — and vice versa. The basic strategy of the Option Short Spread, illustrated in Figure 1.2, is to **sell short** *put* options and *call* options with a *spread* between the strike prices. You receive the premium for the options in your account — less a small commission — at the time the options are *sold*. You want both options to be worthless at expiration — in which case you get to keep the money you received — the poor fellow who *bought* the options you sold gets nothing at expiration. You win, he loses.

But first, we should make one fundamental point in the investment strategy using Option Short Spread trading: the basic idea is that the investor's capital should be invested in whatever financial instruments the investor deems prudent — for example: mutual funds, certificates of deposit, bonds, common stock, or even savings accounts — whatever your broker will accept as collateral. I believe high grade bonds are the safest investment — and most brokers will accept bonds as collateral. You, the investor, then pledge these primary financial assets as collateral for the margin requirements needed for the option trading. The option trading then augments both your capital and the return on your capital with some increased risk — but a risk you can be comfortable with.

FIGURE 1.2 OPTION TRADING STRATEGY: The *SHORT SPREAD*
SHORT SPREAD MAKES MONEY IF MARKET STAYS WITHIN SAFE BOUNDARIES

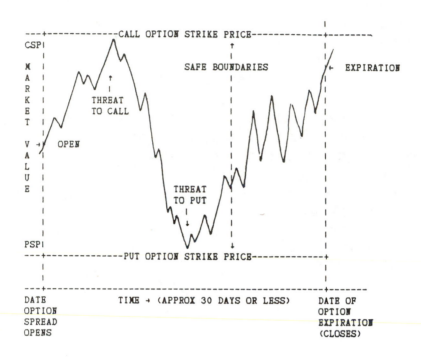

Let's look at one of the oldest types of options: the common stock option. Assume, for example, that you, the investor, believe that UAL stock is going to increase in value and you would like to buy 1000 shares of UAL common stock to benefit from the increase in value you expect the UAL stock to achieve in the future. Refer again to Table 1.1 for purposes of this example. You'll notice that the market value of UAL stock is 151 1/2 dollars per share. If you expect UAL stock to rise in value to 160 dollars per share within one month, what should you, the investor, do?

The conventional thing to do would be to purchase the stock outright, which would require a capital sum of $151,500 for the 1000 shares plus commissions of, say, 2%. Or, if you purchase the shares on a 50% margin account with your broker you put up cash or collateral for half that sum, or $75,750, plus commissions of 2% (on the whole sum of $151,500), so the commission would be $3,030.

As an alternative you could buy an option for UAL stock for a lot less capital outlay and yet still benefit from the expected increase in the stock value — if it happens. Refer to Table 1.1, which shows the UAL option market for May 29, 1990. For our example, you purchase 10 June call options (each option is for 100 shares) for UAL stock at a strike price of $155 per share. In Table 1.1, read under the JUN Calls column at the intersection with the strike price of 155 the figure 4 3/4. This means that the market value for the June call option with strike price 155 (JUN C155) is $4.75 per share. The 10 options represent 1000 shares (100 shares per option). A typical brokerage commission may be $10 per option. The cost of the ten call options is then:

10 (options) x [100 (shares/option) x 4.75 ($/share) + 10 ($/opt)] = $4850

At the time this JUN C155 option is purchased (May 29, 1990) the value of the option is all premium. There is no intrinsic value, since the market price of the stock (151 1/2) is less than the strike price. In other words, the option is *out-of-the-money*. The option can attain intrinsic value *only* if the market value of the underlying UAL stock exceeds the strike price of 155.

The June options expire on the third Friday of the month, June 15, 1990, or 24 days from the option is purchased. On

11

that date UAL stock closed at 156 1/4. Too bad. You lost money. How much? The intrinsic value of the options at expiration was (156 1/4 - 155) x 10 x 100 = $1,250. But you paid $4850 for the options — so you lost $3600. You had the right idea — the market did go up — just not enough to make money.

Note that you spent only $4,850 for the options compared with the $75,750 you would have had to pay for the stock itself on 50% margin. This represents a significant *leverage* on your capital — some 16 to one in this example. Note that in this example the most money you could lose is the amount, or **premium,** that you paid for the **call** option, the $4,850 plus commission. If the market had closed above 159.85 on the expiration of the option, you would have made money. As it turned out, the market just didn't share your optimism — this is often the case. That's why the short spread strategy works much better.

On the other hand, if you had believed the market was going to drop — that in a month UAL stock was going to be worth less than it was on the 22nd of May 1990 — then you could have bought a put option — available for those investors who believe the market is going to go down. Let's refer to Table 1.3 and go through an example for the pessimistic (or bearish) investor.

For the second example, we will use the same day as discussed before, when the UAL stock is worth 151 1/2 dollars per share. You decide the market is going to drop way down, so you buy 10 June **put** options at a strike price of 145. Refer to the UAL option Table 1.3 under the JUN Puts column at the intersection with the 145 strike price where the number 3 1/2 appears. This means the market value of the June put option with the strike price 145 (JUN P145) is $3.50 per share. The cost of the ten options is then

10 (options) x [100 x 3.5 ($/share) + 10 (Commission)] = $3,600

TABLE 1.3 STOCK OPTION TABLE FOR UAL STOCK: Buy Put Option
Tuesday May 29, 1990 — 3 PM New York Time

STRIKE PRICE	CALLS			PUTS		
	JUNE	JUL	AUG	JUN	JUL	AUG
115	s	s	r	s	s	2 3⁄8
120	s	s	38	s	s	3 1/2
125	s	s	r	s	s	4 3/4
130	r	s	r	1 1/4	s	r
135	19 1/8	s	26 1/2	1 1/2	s	7
140	r	s	r	2 3/8	s	8 1/2
145	12 3/8	r	r	3 1/2	r	9 7/8
150	7 1/8	r	15 1/2	4 3/4	r	11 1/4
151 1/2 = MARKET VALUE AT 3 PM OF UAL STOCK						
155	4 3/4	r	12	7	r	13 1/4
160	2 1/2	r	9 1/4	9 1/2	r	r
165	1 3/8	s	7	r	s	17 1/4
170	s	s	4 3/4	s	s	r
175	s	s	3 1/4	s	s	r

s = option doesn't exist   r = option not traded that day

Let us assume now that, instead of rising, the UAL stock drops to 138 on the expiration date of June 15. In this case the intrinsic value of the options at expiration is:

(145 - 138) x 10 x 100 = $7,000 (close out value)

In this hypothetical case your profit for the UAL JUN P145 options would have been:

$7,000 (close-out value) - 3,600 (option cost) - commission ($100) = $3,300

In our example, if UAL dropped below 141.3 at expiration, the investor would make money or at worst break-even. If UAL closed above 145 on the day the option expired, then the investor would lose the total $3,600 he had invested. Unfortunately for the bearish investor, the June market went up — not down — so he lost all $3,600.

Buying options sounds risky, doesn't it? Well it is, because face it, we never really know whether the market is going to rise or fall. In view of this uncertainty in the market, wouldn't it be nice if we could devise a strategy to make money whether the market went up or went down? The principal purpose of this book is to describe just such an option trading *strategy:* to make money whether the market goes up or down — just as long as it doesn't fluctuate outside our pre-selected limits during the option period, typically 30 days or less. We shall refer to this *Option Trading Strategy* as **OPTION SHORT SPREADS.** Let's apply this strategy to the UAL stock options that we considered in the two examples above. Let us assume that you, the investor, are convinced that during the June option period of the 24 days before expiration, UAL will not rise in price above 165 dollars per share nor drop in price below 135 dollars per share (Refer to Table 1.4).

The spread strategy is simple:

sell (short) 10 June **call** options at
strike price 165 (JUN C165)
sell (short) 10 June **put** options at
strike price 135 (JUN P135)

Because you **sold** these options your account will be credited with premiums for the call and put options less commission. For the JUN options expiring in four weeks (see Table 1.4), the premium for the JUN C165 options is 1 3/8 dollars per share; the premium for the JUN P135 options is 1 1/2 dollars per share. Since the 10 options are for a total of 1000 shares, the total amount credited to your account will be (1 3/8 + 1 1/2) x 1000 - 100 (commission) = $2775.

TABLE 1.4 STOCK OPTION TABLE FOR UAL STOCK SHORT SPREAD: Sell Put / Call Options Tuesday May 29, 1990 — 3 PM New York Time

STRIKE PRICE	CALLS			PUTS		
	JUNE	JUL	AUG	JUN	JUL	AUG
115	s	s	r	s	s	2 3/8
120	s	s	38	s	s	3 1/2
125	s	s	r	s	s	4 3/4
130	r	s	r	1 1/4	s	r
135	19 1/8	s	26 1/2	1 1/2	s	7
140	r	s	r	2 3/8	s	8 1/2
145	12 3/8	r	r	3 1/2	r	9 7/8
150	7 1/8	r	15 1/2	4 3/4	r	11 1/4

151 1/2 = MARKET VALUE AT 3 PM OF UAL STOCK

STRIKE PRICE	CALLS			PUTS		
155	4 3/4	r	12	7	r	13 1/4
160	2 1/2	r	9 1/4	9 1/2	r	r
165	1 3/8	s	7	r	s	17 1/4
170	s	s	4 3/4	s	s	r
175	s	s	3 1/4	s	s	r

s = option doesn't exist   r = option not traded that day

If on the third Friday of June (June 15th) the market value of UAL is less than 165 but more than 135, you will keep the $2775 as your trading profit for the month.

Now, how much capital did you have to put up with your broker for this spread position? Since the October 1987 market collapse, brokerage houses have raised their margin or collateral requirements for option trading from about 5% to around 30%. Using this figure, the capital or margin amount needed for the above example would be 151 1/2 x 1000 x 0.3 = $45,450.

In other words you would have had to pledge some $45,450 of your assets to cover this Option Short Spread. Your return on the $45,450 collateral would be $2775, some

6% per month return on your investment, or an annualized return of 72%.

As you may see from this simple example, the return on capital in Option Short Spread trading can be very rewarding — and you don't have to guess whether the market is going to go up or down to make money.

However, you may ask: *How about the downside risk? How much can you lose?* The answer is that, using the trading strategy of Option Short Spreading described in this book, the probability of keeping the initial premium for the options you sold is about 90%. In other words, on a statistical basis, once every 10 months you may have to *give back* some, all, or even more than your initial *profits*. However, we will discuss methods of limiting any such loss by taking appropriate countermeasures when the market begins to approach either the upper (call) limit or the lower (put) limit of your spread.

SUMMARY OF THREE EXAMPLES OF OPTION TRADING:

The UAL stock closed at 157.75 on the third Friday of June . . . June 15, 1990.

CASE A: Bought 10 UAL CALL options, strike price 155, on May 22, 1990, cost $4,850

Value on June 15: (157.75 - 155) x 1000 - comm = $2402

Profit = value at expiration - original cost

= 2402 - 4850 = $-2448 (a loss — not a profit)

CASE B: Bought 10 UAL PUT options, strike price 135, on May 22, 1990, cost $3,600

The 10 UAL P135 options are worthless on June 15 close: loss $3600

CASE C: Sold 10 UAL CALL options, strike price 165 AND sold 10 UAL PUT options, strike price 135, on May 22, 1990 — net amount received on May 22: $2775

Both the 10 C-165 and 10 P-135 June options you sold are worthless — just what the short spread investor wanted. You get to keep everything.

PROFIT: $2775 for the UAL June short spread

As it may be seen by these examples, the bull lost $2448, the bear lost $3600, and the trader who didn't know whether the market was going up or down made a profit of $2775. I think I've shown you the strength of the spread trading strategy. It allows one to make money with a small risk and a high return for your capital.

The generic concept of the **Option Short Spread** trading strategy was shown in Figure 1.2 and I will discuss it in more detail below.

At the time the option(s) are sold, the underlying financial instrument (e.g.: UAL stock) has a given market value **A**. The spread is formed by selling an equal number of call options and put options for the current month at strike prices that are approximately equal distances from the market value **A**. The call strike price **CSP** is greater than **A**: the put strike price **PSP** is less than **A**. In other words, (CSP - A) is approximately equal to (A - PSP).

Two Sigma Short Spread

The width of the spread is CSP - PSP. The safe margin for the call is (CSP - A); correspondingly, the safe margin for the put is (A - PSP). The spread width is selected such that, on a statistical basis, the market value fluctuation expected during the option time period (typically 28 to 32 days) will be less than the spread width. A measure of the fluctuation of a statistical process is the standard deviation, or sigma value, of the fluctuation. For a statistical process (such as the stock market) with a so called normal distribution, the fluctuations will exceed one sigma (1σ) approximately 35% of the time; will exceed two sigma (2σ) approximately 10%

17

of the time; and will exceed 3σ approximately 1% of the time. I believe a 2σ safety margin is a prudent value for CSP - A and A - PSP. I refer to this position throughout the book as a ±2σ **Short Spread.** In other words, about nine months out of ten the market fluctuations would not exceed the safety margins and you will profit from the spread position. Conversely, unless you take countermeasures (which I will explain later), on a statistical basis, you may lose your profit one month out of ten.

A two sigma safety margin appears to be adequate, except for extreme changes like those experienced during the October 1987 market collapse. If such a collapse occurred during the option period and there was no recovery, the short spread trader could experience a huge loss. Following the October 1989 crash — which occurred one week before option expiration, the market bounded back after the first day's drop and by the end of the option month, the ±2σ short spread was safe.

Remember, the **first golden rule** of option spreads is: *Never hold an option short spread position for longer than the current option month* — that means 32 days or less. The shorter the time to expiration, the less the exposure to risk. I nearly always open my new position at close on the Monday after the expiration of the old options (3rd Friday of the month).

The premium component of the option price is a "hope" on the part of the investors who *buy* options that the market will move in the right direction. The investors who buy *calls* hope that the market will go *up.* The investors who buy *puts* hope that the market will go *down.* This *hope factor* or premium is affected by several factors: market value, strike price, market volatility, time to expiration, and interest rates. The greater the market volatility, the greater is the premium. As the time period for the options runs out, *hope* diminishes and so does the premium. The closer the strike price is to the market value the higher the hope. In the end, of course, all hope evaporates when the option expires. So does the premium, leaving nothing but the intrinsic value.

An exception occurs if the market value approaches the strike price during the month. Then the hope factor (premium) jumps up.

The *Option Short Spread investor* takes advantage of the buyers of call options' hope that the market will rise and the buyers of put options' hope that the market will fall. If the *Option Short Spread* investor chooses his limits properly — then, when the *hope* evaporates, the Option Short Spread investor is left holding the bag — full of money. The money bag is full of the hope — the premiums — that the put and call buyers had when the spread investor sold them the puts and calls upon establishing the spread!

Stock Index Option Short Spread Trading Results

Why do you want to do Short Spread Index Option Trading? To make your capital increase! Assume you have $50,000 in capital and you would like to make it grow. How much growth can you expect over a period of, say, 5 years? I devised a simulation program to answer that question: the result of the trial run of the simulation is shown in Figure 1.5. If you started with an initial capital of $50,000 in March 1990, by December 1995, your capital would have grown to a half million dollars — an annualized return on your capital of some 50%. *If you have a safe and better way to make money — close the book and continue what you're doing. If not, continue reading and learn how to do short spread option trading.*

Actual stock index trading results using short spreads with an initial capital of $50,000 are shown in Table 1.6. It is assumed that you invest your capital and profits in high grade low risk bonds (not junk bonds) paying an interest rate

19

of 8.8%. The results in the table are for nine option months: October 1989 through June 1990. This short 9 month period includes the mini-crash of October 1989 and the roaring bull leg of May 1990. The final capital was $74,491 — an increase of $24,491 for an annualized return of 65.31%. The short spread strategy survived the 7% drop in October 1989 and the 3% rise in May, 1990 — *proving it is a robust strategy for making profits*, even when there are huge fluctuations up and down in the market during the option month.

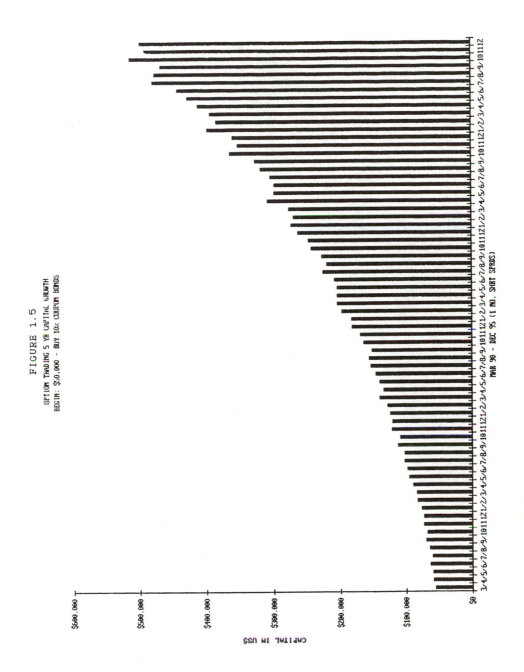

FIGURE 1.5
OPTION TRADING 5 YR CAPITAL GROWTH
BEGIN: $50,000 - BUY 10% COUPON BONDS

TABLE 1.6 ACTUAL OPTION TRADING: OCT 89 – JUN 90
Option Type: OEX S&P 100 STOCK INDEX
REINVEST CAPITAL IN BONDS AT : 8.50%
FILENAME:TRADEEXP.WKS   INITIAL CAPITAL: $50,000

Tr Date	Exp Date	OEX	NOP	CSP	PSP	CPR	PPR	TPR	COMM	OPTION TOT	CUM OPTION	CUM CAPITAL	END INT	CAP RET
18/9/89	20/10/89	323.04	5	335	310	1.750	1.875	3.625	$288.20	$1,582.05	$1,582.05	$51,936	$354	$1,936
20/10/89	17/11/89	324.35	5	335	310	2.000	3.250	5.250	$288.00	$2,514.17	$4,096.22	$54,818	$368	$2,882
20/11/89	15/12/89	316.96	6	330	310	1.125	2.500	3.625	$252.00	$1,837.81	$5,934.04	$57,044	$388	$2,226
18/12/89	19/1/90	323.09	6	345	320	0.438	5.125	5.563	$213.47	$3,060.22	$8,994.26	$60,509	$404	$3,464
19/1/90	19/1/90	319.60	6	345	320	0.000	-0.380	-0.380	$95.36	($335.17)	$8,659.09	$60,602	$429	$93
19/1/90	16/2/90	319.60	6	330	310	1.000	8.000	9.000	$228.82	$5,459.74	$14,118.83	$66,491	$429	$5,889
16/2/90	16/3/90	311.68	7	325	300	0.750	4.000	4.750	$248.51	$3,129.24	$17,248.06	$70,091	$471	$3,600
19/3/90	20/4/90	324.94	7	335	310	1.750	1.750	3.500	$270.18	$2,246.38	$19,494.45	$72,834	$496	$2,743
23/4/90	18/5/90	315.57	8	330	310	1.063	3.875	4.938	$288.27	$3,510.35	$23,004.79	$76,860	$516	$4,026
18/5/90	18/5/90	336.95	8	330	310	-6.950	0.000	-6.950	$144.00	($5,428.46)	$17,576.33	$71,976	$544	($4,884)
21/5/90	15/6/90	340.09	7	350	325	1.938	1.313	3.250	$288.18	$2,004.58	$19,580.91	$74,491	$510	$2,514

TOTAL RETURN: $24,491
FINAL CAPITAL: $74,491
% ANNUAL RETURN: 65.31%

I have not addressed the question of taxes on option trading. Instead, I leave that up to the individual investor and his or her tax advisor.

The monthly trading profits are shown in Figure 1.7 and the cumulative trading profits are shown in Figure 1.8. For the S&P 100 Index (Code: OEX) Option short spreads tabulated in Table 1.6. Added to the option profits is the 8.5% bond interest. Both charts show the option trading results with and without bond interest. The short spreads were selected using the OPTEVAL computer program described in Chapter 10. (The BASIC listing is in Appendix A.) Close out losses occurred in the January 90 and May 90 options. In May 90 the short spread was changed during the month from 330C/310P to 335C/325P because of the huge market surge one week before option expiration. Golden Rule 2: (never change your position based upon a single day market move) saved the day when the market plunged on Friday, October 13, 1989, and reduced the loss when the market surged on Friday, May 11, 1990.

S&P 100 Index Options short spreads for November 89 through June 90 are shown in Figure 1.9, together with the fluctuating OEX market values. You may see clearly the points where the OEX penetrated the call or put strike prices as well as the value at expiration.

RISKS OF OPTION TRADING IN SHORT SPREADS

1. If the market value of the underlying instrument rises above the call strike price or falls below the put strike price, the short spread trader can lose a significant sum of money because of the inherent leverage involved.

2. It is possible that the put and call sides of the short spread are not sold at the same time due to delays in execution. The result could be making less profit than expected.

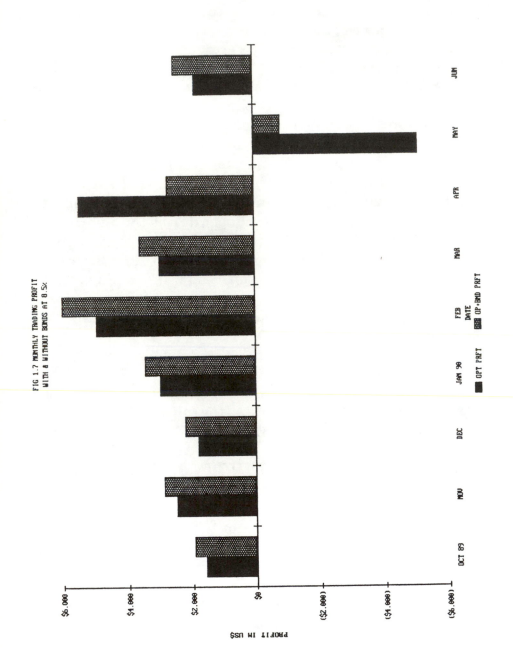

FIG 1.7 MONTHLY TRADING PROFIT WITH & WITHOUT BONDS AT 8.5%

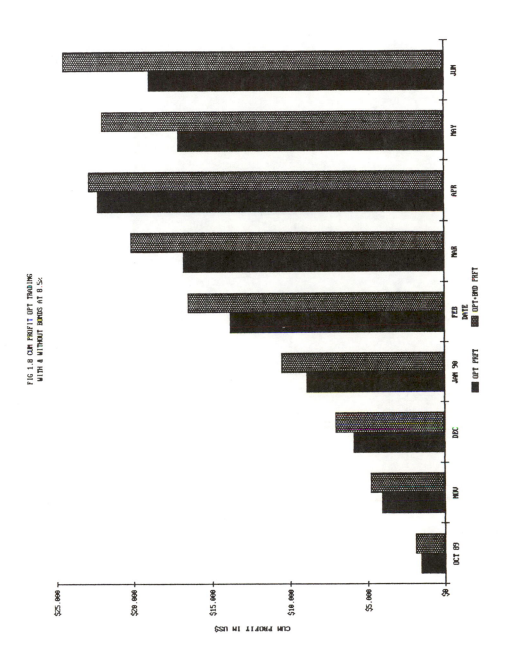

FIG 1.8 CUM PROFIT OPT TRADING
WITH & WITHOUT BONDS AT 8.5%

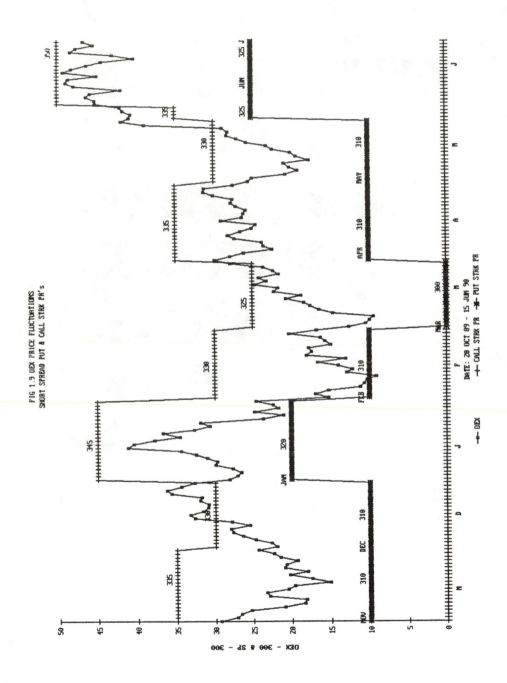

FIG 1.9 OEX PRICE FLUCTUATIONS
SHORT SPREAD PUT & CALL STRK PR's

DATE: 20 OCT 89 - 15 JUN 90

—•— OEX   —+— CALL STRK PR   —⚊— PUT STRK PR

OEX - 300 & SP - 300

3. If the secondary (trading) market in options were to become unavailable, option traders could not close-out their positions before expiration.

4. Lack of investor interest may mean that options with the desired strike prices are not available so that a short spread with sufficient width to have low risk is not available, thus increasing the risk if you take a short spread with put and call strike prices closer together.

5. Market disruptions in the underlying securities could cause losses to the option trader. After a market halt, the prices could jump by an amount that threatens the safety of the put or call component of the spread.

6. If one side of the short spread (put or call) is in-the-money, then that side may be closed out by the process of *early assignment* (see Glossary). Early assignment may prevent you from riding out a temporary market setback, causing you to take an immediate loss.

7. The OCC may, under their authority, prohibit exercise of options before the expiration date. Such action could lock you into a loss position.

8. Insolvency of your broker could represent a risk for the option trader.

I feel that you can live with these risks or I wouldn't have written this book. I only mention them so you will understand what risks there are in option short spread trading.

Chapter 2

PROTECTIVE TRADING

Big profits can be made by buying put options or call options if you are lucky and can predict the direction the market will move but this is a lot like gambling in a casino: you can make a lot of money but you can also lose a lot of money. Buying options is gambling because you never know for sure which direction the market will move. Even the most experienced market analysts are often wrong. How many times have you heard the experts predict that the market is going to go *up* when, in fact, it went *down,* and vice versa? If your trading strategy is to buy *call* options when you expect the market to go *up* or to buy *put* options when you expect the market to go *down,* then you will probably lose in the long run. One factor that would contribute to your losing is the fact that if you buy options, you are paying for *hope* — the premium component of the option price. This hope factor, or premium, *always* evaporates at the expiration of the option. If there is no *intrinsic* value at expiration, the option buyer loses his original investment.

You may make money buying options if you have *inside*

information. But this is illegal according to the US Justice Department, which recently has been busily sending to prison *inside traders* who were caught executing option trades on the basis of insider information — that is, privileged information which is not available to all investors.

Instead I suggest you use ***Protective Trading*** so you can make money whether the market goes up or down. A prudent investor is comfortable when the *risk* is *small,* the *return* on capital is *high,* and the time necessary to *watch* the market is minimal — that's why he uses *protective trading.*

The most important rule of *protective trading* is to *limit the time exposure* of your option position. This rule dictates taking a position in the **current option month** only, **not** in a *future option month.* This means your maximum exposure time is about 30 days. We will examine six different option markets in Chapter 3. Stock index options and common stock options prove to be the best for protective trading strategies.

The October '87 market collapse provided an unforgettable lesson for those option traders who were holding short put positions for November options which they had assumed before the close of the October options on Friday the 16th of October. The market collapse of 508 points occurred on Monday the 19th of October, the first trading day after the October expiration date. The sudden drop on that single day, now called Black Monday, was statistically so large that no one could have expected it. A short November put position open before October 19th would have been disastrous. However, by limiting your position to the current option month you would have been safely out of the market.

It is not possible to make a big killing using the strategies of protective trading. One must be content with the regular monthly investment income, not the big splash!

Table 2.1 is a spreadsheet generated on a personal computer (PC) which compares the six protective strategies

TABLE 2.1 PROTECTIVE STRATEGIES – UAL STK OPTION EXAMPLES:

EXECUTION DATE: 22 MAY 1990
EXPIRATION DATE: 15 JUNE 1990   MARGIN   30%
FILENAME: UALPRSTG.WKS
CAPITAL: $50.000

UAL COMMON STOCK OPTION TABLE: 22 MAY 1990   NOTES: r no price, s no option

PRICE	STRK	JUN C	JUN P
151.50	115	s	s
151.50	120	s	s
151.50	125	s	s
151.50	130	r	1.250
151.50	135	19.125	1.500
151.50	140	r	2.375
151.50	145	12.375	3.500
151.50	150	7.125	4.750
151.50	155	4.375	7.000
151.50	160	2.500	9.500
151.50	165	1.375	r
151.50	170	s	s
151.50	175	s	s

PROTECTIVE STRATEGIES – OPTION TRADING

	SK PR NrMKT	NO. OPT	2SIG	SELL CALL	SELL PUT	NO. P/C	CPRM	PPRM	BUY CALL	BUY PUT	NO. P/C	CPRM	PPRM	SELL CALL	SELL PUT	SELL NO. P/C	CPRM	PPRM	TOTPRM	INITIAL CREDIT
SHORT SPREAD	150	12	10.49	160	140	12	2.500	2.375	155	145	12	4.375	3.5						4,875	$5.801
PROTECTED STRADDLE	150	12	10.49	150	150	12	7.125	4.750	160	140	12	2,5	2,38						4,000	$4.702
PROTECTED STRADDLE	150	12	10.49	150	150	12	2.500	2.375	150	150	6	7.125	4.75						7,000	$8.302
RATIO SPREAD	150	12	10.49	160	140	12	2.500	2.375	150	150	6	7.125	4.75						-1,063	($1.349)
RATIO SPREAD	150	12	10.49	155	145	12	4.375	3.500	150	150	4	7.125	4.75						1,938	$2.251
COMBINATION SPREAD	150	12	10.49	160	140	4	2.500	2,375	150	150	4	7.125	4.75	155	145	8	4.375	3,500	2,917	$3.435
BULLISH BUTTERFLY	150	12	10.49	155		12	4.375		160	150	6	7.125		160	140	6	-2,500		-0,438	($623)
BEARISH BUTTERFLY	150	12	10.49		145	12		3,500	150		6		4.75	140	6		-2,375		-0,063	($173)

PROFIT VERSUS MARKET PRICE AT OPTION EXPIRATION

	P130	P135	P140	P145	P150	P155	P160	P165	P170
SHORT SPREAD	($6.199)	($6.199)	$5.801	$5.801	$5.801	$5.801	$5.801	($6.199)	($6.199)
PROTECT STRADDLE	($3.698)	($3.698)	($3.698)	$2.302	$8.302	$2.302	($3.698)	($3.698)	($3.698)
RATIO SPREAD	$3.749	($749)	$2.251	$5.251	$2.251	$5.251	$3.749	$3.749	$3.749
COMBINATN SPREAD	$4.565	($565)	$3.435	$5.435	$3.435	$5.435	$3.435	$565	$4.565
BULLISH BUTTERFLY	($623)	($623)	($623)	($623)	($623)	$2.377	($623)	($623)	($623)
BEARSH BUTTERFLY	($173)	($173)	($173)	$2.827	($173)	($173)	($173)	($173)	($173)

DESCRIPTION:

SHORT SPREAD	Sell equal no. Calls/Puts +/- 2 Sig above & below Mkt
PROTECTED STRADDLE	Sell equal no. Calls/Puts at MKT, Buy Same no. Calls/Puts above/below MKT
RATIO SPREAD	Sell equal no. Calls/Puts above/below MKT, buy half as many Calls/Puts at MKT
COMBINATION SPREAD	Sell equal no. Calls/Puts above/below MKT, Sell half as many C/P at higher/lower SP, Buy half as many C/P at MKT
BULLISH BUTTERFLY	Sell a no. of Calls above Mkt, Buy half as many Calls at Mkt and half as many Calls at SP higher than Sell SP
BEARISH BUTTERFLY	Sell a no. of Puts below MKT, Buy half as many Puts at MKT, Buy half as many Puts at a SP lower than Sell SP

which will be discussed in this chapter. These examples assume an initial capital of $50,000 and a margin requirement of 30%, which determines the number of options that may be traded.

The June UAL stock option is used for the trading strategies illustrated. The protective strategies are described and defined in the table. Also included are the strike prices, premiums, and the number of options involved in each strategy. The initial credit is computed based on the put and call premiums and the number of options in the spread. The final profit is computed as a function of the UAL market price at option expiration. The range of expiration prices goes from 130 to 170 (labeled P130 to P170 in the figure at the bottom of Table 2.1).

The same spreadsheet was also used to generate all the figures shown in this chapter.

For the Option Short Spread described in Chapter 1, the profit is realized at the time the trade is made. You get to *keep* this profit if the market fluctuations remain between your call strike price at the top and your put strike price at the bottom. However, if there should be a large adverse move in the market, it is possible to lose a large sum if some counter-action is not taken.

This potential loss is illustrated in Figure 2.2 for the UAL Option Short Spread.

The June 1990 Option Short Spread of 12 options from Table 2.1 is: call strike price of 160 (or C160), put strike price of 140 (or P140). On May 22, 1990, when the spread position was opened, the C160 premium was 2 1/2 and the P140 premium was 2 3/8 for a profit (after commission) of $5,801. As may be seen from the figure, you get to keep that profit so long as the market price of UAL stock stays within the safe limits of 160 high and 140 low at the expiration date of June 15, 1990. However, if on the expiration date the market closes at 135 1/4 or lower, then you lose all the profit on the

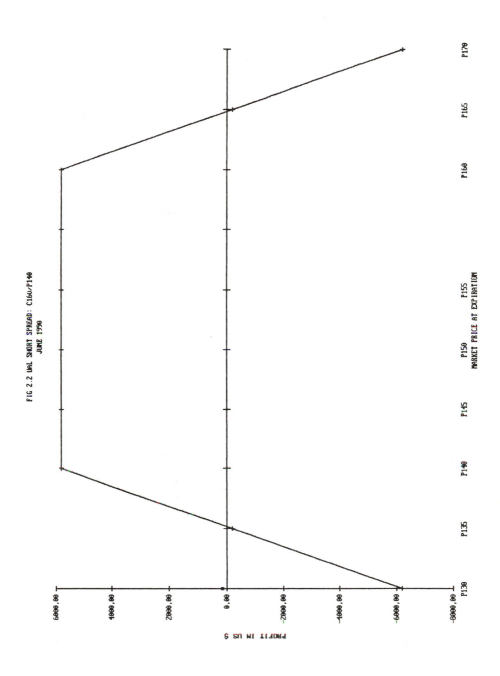

FIG 2.2 UAL SHORT SPREAD: C160/P140
JUNE 1990

put side of the spread. And if the market closes at 164 3/4 or higher, then you lose all the profit on the call side of the spread. (Fortunately, the market closed at 156 1/4, well within the safe limits of the short spread.) As you may see from the steep slope of the curve *outside* the safe limits for this example of 1200 shares (12 options), you will lose at the rate of $1200 per point of market movement outside your safe limits (140 to 160). The leverage that works to your advantage within the safe limits works to your disadvantage outside the safe limits.

WHAT STRATEGIES CAN BE USED TO PROTECT YOUR SPREAD IF EITHER THE PUT SIDE OR THE CALL SIDE IS THREATENED?

One technique you can use to limit your possible loss is to place a ***Stop Loss Order*** with your broker when you first place the sell orders for your short spread. The stop loss order for protecting the UAL short spread we have used in our example would be:

Buy back 12 JUN C160 if UAL market price reaches ***161,***
AND
Buy back 12 JUN P140 if UAL market price reaches ***139.***

In this example, ***161*** and ***139*** are your stop loss levels, one point higher and one point lower than your original positions for the call and put, respectively.

Assuming that your broker executes this stop loss order perfectly, you would limit your loss to one point *plus* the premium that exists when the stop loss order is executed. As an example, the premium on the 160 call would be about 4 7/8 if the market jumped to 161 and your loss on the spread (ignoring commissions) would be:

(4 7/8 + 1) x 1200 — 5801 (your initial profit) = $1249

The big problem with the automatic stop loss order is that it takes away your decision—making power and puts it in your broker's hands. Also, he may not execute it properly. Besides, in times of extreme market volatility, your broker will probably refuse to accept a stop loss order. It is much better for you to use a "mental" stop loss. In other words, watch the market yourself and when the **put** or **call** side of your short spread is threatened, then take the appropriate countermeasures against the threat.

The best strategy I have found to protect a threatened put or call is to buy back the threatened position and move the strike price **higher** for a threatened **call** or **lower** for a threatened **put**. The non-threatened side of your spread is safer than it needs to be and can be adjusted to reduce the cost of the change on the threatened side without greatly increasing your risk. This strategy is illustrated by the following example:

At close on June 4 the market value of UAL reached 160 3⁄4, a three point rise since the market closed on Friday, June 1, which threatened the call at 160. The option table in your newspaper gave the market value for the June option:

Strike Prices	JUNE CALL	JUNE PUT
140		5/16
145		11/16
150		1
160	5 5⁄8	
165	2 15/16	
170	1 1⁄2	

Change your open position by raising your threatened call from 160 to 165 and at the same time raising your safe put from 140 to 145. You can achieve this change by calling your broker early June 5, and placing the following order for

35

June UAL stock options:

Buy 12 JUN calls, strike price 160
Sell 12 JUN calls, strike price 165
Buy 12 JUN puts, strike price 140
Sell 12 JUN puts, strike price 145

After this order is executed your new position is C165/ P145.

The cost of this change is:

$1200 \times (5\ 5/8 - 2\ 15/16) - 1200\ (11/16 - 5/16) + 10 \times 12 = \$2,775$

Your net profit for your June short spread after this change is:

JUN Net Profit = 5801 - 2775 = $3026

You gave back some of your original profit, but now you are protected against a further market rise of 4 1/4 points in the UAL stock. You are much better off changing your position than closing out the call with a stop loss order. By changing, you have increased your risk against a market drop, but you still have a safe margin for your new put position (P145) of 15 3/4 points. This is the strategy I recommend when you have to make a change.

Using the *mental stop loss* coupled with my recommended loss protection strategy requires up-to-date market information, vigilance and resolve on your part to modify your threatened position. But remember Golden Rule No. 2 — wait one day before you change your position. In the above example, if you had waited, you would have seen the market drop back, making your call safe once again. Your change in position was premature, and unnecessary.

An added risk of holding a short in-the-money option — such as the C160 when the market goes to 160 3/4 — is the possibility of an early assignment by the OCC which would force you to buy stock to settle the assignment. While not a common occurrence, you should be aware of this possibility.

The Protected Straddle is a trading strategy that reduces the investor's potential profit, but also limits the downside risk and loss to a very small amount. The protected straddle is defined in Table 2.1 using June 1990 UAL options. The protected straddle is established by selling equal numbers of calls and puts at the strike prices nearest the market and buying the same number of calls and puts at the strike prices at ±2 sigma above and below the market; give your broker the following order:

Market Value

Sell 12 JUN calls, strike price 150, C150   7 1/8
Sell 12 JUN puts, strike price 150, P150   4 3/4
Buy 12 JUN calls, strike price 160, C160   2 1/2
Buy 12 JUN puts, strike price 140, P140   2 3/8

The initial amount credited to your account assuming $98 commission is:

(# straddles) x 100 [(CPRM (150) + PPRM (150)) - (CPRM (160) + PPRM (140))] - COMM

or: 12 x 100 x [(7 1/8 + 4 3/4) - (2 1/2 + 2 3/8)] - $98 = $8,302

The protected straddle profit/loss versus the UAL stock price at option expiration is depicted in Figure 2.3. On the same figure the JUN C160/P140 short spreads' profit/loss is shown for comparison. Note that in this example the protected straddle has less risk with a maximum loss of $3698, but the profit goes to zero if the UAL market price closes on the option expiration date greater than 157 or less than 143, a very narrow range considering the market volatility. In comparison, the 12 option short spread C160/P140 makes profit over a considerable greater spread of market values: between 135 1/2 and 164 1/2. However, the 12 short spreads' loss rate of $1200 per point means you could suffer a much greater loss should the market price at expiration experience

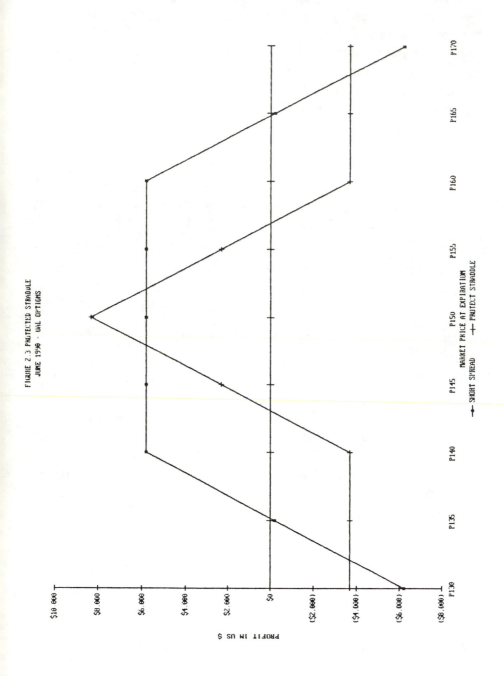

FIGURE 2.3 PROTECTED STRADDLE
JUNE 1990 - UAL OPTIONS

a huge rise or drop. I believe the short spread is a more robust profit maker than the protective straddle.

The Ratio Spread is another technique which reduces the rate of loss beyond the safe limits by using a combination of buying and selling puts and calls. Sell an equal number of puts and calls below and above the market value. Buy half as many puts and calls at the strike price nearest the market value. To establish a ratio spread using the June UAL stock options, place the following order with your broker (using prices from Table 2.1):

Sell 12	JUN C155	+ 4 3/8 x 1200	= $5250
Buy 6	JUN C150	- 7 1/8 x 600	= -4275
Buy 6	JUN P150	- 4 3/4 x 600	= -2850
Sell 12	JUN P145	+ 3 1/2 x 1200	= + 4200
	less commission		- 74
	Initial Credit		= $+2251

The profit//loss for this ratio spread position is compared with the ±2 sigma short spread as a function of the market value at option expiration time (see Figure 2.4). The figure shows clearly that the ratio spread provides less profit than the short spread but the loss rate beyond the safe limits is one half that of the short spread; that is $600 per point compared with $1200 per point. As you can see from this example, the short spread provides a larger, uniform profit over a greater range than the ratio spread.

The Combination Spread is another strategy for protective trading that combines the ratio spread with the short spread. To establish the combination spread, sell 4 calls and 4 puts at ±2 sigma above and below the market. Sell twice as many calls at the next strike price higher and twice as many puts at the next strike price lower than the first position. Then buy 4 calls and 4 puts *at the strike price nearest the*

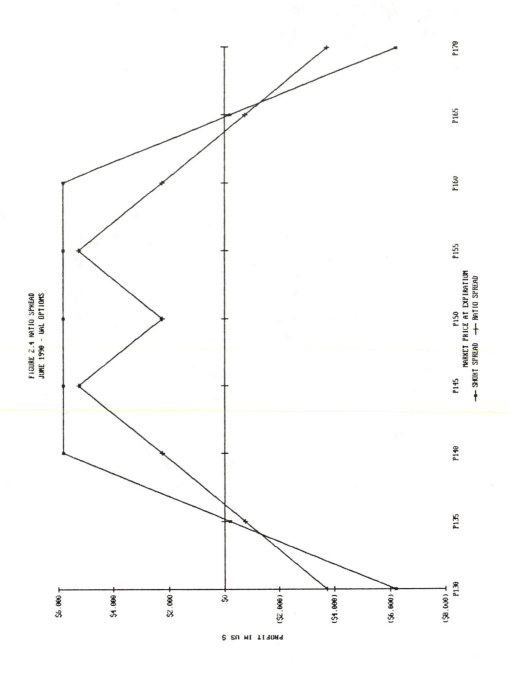

FIGURE 2.4 RATIO SPREAD
JUNE 1990 - VAL OPTIONS

market. The numbers are based on $50,000 capital and a 30% margin. Place the following order with your broker, using prices from Table 2.1.

Combination Spread for UAL Stock Options

+2σ	Sell	4 JUN C160	+2 1/2 x 400	= $1000
Next higher	Sell	8 JUN C155	+4 3/8 x 800	= $3500
Nearest market	Buy	4 JUN C150	-7 1/8 x 400	= -2850
value	Buy	4 JUN P150	-4 3/4 x 400	= -1900
Next lower	Sell	8 JUN P145	+3 1/2 x 800	= +3800
-2σ	Sell	4 JUN P140	+2 3/8 x 400 =	+950
			commission	-65
			Initial credit=	$3435

The profit/loss for this combination spread is shown in Figure 2.5 as a function of the UAL stock market value at expiration time. The combination spread has two peaks. Outside the safe limits the loss rate is 2/3 that of the short spread, or $800 per point for the example. The combination spread has inferior profit/loss characteristics compared with the short spread, except for the slight advantage of a lower loss rate. The short spread has a more robust profit profile and, of course, is simpler to execute and to monitor. The margin capital requirements are the same as for the combination spread, since both have the same number of short options as the short spread.

The Butterfly Spread is another protective trading strategy that you can use if you are feeling either **bullish** or **bearish**. If you feel that the market is going **up** during the option month, then you can execute a *Bullish Butterfly Spread*. If you feel the market is going **down**, then you execute a *Bearish Butterfly Spread*. In either case, the maximum profit occurs at the market value you expect the market to close at on expiration day. The loss is limited so

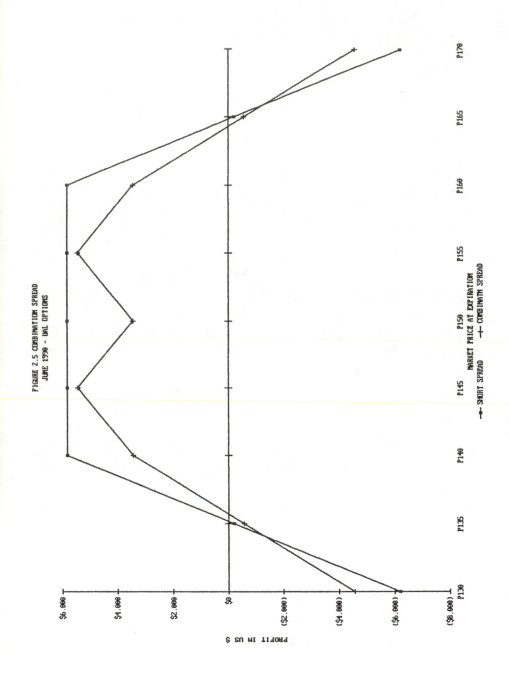

FIGURE 2.5 COMBINATION SPREAD
JUNE 1990 - UAL OPTIONS

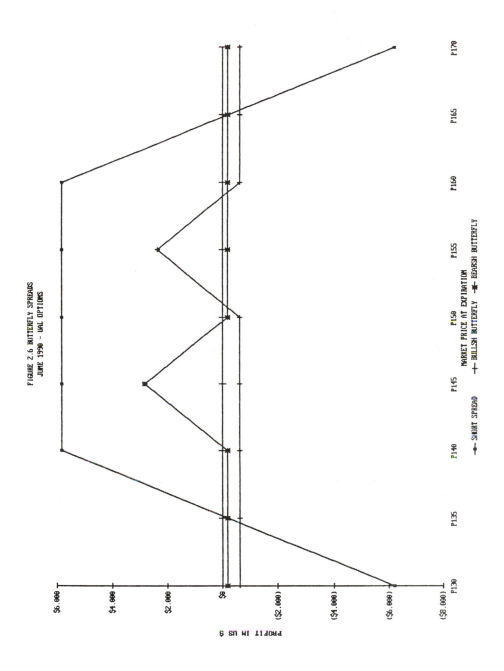

FIGURE 2.6 BUTTERFLY SPREADS
JUNE 1990 - UAL OPTIONS

that the risk is very small. Table 2.1 illustrates both of these butterfly spreads and compares them with the *short spread*. Figure 2.6 compares them graphically. To execute a bullish butterfly spread, sell a number of call options at the strike price higher than the one nearest the market, and buy half as many calls at the strike price nearest the market and at +2 sigma above the market; place the following order with your broker for June UAL options:

Sell 12	UAL JUN C155	Premium 4 3/8 =	$ 5250
Buy 6	UAL JUN C150	7 1/8 =	-4275
Buy 6	UAL JUN C160	2 1/2 =	-1500
	less commission		- 98
	Initial Credit	=	$ -623

The bearish butterfly spread is the mirror image of the bullish butterfly; place the following order:

Sell 12	UAL JUN P145	Premium 3 1/2 =	$+4200
Buy 6	UAL JUN C150	4 3/4 =	-2850
Buy 6	UAL JUN C160	2 3/8 =	-1425
	less commission		- 98
	Initial Credit	= $	-173

You may see by studying Figure 2.6 that both the butterfly spreads provide profits over a very limited range of expiration prices but have very little risk if the market moves sharply up or down. Neither butterfly spread is as profitable as the short spread. The only advantage of the two butterfly spreads is that they have a very limited loss potential. Unless you are good at predicting whether the market is going up or down, you better stick with the short spread — which has a much more robust profit profile.

Selecting the Proper Strategy

Depending upon the circumstances, the prudent investor may wish to select one of the trading strategies that limits the loss for large movements of the market. The short spread has the disadvantage of large losses if the market moves outside the safe limits selected. However, it is my experience that if the short spread is selected with statistically safe 2σ (see chapter 1) limits, the risk versus return trade-off favors the short spread strategy over the other protective strategies. One primary reason is that the short spread generates more income, so an occasional loss can be absorbed. And as previously discussed, protective changes to the short spread may be taken if the market threatens either the short put or call side of the spread.

The UAL stock had a market value of 157.75 at expiration. The results for the protective trading strategies given in this chapter are summarized below:

Profit / Loss
Market Close at 157.75

Short Spread	Sell 12 C160/P140	$5,801
Protected Straddle	Sell 12 C150/P150	
	Buy 12 C160/P140	- 998
Ratio Spread	Sell 12 C155, Sell 12 P145	
	Buy 6 C150, Buy 6 P150	3,601
Combo Spread	Sell 4 C1670/P140	
	Sell 8 C155/P145	
	Buy 4 C150/P150	4,335
Bullish Butterfly	Sell 12 C155	
	Buy 6 C150/C160	727
Bearish Butterfly	Sell 12 P145	
	Buy 6 P150/P140	-173

All of the protective strategies discussed above are summarized in Figure 2.7. The more robust profit charac-

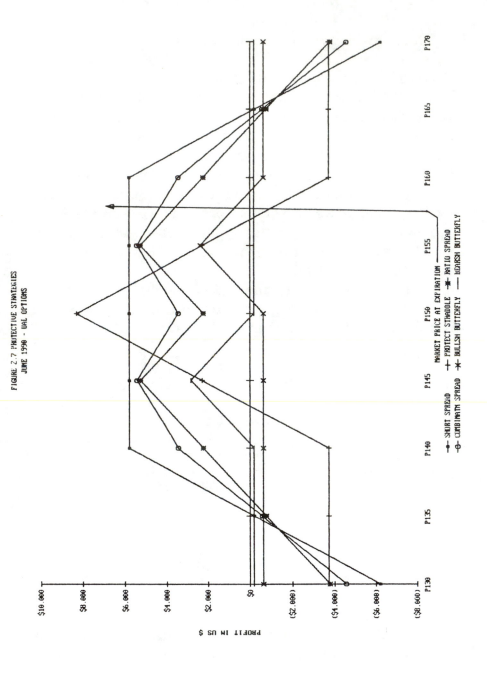

FIGURE 2.7 PROTECTIVE STRATEGIES
JUNE 1990 - UAL OPTIONS

teristics of the short spread made it the clear winner. I recommend using the short spread over these other more complex protective strategies because of its profit potential for a broader range of fluctuations in the market.

The **Early Assignment Problem** must be considered for those protective trading strategies that utilize in-the-money puts or calls, such as may occur in the *protected straddle,* the *ratio spread,* and the *butterfly spreads.* The *early assignment* is the process of an automatic close-out of your position that is **in-the-money.** The *protected straddle* and the *butterfly spreads* are particularly dependent upon in-the-money *long* positions (the options you *bought* to protect your position). Early assignment occurs when there is a disparity or discount of futures versus options of the same underlying financial instrument. Typically, the OCC will select, say, 25% of the outstanding in-the-money options on a random basis and close them out. Now you are left with an exposed, unprotected short position. In other words, part of the protected position you established is closed out by the OCC with no order from you *before* the expiration time. This *early assignment problem* adds risk to a position that otherwise has little or none.

The *early assignment problem* is one more factor that tips the scales in favor of the *short spread.* So long as the market price of the underlying financial instrument is between the *put* and *call* strike prices for the short spread, neither the puts nor the calls are in-the-money. Therefore, the position is not subject to early assignment. However, should the market move outside your safe limits, then the *put* or the *call* would have an intrinsic value and thus might be closed out (bought back) through the process of early assignment. In this case, you could be closed out with a significant loss.

IN SUMMARY: The short spread proves to be the best protective trading strategy in the June 1990 examples using UAL stock options — as long as you select safe ±2 sigma limits for the call and put strike prices. The selection of these safe limits will be discussed in more detail in Chapters 3 and 9 of this book. A computer program and spread sheets for selecting safe put and call values are described in Chapter 10 and Chapter 7, respectively.

Chapter 3

How To Get Started Trading Options

The secret to successful option trading is to select a particular option and specialize — become an expert in your selected option market. This way it will be less work, less worry, and more money. My philosophy is to make a reasonable monthly income from option trading, with a minimum of watching and worrying. By specializing in a particular option market, you need watch only one number — the market value of the underlying security — to make sure it stays within the safe limits for the *short spread* position. I am assuming that Chapter 2 has convinced you that the *short spread* is the best trading strategy to be used — a reasonable trading-profit-to-risk ratio. This chapter examines six Option Markets and identifies those markets that meet the criteria for making money safely in option trading. Then from the suitable market you can select that particular option in which to specialize and become an expert. You should select a financial market in which you feel comfortable. Again the six option markets are:

- Stock Market Index Options
- Common Stock Options
- Foreign Currency Options
- US Treasury Bills/Notes Options
- Precious Metal Options
- Commodity Futures Options

Those option markets that pass the criteria screening in this chapter will be discussed in detail in Section 2 of this book, starting with Chapter Four. Whatever option you select, there are some generic questions for which you need answers before you start trading. These questions will be addressed during the remainder of this chapter.

HOW MANY SHORT SPREAD POSITIONS CAN I ASSUME?

Your first step is to select a broker, if you don't already have one. Your broker will be able to tell you what the current margin requirements are for trading in options. Before *Black Monday,* the margin requirements for options were typically 5%. The minimum margin requirements for the S&P 100 were raised from 10% to 15% in April 1988. Some brokerage house have established even higher collateral requirements, some as high as 50%. In June 1990 a 30% margin on short spread trading was typical and that is the figure I used in all examples, which should be close to the requirements of your broker. The column **NO. OPTS** in Table 3.1 gives the number of short spreads you may open with an initial capital of $50,000 and a margin requirement of 30%. There are a total of 15 different options in the six markets covered. For example, you may open 5 S&P 100 Index June 1990 short spreads with 5 calls and 5 puts; you may open 32 silver (EOE) June 1990 short spreads with 32 calls and 32 puts. The market values on May 22, 1990 were used as the basis for the table. The number of options was rounded off to the nearest whole number.

TABLE 3.1: HOW MANY SHORT SPREADS CAN I ASSUME?
SIX OPTION MARKETS:
SHORT SPREADS
EXECUTION DATE: MAY 22, 1990

	EXPIR DTE	QTY	UNITS	MKT VAL	NO OPTS
STOCK INDEX OPTIONS:					
S&P 100 INDEX (OEX)	15/6/90	100	SHARES	$340.00	5
NYSE INDEX (NYA)	15/6/90	100	SHARES	$195.00	9
AMEX MAJ MKT INDEX (XMI)	15/6/90	100	SHARES	$580.00	3
COMMON STOCK OPTIONS:					
UAL	15/6/90	100	SHARES	$151.00	11
IBM	15/6/90	100	SHARES	$117.00	14
MICROSOFT	15/6/90	100	SHARES	$118.00	24
CURRENCY OPTIONS (PHIL):					
W. GERMAN MARKS	15/6/90	62500	DM	$0.5986	4
JAPANESE YEN	15/6/90	6250000	YEN	$0.0066	4
SWISS FRANCS	15/6/90	31250	LBS SLG	$1.6926	4
PRECIOUS METAL OPTIONS:					
GOLD (CMX)	20/7/90	100	TR OZ	$376.00	4
SILVER (EOE)	15/6/90	1000	TR OZ	$5.20	32
TREASURY FUTURES OPTIONS:					
T-BONDS (CBT)	21/9/90	100000	US$	92.56%	2
T-NOTES (CBT)	21/9/90	100000	US$	95.63%	2
COMMODITY FUTURES OPTIONS:					
SOYBEANS (CBT)	20/7/90	5000	BUSHELS	$5.8350	6
WORLD SUGAR (CSCE)	20/7/90	112000	LBS	$0.1446	10

The equations for computing the number of short spreads you can purchase for a given amount of capital are given below:

MV = Market Value for one option

MGN = Margin Requirements

NS = Number of Spreads = CAPITAL ÷ (MV x MGN)

The general equation is:

$$NS = \frac{CAPITAL}{MV \times MGN}$$

1. EXAMPLE for NYA: $50,000 CAPITAL, 30% Margin
    MV (NYA) = NYA x 100 For NYA = 195, MV(NYA) = $19,500

    $$NS\ (NYA) = \frac{\$50,000}{\$19,500 \times 0.3} = 8.55;\ \text{round off to } 9$$

2. EXAMPLE for UAL: $50,000 CAPITAL, 30% Margin
    MV (UAL) = UAL x 100 For UAL = 151, MV (UAL) = $15,100

    $$NS\ (UAL) = \frac{\$50,000}{\$15,100 \times 0.3} = 11.04;\ \text{round off to } 11$$

3. EXAMPLE for DM, MV (DM) = $0.60/DM X 62,500 = $37,500

    $$NS(DM) = \frac{\$50,000}{\$37,500 \times 0.3} = 4.44;\ \text{round off to } 4$$

4. EXAMPLE for Gold (CMX), MV (GOLD) = $376/oz. x 100 oz. = $37,600

    $$NS(GOLD) = \frac{\$50,000}{\$37,600 \times 0.3} = 4.43;\ \text{round off to } 4$$

5. EXAMPLE for T-Bonds (CBT), MV = $100,000 face value x 92% = $92,000

    $$NS(T\text{-}BONDS) = \frac{\$50,000}{\$92,000 \times 0.3} = 1.81;\ \text{round off to } 2$$

6. EXAMPLE for Soybeans (CBT) MV = 5000 bushels x $5.83/bu = $29,150

$$NS(SB) = \frac{\$50,000}{\$29,150 \times 0.3} = 5.72; \text{ round off to } 6$$

You may use Table 3.1 to estimate how many short spreads you should open for various types of options, but your broker will determine exactly how many short spreads you are allowed. I advise you to open as many as your capital will permit. The more spreads the more money you can make. The other side of the coin is: the more spreads you have the more money you may lose if the market moves outside your spread limits.

HOW WIDE SHOULD MY SHORT SPREAD BE? WHAT SHOULD THE CALL AND PUT STRIKE PRICES BE?

As mentioned in Chapter 2, the spread between the put and call strike prices should be ±2σ. Sigma (σ) is a measure of the statistical fluctuation of the particular option. The details of computing sigma for options are presented in Chapter 9. You should update the value you use for sigma at least once per year to account for long term changes in market volatility. Table 3.2 shows the 2σ spread widths for the options of the six different markets, using 2 or 3 examples for each market—a total of 15 different options. The value of 2σ varies from 2.07 for W. German Marks to 53 for silver options.

This table also shows the market values of the underlying financial instruments for each of the options listed. The stock index, common stock, currency, and silver options expired June 15, 1990. The Treasury issue options had September 1990 expirations and both the gold and commodity futures options had July expiration dates. All the Short

Spreads were opened on May 22, 1990, and the market values are shown under the **MKT VAL** column.

TABLE 3.2: HOW WIDE SHOULD MY SPREAD BE?
SIX OPTION MRKTS: WHAT SHOULD THE
CALL & PUT STRIKE PRICES BE?
SHORT SPREADS
EXECUTION DATE: MAY 22, 1990

	EXPIR DTE	MKT VAL	2SIG	SHORT CALL	SPREAD PUT
STOCK INDEX OPTIONS:					
S&P 100 INDEX (OEX)	15/6/90	340.12	9.87	350	330
NYSE INDEX (NYA)	15/6/90	195.58	4.82	200	190
AMEX MAJ MKT INDEX (XMI)	15/6/90	572.82	17.04	590	555
COMMON STOCK OPTIONS:					
UAL	15/6/90	151.5	10.49	160	140
IBM	15/6/90	117.125	4.7	120	110
MICROSOFT	15/6/90	70.625	6.29	75	65
CURRENCY OPTIONS (PHIL):					
W. GERMAN MARKS	15/6/90	59.85	2.07	62	58
JAPANESE YEN	15/6/90	66.1	2.19	68	64
SWISS FRANCS	15/6/90	70.54	2.27	72.5	67.5
PRECIOUS METAL OPTIONS:					
GOLD (CMX)	20/7/90	376	20	400	360
SILVER (EOE)	15/6/90	5.2	53	550	450
TREASURY FUTURES OPTIONS:					
T-BONDS (CBT)	21/9/90	0.92563	4.2	96	88
T-NOTES (CBT)	21/9/90	0.95625	2.3	98	93
COMMODITY FUTURES OPTIONS:					
SOYBEANS (CBT)	20/7/90	5.835	52.7	625	525
WORLD SUGAR (CSCE)	20/7/90	0.1446	2.05	17	12

The general equations for computing the safe ±2σ short spread call and put strike prices are:

Call Strike Price (2σ) = round-off (MV + 2σ)
Put Strike Price (-2σ) = round-off (MV - 2σ)
where MV = market value for the option's underlying financial instrument

2σ = 2 times the statistical fluctuation of the option's underlying financial instrument

Round-off means round-off to the nearest available strike price.

GOLDEN RULE 3 OF OPTION TRADING

Make your spread positions wide enough to be safe - don't get greedy and narrow your spread. You may make more money when you open your positions with a narrow spread width, but the statistics of market volatility will take the money back. *Trade safely, not greedily!*

HOW MUCH MONEY
WILL THE SHORT SPREAD MAKE?

The column **INITIAL CREDIT** of Table 3.3 shows the amount received at the beginning of the option month. You get to keep this amount if the market value is within your spread limits at expiration:

Initial Credit = No.Opts x Qty x TPRM - COMM
         TPRM = Total Premium = PPRM + CPRM
where: No.Opts = the number of spreads (puts/calls)
          Qty = quantity of the underlying financial
                instrument per option
         PPRM = Put premium
         CPRM = Call premium
         Comm = Commission
Example: S&P 100 Index (OEX) spread
Initial credit = 5 x 100 x 3.875 - 37.50 = $1,900

55

TABLE 3.3: HOW MUCH MONEY WILL THE SHORT SPREADS MAKE?
SIX OPTION MRKTS: SHORT SPREADS
EXECUTION DATE: MAY 22, 1990

	EXP DTE	NO. OPTS	PREMIUMS CPRM	PPRM	TPRM	INITIAL CREDIT
STOCK INDEX OPTIONS:						
S&P 100 INDEX (OEX)	15/6/90	5	1.9375	1.9375	3.88	$1.899
NYSE INDEX (NYA)	15/6/90	9	1	1	2	$1,704
AMEX MAJ MKT INDEX (XMI)	15/6/90	3	4.75	2.57	7.25	$2,109
COMMON STOCK OPTIONS:						
UAL	15/6/90	11	2.5	2.375	4.88	$5,363
IBM	15/6/90	14	1	0.25	1.25	$1,779
MICROSOFT	15/6/90	24	1.875	1.1875	3.06	$7,227
CURRENCY OPTIONS (PHIL):						
W. GERMAN MARKS	15/6/90	4	0.08	0.09	0.17	$473
JAPANESE YEN	15/6/90	4	0.13	0.09	0.22	$555
SWISS FRANCS	15/6/90	4	0.12	0.12	0.24	$567
PRECIOUS METAL OPTIONS:						
GOLD (CMX)	20/7/90	4	0.7	0.5	1.2	$532
SILVER (EOE)	15/6/90	32	6	4	10	$3,205
TREASURY FUTURES OPTIONS:						
T-BONDS (CBT)	21/9/90	2	0.45313	0.375	0.83	$1,491
T-NOTES (CBT)	21/9/90	2	0.40625	0.3125	0.72	$1,253
COMMODITY FUTURES OPTIONS:						
SOYBEANS (CBT)	20/7/90	6	8.5	0.25	8.75	$2,499
WORLD SUGAR (CSCE)	20/7/90	10	0.01	0.01	0.02	$231

HOW MUCH MONEY CAN I KEEP AT EXPIRATION?

The profit for each option short spread at expiration on June 15, 1990, is given in the last column of Table 3.4. Please note that several of the options opened have expiration dates later than June 15 — namely Gold, T-Bonds and T-Notes, Soybeans, and World Sugar. For these options the close-out costs based upon the premium existing on June 15 were used to compute the June expiration profit or loss. I don't use options without monthly expirations in my trading because I think it's too risky to leave short spreads open for more than a month — the risk being that the market may more easily fluctuate outside your spread limits.

TABLE 3.4: HOW MUCH OF THE MONEY CAN I KEEP AT EXPIRATION?
SIX OPTION MRKTS: SHORT SPREADS
EXECUTION DATE: MAY 22, 1990

	EXPIR DTE	SHORT CALL	SPREAD PUT	MKT VAL JUN EXP	INITIAL CREDIT	PROFIT JUN EXP
STOCK INDEX OPTIONS:						
S&P 100 INDEX (OEX)	15/6/90	350	330	346.42	$1,899	$1,899
NYSE INDEX (NYA)	15/6/90	200	190	197.86	$1,704	$1,704
AMEX MAJ MKT INDEX (XMI)	15/6/90	590	555	586.14	$2,109	$2,109
COMMON STOCK OPTIONS:						
UAL	15/6/90	160	140	157.75	$5,363	$5,363
IBM	15/6/90	120	110	121.19	$1,779	$82
MICROSOFT	15/6/90	75	65	76.00	$7,227	$4,867
CURRENCY OPTIONS (PHIL):						
W. GERMAN MARKS	15/6/90	62	58	59.19	$473	$473
JAPANESE YEN	15/6/90	68	64	64.94	$555	$555
SWISS FRANCS	15/6/90	73	68	69.76	$567	$567
PRECIOUS METAL OPTIONS:						
GOLD (CMX)	20/7/90	400	360	346.90	$532	($5,275)
SILVER (EOE)	15/6/90	550	450	481.10	$3,205	$3,205
TREASURY FUTURES OPTIONS:						
T-BONDS (CBT)	21/9/90	96	88	0.94	$1,491	($281)
T-NOTES (CBT)	21/9/90	98	93	0.97	$1,253	($191)
COMMODITY FUTURES OPTIONS:						
SOYBEANS (CBT)	20/7/90	625	525	586.00	$2,499	$2,232
WORLD SUGAR (CSCE)	20/7/90	17	12	15.28	$231	$231

Note that for all the short spreads, except IBM and MSFT, that expired on June 15 you were able to keep all the initial credit. Both IBM and MSFT finished slightly higher than the call strike price — instead of being worthless, the

IBM and MSFT call options finished with intrinsic values of 3/8 and 1, respectively. The general equation for computing the amount of money you get to keep for an in-the-money call at expiration (like IBM and MSFT) is:

$$\text{Profit at Expiration} = \text{Initial Credit} - (\text{MV (exp)} - \text{SP}) \times \text{No.Opts} \times \text{Qty}$$

$$\begin{aligned}
\text{where MV (exp)} &= \text{market price of call side of spread} \\
\text{SP} &= \text{strike price of call side of spread} \\
\text{Profit at Expiration} &= \$1781 - (120.375 - 120) \times 14 \times 100 \\
&= \$1256
\end{aligned}$$

Gold had a huge loss because of an unusual drop in gold prices during June 1990. A rumor circulated that the drop was caused by the Saudis and the Soviets selling gold to pay their hard currency debts. I would not have used the gold option, since it did not have a June expiration.

You would have lost money closing out the Treasury issue options, because changes in interest rates made your spread more valuable than when you opened it — another example of the hazards of options that expire more than month away.

HOW DO I PLACE MY ORDER?

The easiest way to place your order is by a short telephone call to your broker. It is assumed that you have discussed your option trading plans with your broker so he or she will understand what you are doing. The order should include the following:

- Type of option. For example, NYSE Index Option.
- Month option expires: always the current option month. For example, on May 22, 1990, the NYSE Index Option month is June 90, with expiration on June 15, 1990. (Remember, options expire on the third Friday of each month, called the witching hour.)

• Specify the **number** of options to be sold at either the market **open** or **close**. I prefer to use the close so I can check the prices I get versus what is reported in the newspaper. Sometimes I am surprised at the discrepancy and complain to my broker. This helps to keep the system honest.

Your telephone order should be confirmed by a written order to avoid any misunderstanding. Ask your broker to repeat back your order to make sure he understood all the numbers.

A few examples will be given to make sure you understand how to give the order exactly and unambiguously. **A misunderstanding could be costly!**

EXAMPLE ORDERS: All assume a 30% margin and refer to the specific cases in Tables 3.1 through 3.3.

1. Stock Index Options: "Sell 9 June NYSE Index options at call strike price 200 (C200) at close today and at the *same time* sell 9 June NYSE Index options at put strike price 190 (P190)."

2. Stock Options: "Sell 14 June IBM options at call strike price 120 (C120) at close today and at the same time sell 14 June IBM options at put strike price 110 (P110)."

3. Currency Options: "Sell 4 June DM62,500 options at call strike price 62 (C62) at close today and at the same time sell 4 June DM62,500 options at put strike price 57 1/2 (P57 1/2)."

4. Precious Metal Options: "Sell 32 June EOE silver options (1000 oz) at call strike price 550 (C550) at close today and at the same time sell 32 June EOE silver options at put strike price 450 (P450)."

5. Treasury Issue Options: "Sell 2 March T-Bond (CBT) $100,000 options at call strike price 96 (C96) at close today and at the same time sell 2 March T-Bond (CBT) options at put strike price 88 (P88)."

6. Commodity Futures Options: "Sell 6 July CBT Soy-

bean options at call strike price 625 (C625) at close today and at the same time sell 6 July CBT Soybean options at put strike price 525 (P525)."

The first time you place an order remind your broker that the call and put options must be *sold* at the same time to make sure you have a spread position, not naked options. The margin amount for *naked* put and call options would be approximately twice the amount as for the put/call spread. The spread costs less because even if the market should move adversely against your short spread, you can lose money on either the put or the call but *not both!*

WHAT DO I DO DURING THE MONTH MY SHORT SPREAD POSITION IS OPEN?

As any prudent trader should, you monitor the market value of the underlying financial instrument for your short spread option position. You will, of course, check to make sure the market value is within your safe limits. For your short spread to be **safe** the market value should be less than your **call strike price** and **greater** than your **put strike price.** In other words, it is only necessary to monitor a *single* number — the market value. As an example, consider the *S&P 100 Index Option Short Spread* with C350/P330. So long as the S&P 100 Index is less than 350 and greater than 330, your short spread is *safe.* If, for example, during the option month the S&P 100 Index should go over 350 — and stays over for one day — you should call your broker and close out (buy back) your C350 options and sell C355 options. To reduce the cost of this change you should also buy back the P330 options and sell P335. Remember the mental stop numbers — call 350 and put 330 allow you to take action if either your put or call is threatened by a market change. You may have to give back some of your initial credit, but you can avoid a disastrous loss by watching and acting. Never let your losses run. Conserve your capital and return next month to trade again.

HOW DO I CLOSE OUT MY POSITION ON THE OPTION EXPIRATION DATE?

The answer to this question is easy. **You do nothing.** If the market value is between your safe call strike price and put strike price at time of expiration, then you get to keep *all* the money you received when you sold the options on the day you opened your short spread position. It requires no action on your part — it's automatic. Also, there is no close out commission if the close is within your safe limit. Otherwise, there will be a commission on the in-the-money *put* or *call* (never both).

If your put or call finishes in-the-money for options other than index options, the expiration is more complicated. You must take delivery of or furnish the underlying financial instrument and pay commissions (larger than for options alone) for the transaction. You may, of course, immediately sell the instrument (if you take delivery) but there are inevitable costs and risks for such settlements.

TRADING TOOLS

The trading in short spread options is straightforward, and the numerical calculations to establish a safe short spread are easy to make using a small hand-held calculator and the tables presented in this chapter (Tables 3.1 and 3.2). Nevertheless, a computer program or spreadsheet to make these computations would make it easier for you to select your safe position at the beginning of the option month. Such a computer program or spreadsheet would also facilitate the monitoring of the position during the month to evaluate the potential threats to your short spread position.

I have developed spread sheets for evaluating short spreads in index options, stock options, and currency options, and they are described in Chapter 7. I've also developed software for evaluating short spreads for the three index options plus UAL stock options, and it is described in Chapter 10. The software is written in the language **BASIC** using the version 3.2 GW BASIC by Microsoft. The BASIC listing is provided in Appendix A. The spreadsheet listings are provided in Appendix B. The statistics for each type of option listed in the tables of this chapter (Tables 3.1 and 3.2) are embedded in the program to assist the software user in selecting and monitoring the short spread positions. The program allows the evaluation of a large number of option positions in a short time (a few minutes). This program permits the option trader to make profit/risk trade-offs very rapidly.

WHICH OPTIONS WORK
FOR THE SHORT SPREAD STRATEGY?

To answer this question please refer to Table 3.5, which shows the annual returns for option trading in the six option markets for the 15 different options used as examples in this chapter. The percent annual return — based upon the initial credit and displayed under the column ANNUAL RETURN — ranges from a low of 5.5% for Sugar to 173% for MSFT stock.

The *first criterion* for selection should be making an annual return *greater than 25%*. Eight of the 15 examples meet this criterion and are listed in the table.

The *second criterion* is that the options market should *have monthly expirations*. You are trying to earn a monthly income from your trading. Also, the longer the trading period, the greater the chance of wild market fluctuations. This second criterion reduces the list of candidates to only

Table 3.5   **WHICH OPTIONS WORK FOR SHRT SPRD STRATEGY**
CRITERIA 1:   **ANNUAL RETURN GREATER THAN 25%**
CRITERIA 2:   **MONTHLY EXPIRATION DATES YEAR ROUND**
CRITERIA 3:   **IN-THE-MONEY SETTLEMENT IN CASH**

	EXPIR DTE	INITIAL CREDIT	PROFIT JUN EXP	ANNUAL RETURN
STOCK INDEX OPTIONS:				
S&P 100 INDEX (OEX)	15/6/90	$1,899	$1,899	45.6%
NYSE INDEX (NYA)	15/6/90	$1,704	$1,704	40.9%
AMEX MAJ MKT INDEX (XMI)	15/6/90	$2,109	$2,109	50.6%
COMMON STOCK OPTIONS:				
UAL	15/6/90	$5,363	$5,363	128.7%
IBM	15/6/90	$1,779	$82	42.7%
MSFT	15/6/90	$7,227	$4,867	173,5%
CURRENCY OPTIONS (PHIL):				
W. GERMAN MARKS	15/6/90	$473	$473	11.4%
JAPANESE YEN	15/6/90	$555	$555	13.3%
SWISS FRANCS	15/6/90	$567	$567	13.6%
PRECIOUS METAL OPTIONS:				
GOLD (CMS)	20/7/90	$532	($5,275)	12.8%
SILVER (EOE)	20/7/90	$3,205	$3,205	76.9%
TREASURY ISSUE OPTIONS:				
T-BONDS (CBT)	21/9/90	$1,491	($281	11.9%
T-NOTES (CBT)	21/9/90	$2,253	($191)	10.0%
COMMODITY FUTURES OPTIONS:				
SOYBEANS (CBT)	20/7/90	$2,499	$2,232	60.0%
WORLD SUGAR (CSCE)	20/7/90	$231	$231	5.5%
THOSE OPTIONS THAT MEET CRITERIA 1:				
STOCK INDEX OPTIONS:				
S&P 100 INDEX (OEX)	15/6/90	$1,899	$1,899	45.6%
NYSE INDEX (NYA)	15/6/90	$1,704	$1,704	40.9%
AMEX MAJ MKT INDEX (XMI)	15/6/90	$2,109	$2,109	50.6%
COMMON STOCK OPTIONS:				
UAL	15/6/90	$5,363	$5,363	128.7%
IBM	15/6/90	$1,779	$82	42.7%
MSFT	15/6/90	$7,227	$4,867	173.5%
PRECIOUS METAL OPTIONS:				
SILVER (EOE)	20/7/90	$3,205	$3,205	76.9%
COMMODITY FUTURES OPTIONS:				
SOYBEANS (CBT)	20/7/90	$2,499	$2,232	60.0%
THOSE OPTIONS THAT MEET CRITERIA 2:				
STOCK INDEX OPTIONS:				
S&P 100 INDEX (OEX)	15/6/90	$1,899	$1,899	45.6%
NYSE INDEX (NYA)	15/6/90	$1,704	$1,704	40.9%
AMEX MAJ MKT INDEX (XMI)	15/6/90	$2,109	$2,109	50.6%
COMMON STOCK OPTIONS:				
UAL	15/6/90	$5,363	$5,363	128.7%
IBM	15/6/90	$1,779	$82	42.7%
MSFT	15/6/90	$7,227	$4,867	173.5%
THOSE OPTIONS THAT MEET CRITERIA 3:				
STOCK INDEX OPTIONS:				
S&P 100 INDEX (OEX)	15/6/90	$1,899	$1,899	45.6%
NYSE INDEX (NYA)	15/6/90	$1,704	$1,704	40.9%
AMEX MAJ MKT INDEX (XMI)	15/6/90	$2,109	$2,109	50.6%

six of the original 15 different options and only two of the six option markets — stock index options and stock options.

The *third criterion* is that *in-the-money settlements* should be made *in cash* to avoid the special risks and costs involved in the forced buying and selling of the underlying financial instrument. Only the three index options survive this last criterion. You may choose to ignore this criterion and assume the special costs of any in-the-money settlements — particularly for some of the high flying common stock options that have enormous profit potential.

I recommend that you limit your option trading to stock index options and common stock options. For this reason the remainder of the book will focus primarily on these two markets. Section two will detail reasons why these are the two best markets for your protective option trading.

Naturally, market situations will change. As trading increases in the other markets, they may very well become more profitable. As you trade, you should keep these other markets in mind. It is likely they will be worthwhile at some point in the future.

Table 3.6 summarizes the information about all six options markets, which was presented in Tables 3.1 thru 3.4, as a handy reference.

TABLE 3.6: SIX OPTION MARKETS:
+/- 2 SIGMA SHORT SPREADS
EXECUTION DATE: 22 MAY 1990
INITIAL CAPITAL: $50,000   MARGIN: 30%
FILENAME: OPTMKTS1.WKS

	EXPIR DTE	QTY	UNITS	MKT VAL	NO. OPTS	2SIG	SHORT SPREAD CALL	PUT	INIT PREMIUMS CPRM	PPRM	TPRM	INITIAL CREDIT	AMT EXPIR	VALPROFIT EXPIR	3FRL VALUE	ANNUAL RETURN
INDEX OPTIONS:																
OEX	15/6/90	100	SHARES	340.12	5	9.87	350	330	1.94	1.94	3.88	$1.899	340.42	$1.899	$0	45.6%
NYA	15/6/90	100	SHARES	195.58	9	4.82	200	190	1.00	1.00	2.00	$1.704	197.86	$1.704	$0	40.9%
XMI	15/6/90	100	SHARES	572.82	3	17.04	590	555	4.75	2.50	7.25	$2.109	586.14	$2.109	$0	50.6%
STOCK OPTIONS:																
UAL	15/6/90	100	SHARES	151.50	11	10.49	160	140	2.50	2.38	4.88	$5.363	157.75	$5.363	$0	128.7%
IBM	15/6/90	100	SHARES	117.13	14	4.70	120	110	1.00	0.25	1.25	$1.779	121.19	$82	$1.693	42.7%
MSFT	15/6/90	100	SHARES	70.63	24	6.29	75	65	1.88	1.19	3.06	$7.227	76.00	$4.867	$2.360	173.5%
CURR OPTIONS:																
DM	15/6/90	62500	DM	59.85	4	2.07	62	58	0.08	0.09	0.17	$473	59.19	$473	$0	11.4%
YEN	15/6/90	62500	YEN	66.10	4	2.19	68	64	0.13	0.09	0.22	$555	64.94	$555	$0	13.3%
SF	15/6/90	62500	SF	70.54	4	2.27	73	68	0.12	0.12	0.24	$567	69.76	$567	$0	13.6%
AU & AG OPTIONS:																
GOLD (CMX)	20/7/90	100	TR OZ	376.00	4	20.00	400	360	0.70	0.50	1.20	$532	346.90	($5.275)	$6.012	12.8%
SILVER (BDE)	15/6/90	1000	TR OZ	5.20	32	53.00	550	450	6.00	4.00	10.00	$3.205	481.10	$3.205	$0	76.9%
T-OPTIONS:																
T-BONDS (CBT)	21/9/90	100000	US$	92.56%	2	4.20	90	88	0.45	0.38	0.83	$1.491	94.48%	($281)	$1.772	11.9%
T-NOTES (CBT)	21/9/90	100000	US$	95.63%	2	2.30	98	93	0.41	0.31	0.72	$1.253	97.19%	($191)	$1.443	10.0%
COMM OPTIONS:																
SOYBEANS (CB)	20/7/90	5000	BUSHELS	5.84	6	52.70	625	525	8.50	0.25	8.75	$2.499	586.00	$2.232	$268	60.0%
SUGAR (CSCE)	20/7/90	112000	LBS	0.14	10	2.05	17	12	0.01	0.01	0.02	$231	15.28	$231	$0	5.5%

PART 2

OPTION MARKETS

Chapter 4

Stock Index Options

If you examine the *Wall Street Journal* you will find a number of options listed under the heading *Index Options*. As a trader in stock index options, it is only necessary to select one. In this chapter we will consider three of the options that are suitable for the protective trading strategies discussed in SECTION 1. These are the same three options presented in the tables of Chapter 3 in which the profits were compared: namely the Chicago Board S&P 100 Index (OEX), the NY Stock Exchange NYSE Index (NYA), and the American Stock Exchange Major Market Index (XMI). I recommend the S&P 100 Index as the best index option to use for protective option trading, for reasons to be detailed in this chapter.

OPEN INTEREST

It is important to select index options that have a large *open interest*. Open interest is defined as the total number of positions that are open for a given option on any one date. For each option position there must be a *buyer* and a *seller*. So the open interest is a measure of the *size* of the market — the larger the open interest, the larger the market *size*. It is important for you, the trader in options, to operate in a *large* market to be sure the market will have a wide range of strike prices and to be able to change your position easily if necessary. If the market size is too small, you may not be able to change your threatened put or call because the desired new strike price is unavailable. If the market is large, the strike prices needed for protective actions will most likely be available. A large open interest is to your advantage in short spread trading.

Table 4.1 shows the OEX open interest and volume of trading for selected dates from September 18, 1989, to May 21, 1990, on days a short spread was opened or modified. The S&P 100 Index Options have the largest open interest, making it likely to be the safest vehicle for trading. For a given option the majority of open interest is in the current month — typically 80% in the current month, about 15% in the next month and 5% in the month after next — another reason for trading in one option month at a time.

TABLE 4.1 STOCK INDEX MARKET SIZE — OEX INDEX OPTIONS

Tr Date	TRADING VOL CALLS	PUTS	OPEN INTEREST CALLS	PUTS	OI RATIO PUT/CALL	MARKET SENTIMENT
18/9/89	54363	51042	389413	572431	1.47	BEARISH
20/10/89	164251	212860	443769	604717	1.36	BEARISH
20/11/89	75790	97885	398951	444230	1.11	BEARISH
18/12/89	88996	127906	283492	489202	1.73	BEARISH
19/1/90	160176	161433	452545	457125	1.01	BEARISH
19/1/90	160176	161433	452545	457125	1.01	BEARISH
16/2/90	190755	186171	3331750	1773804	0.53	BULLISH
19/3/90	108516	131442	315971	345503	1.09	BEARISH
23/4/90	117867	136247	455436	575985	1.26	BEARISH
15/5/90	143058	132972	408610	572082	1.40	BEARISH
18/5/90	187143	158222	417246	636606	1.53	BEARISH
21/5/90	118973	108739	324280	666500	2.06	BEARISH

On June 6, 1990, the OEX open interest was 871,709 options, XMI had 125,303, and NYA only 13,449 — these figures make the OEX the clear winner in open interest. Remember, high open interest means a safer market with a wider range of strike prices to use for the short spread trading strategy.

Market Sentiment can be measured by examining the open interest ratio between puts and calls — which nearly always showed a bearish sentiment (see column OI RATIO PUT/CALL in Figure 4.1). The ratio of put premiums to call premiums (see column PRM RAT PUT/CALL) also showed a bearish sentiment: the put premiums were almost always greater than the call premiums — except in May 1990, after a huge bull leg in the stock market. I don't use these ratios to make my trading decisions, but they do show the market is always expecting a precipitous drop. Over the last year such sudden drops have occurred frequently — but the ±2 sigma spread has protected my trading.

The Expiration Date for the *stock market options* is on the third Friday of each month. The S&P index options that I used in 1990 expire at the close. The NYSE index options expire at the open. Quite often the stock markets and indexes suffer **extreme volatility** during the last several minutes before the third Friday expirations. The market volatility has usually been more extreme on the quarterly expirations (third Friday in March, June, September, and December). This is the so called *triple witching hour* when stock options, stock index options, and stock index futures all expire.

Correlation among stock index market values is relatively high. The most widely reported stock index, the Dow Jones Industrial Average (DJIA), does not have an associated index option; however, the AMX Major Market Index, with 20 of the DJIA's 30 stocks, is fashioned to emulate the DJIA. The correlation factor with the DJIA is a handy tool to estimate the stock index for which you have an open trading position when that index is missing from your newspaper — a too frequent occurrence. For example, during the month that you are monitoring your short spread position, say in S&P 100 index options, you might be able to obtain the current value of the DJIA but not the OEX index. The DJIA is reported nightly on many TV programs, but the other indexes are not reported. If you knew the correlation factor between the two indexes you could estimate the current value of the OEX index from the current value of the DJIA. Table 4.2 shows the correlation ratios (DJIA/index) for the three indexes OEX, NYA, and XMI from September 18, 1989, through May 21, 1990. By listening to the radio on Friday, June 22, 1990, I learned that the DJIA closed at 2857, but I didn't have the OEX for that date. I estimated the OEX using the formula:

OEX (est.) = DJIA (close)/OEX Ratio

OEX Ratio = 8.4465   (The most recent ratio I had based upon June 20, 1990, data)

OEX (est.) = 2958/8.4465 = 338.24

Similarly, NYA (est.) = 2857/14.7840 = 193.25

XMI (est.) = 2857/5.0120 = 570.03

TABLE 4.2 RATIOS BETWEEN DJIA AND OEX, NYA, XMI USEFUL FOR ESTIMATING INDEX FROM DJIA

Tr Date	DJIA	DJIA/OEX	DJIA/NYA	DJIA/XMI
18/9/89	2688.00	8.3210	13.9687	N/A
20/10/89	2689.00	8.2904	13.9965	N/A
20/11/89	2632.00	8.3039	13.9978	5.0343
18/12/89	2697.50	8.3491	14.2333	5.0044
19/1/90	2677.90	8.3789	14.2776	N/A
19/1/90	2677.90	8.3789	14.2776	N/A
16/2/90	2635.59	8.4561	14.2773	4.9848
19/3/90	2755.77	8.4809	14.6071	N/A
23/4/90	2666.67	8.4503	14.6577	N/A
15/5/90	2822.45	8.4067	14.6006	N/A
18/5/90	2819.91	8.3689	14.6003	N/A
21/5/90	2844.64	8.3644	14.5670	5.0144
AVERAGE:		8.3791	14.3385	5.0095

These ratios do not remain exactly the same, but change with time. Figure 4.3 shows the correlation between the DJIA and the S&P 100 stock index from June 16, 1989 to July 20, 1990. You will note the DJIA tends to fluctuate more than the OEX. For this reason you should continually update your ratio, so your estimate of your index from the Dow Jones will be as accurate as possible.

HOW TO COMPUTE SAFE STOCK INDEX SHORT SPREAD POSITIONS

The mechanics of computing the short spread strike prices have been detailed in Part 1. Here I would like to point out a procedure that can earn you money. Very often there is a significant *drop* in the market the day after expiration — 9 times out of the last 13 expirations. Whenever there's a big change in the market, there is an accompanying surge in the values of the put or call premiums. If there's a big drop on the day after expiration, you can benefit from the jump in the put premium which will give you a larger initial credit.

The question is: what market price should I use for computing my safe short spread prices, the Friday expiration value or the Monday close value? The practical answer is to use the Friday market close value. This means the short spread you establish at close on Monday, the first trading day after expiration, will use *stale market data*. There are two reasons for using the Friday expiration market value:

1. You have the information available over the weekend after the expiration and can decide on your position before the market opens on Monday.

2. Statistical analysis shows you are better off using expiration-to-expiration spread widths. You'll make more money in the long run.

The stale data effect on short spread strike prices is illustrated by Table 4.4, a PC generated spread sheet, for two option months (June 1990 and July 1990) for the OEX, NYA, and XMI options.

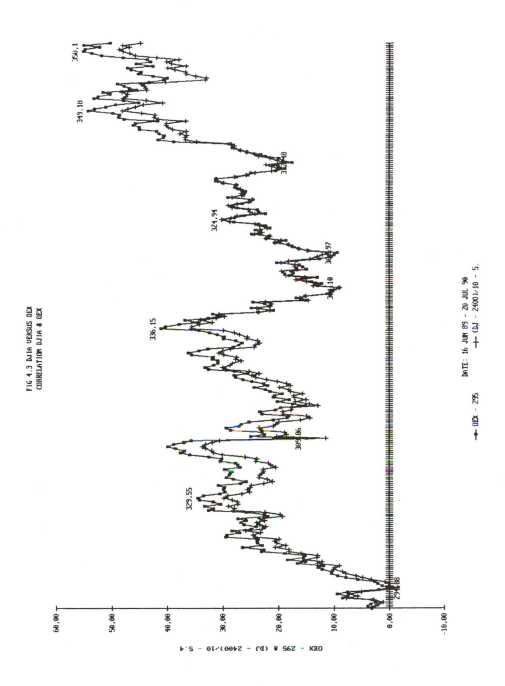

FIG 4.3 DJIA VERSUS OEX
CORRELATION DJIA & OEX

DATE: 16 JUN 89 - 20 JUL 90

TABLE 4.4: STOCK INDEX OPTIONS: STALE DATA EFFECT
INITIAL CAPITAL $50,000
MARGIN: 30%
FILENAME: INDXOPT. WKS

SHORT SPREADS: BASED ON MKT VAL ON EXEC DTE

EXPIR: 15/6/90	EXEC DTE	MKT VAL	NO. OPT	2SIG	SHRT SPRD CALL	PUT
OEX	22/5/90	340.12	5	9.72	350	330
NYA	22/5/90	195.58	9	5.81	200	190
XMI	29/5/90	576.49	3	18.43	595	560
EXPIR:	20/7/90					
OEX	18/6/90	340.60	5	9.72	350	330
NYA	18/6/90	194.93	9	5.81	200	190
XMI	18/6/90	575.80	3	18.43	595	555

SHORT SPREADS: BASED ON MKT AT CLOSE DAY BEFORE TRADE

EXPIR:	15/6/90					
OEX	22/5/90	340.09	5	9.72	350	330
NYA	22/5/90	195.28	9	5.81	200	190
XMI	27/5/90	566.21	3	18.43	585	550
EXPIR:	20/7/90					
OEX	18/6/90	346.47	5	9.72	355	335
NYA	18/6/90	197.86	8	5.81	205	190
XMI	18/6/90	586.14	3	18.43	600	570

Two cases are presented: (1) short spreads based upon the market value at close on the day executed, and (2) short spreads based upon the market value at close the day before. For each case, two option months, June 1990 and July 1990, are included for each of the three index options, OEX, NYA, and XMI. You can examine the MKT VAL column for those two cases to see how much the index market value changed in one day — very little for the OEX and NYA, but some 10 points for the XMI, executed a week later.

When the May (expiration date June 15) safe ±2 sigma spread strike prices were computed, they came out the same for the OEX and NYA: C350/P330 and C200/P195, but different for the XMI C595/P560 versus C585/P550. The July (expiration date July 20) spread strike prices were different for all three index options (see Table 4.4 SHRT

SPRD CALL/PUT).

The effect on profit of these two cases is given in Table 4.5. For the June options the OEX and NYA profits were essentially the same for both cases, but the XMI made more for case (2). Statistically speaking, I have found case (2) to make more profit. For the July options more initial credit was made and more closed out profit for all three indexes when using case (2).

In summary, I recommend that you use the Friday expiration market values to compute your spread values for the next option month, to be executed at close on the Monday after expiration.

TABLE 4.5: STOCK INDEX OPTIONS: STALE DATA EFFECT ON PROFIT
INITIAL CAPITAL $50,000
MARGIN: 30%
FILENAME: INDXOPT. WKS

	EXEC DTE	MKT VA	NO. OPT	2SIG	SHRT SPRD CALL	PUT	INIT CREDIT	MKT AT EXPIR	PROFIT EXPIR
SHORT SPREADS: BASED ON MKT VAL ON EXEC DTE									
EXPIR:	15/6/90								
OEX	22/5/90	340.12	5	9.72	350	330	$1,900	346.42	$1,900
NYA	22/5/90	195.58	9	5.81	200	190	$1,705	198.50	$1,705
XMI	29/5/90	576.49	3	18.43	595	560	$1,320	583.75	$1,320
EXPIR:	20/7/90								
OEX	18/6/90	340.60	5	9.72	350	330	$2,693	346.20	$2,693
NYA	18/6/90	194.93	9	5.81	200	190	$2,513	197.20	$2,513
XMI	18/6/90	575.80	3	18.43	595	555	$2,064	595.88	$1,809
SHORT SPREADS: BASED ON MKT AT CLOSE DAY BEFORE TRADE									
EXPIR:	15/6/90								
OEX	22/5/90	340.09	5	9.72	350	330	$1,900	346.42	$1,900
NYA	22/5/90	195.28	9	5.81	200	190	$1,708	198.50	$1,708
XMI	27/5/90	566.21	3	18.43	585	550	$1,878	583.75	$1,878
EXPIR:	20/7/90								
OEX	18/6/90	346.47	5	9.72	355	335	$2,467	346.20	$2,467
NYA	18/6/90	197.86	8	5.81	205	190	$1,633	197.20	$1,212
XMI	18/6/90	586.14	3	18.43	600	570	$2,561	595.88	$2,561

CAN I MAKE MORE MONEY BY TAKING A NARROWER SHORT SPREAD?

The safest short spread is ±2 sigma wide, but a narrower short spread will pay you more initial credit.

There are two strategies for narrowing your short spread: (1) if you feel bullish — that the market is going to rise — then you may want to raise your put strike price to the next higher value than the -2 sigma value computed; and (2) if you feel bearish — that the market is going to drop — then you may want to lower your call strike price to the next lower value than the +2 sigma value computed. Table 4.6 presents examples for narrower short spreads for the bullish/bearish bias cited above. The same examples are used as for the ±2 sigma spreads discussed in Tables 4.4 and 4.5: the OEX, NYA, and XMI for June and July 1990 options. Compare Table 4.6 with Table 4.4 and you will see that the June bullish bias spread for OEX is C350/P335, compared with the corresponding ±2 sigma spread of C350/P330.

For these two OEX examples the ±2 sigma spreads were 20 points wide, and the narrower spreads were only 15 points wide. The bullish bias spread had the put closer to the market value; conversely the bearish bias spread had the call closer to the market.

BUT HOW ABOUT PROFIT AT EXPIRATION FOR THE NARROWER SPREADS?

In all cases, the narrower spreads yielded more initial credit than the ±2 sigma spread, but if the market moved in the opposite direction to the bias, then the profit at expiration was less. If the bias was in the right direction, then you got to keep the extra money.

TABLE 4.6: STOCK INDEX OPTIONS: BULLISH BEARISH BIAS
INITIAL CAPITAL $50,000
MARGIN: 30%
FILENAME: INDXOPT. WKS

SHORT SPREADS: NARROWER THAN +/- 2 SIGMA: BULLISH
BASED ON MKT AT CLOSE DAY BEFORE TRADE
EXPIR: 15/6/90

	EXEC DTE	MKT VAL	NO. OPT	2SIG	SHRT SPRD CALL	PUT	CPRM	PPRM
OEX	22/5/90	340.09	5	9.72	350	335	1.94	2.94
NYA	22/5/90	195.28	9	5.81	200	193	1.00	1.75
XMI	22/5/90	567.30	3	18.43	585	560	4.75	2.38
EXPIR:	20/7/90							
OEX	18/6/90	346.47	5	9.72	355	340	1.63	5.13
NYA	18/6/90	197.86	8	5.81	205	195	0.50	3.06
XMI	18/6/90	586.14	3	18.43	600	580	2.75	10.38

SHORT SPREADS: NARROWER THAN +/- 2 SIGMA: BEARISH
BASED ON MKT AT CLOSE DAY BEFORE TRADE

EXPIR:	15/6/90							
OEX	22/5/90	340.09	5	9.72	345	330	3.63	1.94
NYA	22/5/90	195.28	9	5.81	200	190	1.00	1.00
XMI	27/5/90	567.30	3	18.43	575	550	5.63	1.63
EXPIR:	20/7/90							
OEX	18/6/90	346.47	5	9.72	350	335	3.00	3.50
NYA	18/6/90	197.86	8	5.81	200	190	1.50	1.44
XMI	18/6/90	586.14	3	18.43	595	570	4.00	6.25

The results are given in Table 4.7. For example, the June
OEX ±2 sigma had a profit at expiration of $1900. The
bullish bias spread made $2,391 because the market went up
from the May expiration to the June expiration. The bearish
bias spread had an initial credit of $2728. At expiration the
market value finished higher than the call at 145, so you had
to give back some of the original credit, ending with a profit
of $2031. This is still more than the ±2 sigma spread. On the
other hand, the bearish bias June XMI spread finished so far
in-the-money on the call side that the spread lost $441.

The examples show the narrower spreads are more risky,
even though the initial credit is higher. If you are **lucky**

enough to predict the direction the market is going to move you can make more profit.

I don't advise using narrower spreads unless you have a relatively accurate determinant of market direction. Don't be greedy. Settle for the profit from the ±2 sigma wide spreads. It's safer.

Table 4.7: STOCK INDEX OPTIONS: BULLISH/BEARISH BIAS
EFFECT ON PROFIT
INITIAL CAPITAL $50,000
30%

FILENAME: INDXOPT. WKS	INITIAL CREDIT	MKT VAL EXPIR	PROFIT EXPIR	SHRT 2 SIG	SPRD CALL	PUT
SHORT SPREADS: BASED ON MKT VAL ON EXEC DTE						
EXPIR: 15/6/90						
S&P 100 INDEX (OEX)	$1,900	346.42	$1,900	9.72	355	335
NYSE INDEX (NYA)	$1,705	195.58	$1,705	5.81	200	190
AMEX MAJ MKT INDEX (XMI)	$1,320	576.49	$1,320	18.43	595	560
EXPIR: 20/7/90						
S&P 100 INDEX (OEX)	$2,693	340.60	$2,693	9.72	350	330
MYSE INDEX (NYA)	$2,513	194.93	$2,513	5.81	200	190
AMEX MAJ MKT INDEX (XMI)	$2,064	575.80	$1,809	18.43	595	555
SHORT SPREADS: BASED ON MKT AT CLOSE DAY BEFORE TRADE						
EXPIR: 15/6/90						
S&P 100 INDEX (OEX)	$1,900	340.09	$1,900	9.72	350	330
NYSE INDEX (NYA)	$1,708	195.28	$1,708	5.81	200	190
AMEX MAJ MKT INDEX (XMI)	$1,878	566.21	$1,878	18.43	585	550
EXPIR: 20/7/90						
S&P 100 INDEX (OEX)	$2,467	346.47	$2,467	9.72	355	335
NYSE INDEX (NYA)	$1,633	197.86	$1,212	5.81	205	190
AMEX MAJ MKT INDEX (XMI)	$2,561	586.14	$2,561	18.43	600	570
SHORT SPREADS: NARROWER THAN +/-2 SIGMA: BULLISH						
BASED ON MKT AT CLOSE DAY BEFORE TRADE						
EXPIR: 15/6/90						
SUP 100 INDEX (OEX)	$2,391	346.42	$2,301	9.72	355	335
NYSE INDEX (NYA)	$2,348	198.50	$2,348	5,81	205	193
AMEX MAJ MKT INDEX (XMI)	$2,095	583.75	$2,095	D18.43	600	560
EXPIR: 20/7/90	$0	0.00	$0			
S&P 100 INDEX (OEX)	$3,249	346.20	$3,249	9.72	355	340
NYSE INDEX (NYA)	$3,003	197.20	$2,581	5.81	205	195
AMX MAJ MKT INDEX (XMI)	$3,734	595.88	$3,734	18.43	600	580
SHORT SPREADS: NARROWER THAN +/-2 SIGMA: BEARISH						
BASED ON MKT AT CLOSE DAY BEFORE TRADE						
EXPIR: 15/6/90						
S&P 100 INDEX (OEX)	$2,728	346.42	$2,031	9.72	345	335
NYSE INDEX (NYA)	$1,708	198.50	$1,708	5.81	205	195
AMEX MAJ MKT INDEX (XMI)	$2,131	583.75	($441)	18.43	575	565
EXPIR: 20/7/90	$0	0.00	$0			
S&P 100 INDEX (OEX)	$3,129	346.20	$1,834	9.72	350	335
NYSE INDEX (NYA)	$2,476	197.20	($2,160)	5.81	200	190
AMEX MAJ MKT INDEX (XMI)	$2,916	595.88	$2,916	18.43	595	575

TABLE 4.8: STOCK INDEX OPTIONS: SUITABLE FOR SHORT SPREADS

INITIAL CAPITAL: $50.000
MARGIN: 30%
FILENAME: INDXOPT.WKS

SHORT SPREADS: BASED ON MKT VAL ON EXEC DTE

	EXEC DTE	MKT VAL	NO. OPT	2SIG	SHRT CALL	SHRT PUT	SPRD CPRM	SPRD PPRM	INIT CREDIT	MKT AT EXPIR	PROFIT EXPIR	EXPIR CPRM	EXPIR PPRM	SPRD VALUE	ANNUAL RETURN
EXPIR: 15/6/90															
OEX	22/5/90	340.12	5	9.72	350	330	1.94	1.94	$1.900	346.42	$1.900	0.00	0.00	$0	45.6%
NYA	22/5/90	195.58	9	5.81	200	190	1.00	1.00	$1.705	198.50	$1.705	0.00	0.00	$0	40.9%
XMI	29/5/90	576.49	3	18.43	595	560	2.19	2.38	$1.320	583.75	$1.320	0.00	0.00	$0	31.7%
EXPIR: 20/7/90															
OEX	18/6/90	340.60	5	9.72	350	330	3.00	2.50	$2.693	346.20	$2.693	0.00	0.00	$0	64.6%
NYA	18/6/90	194.93	9	5.81	200	190	1.50	1.44	$2.513	197.20	$2.513	0.00	0.00	$0	60.3%
XMI	18/6/90	575.80	3	18.43	595	555	4.00	3.13	$2.064	595.88	$1.809	0.88	0.00	$.255	43.4%

SHORT SPREADS: BASED ON MKT VAL AT CLOSE DAY BEFORE TRADE

	EXEC DTE	MKT VAL	NO. OPT	2SIG	SHRT CALL	SHRT PUT	SPRD CPRM	SPRD PPRM	INIT CREDIT	MKT AT EXPIR	PROFIT EXPIR	EXPIR CPRM	EXPIR PPRM	SPRD VALUE	ANNUAL RETURN
EXPIR: 15/6/90															
OEX	22/5/90	340.09	5	9.72	350	330	1.94	1.94	$1.900	346.42	$1.900	0.00	0.00	$0	45.6%
NYA	22/5/90	195.28	9	5.81	200	190	1.00	1.00	$1.708	198.50	$1.708	0.00	0.00	$0	41.0%
XMI	22/5/90	566.21	3	18.43	585	550	4.75	1.63	$1.878	583.75	$1.878	0.00	0.00	$0	45.1%
EXPIR: 20/7/90															
OEX	18/6/90	346.47	5	9.72	355	335	1.63	3.50	$2.467	346.20	$2.467	0.00	0.00	$0	59.2%
NYA	18/6/90	197.86	8	5.81	205	190	0.50	1.44	$1.633	197.20	$1.212	0.00	0.50	$421	29.1%
XMI	18/6/90	586.14	3	18.43	600	570	2.75	6.25	$2.561	595.88	$2.561	0.00	0.00	$0	61.5%

SHORT SPREADS: NARROWER THAN +/- 2 SIGMA :BULLISH
: BASED ON MKT AT CLOSE DAY BEFORE TRADE

	EXEC DTE	MKT VAL	NO. OPT	2SIG	SHRT CALL	SHRT PUT	SPRD CPRM	SPRD PPRM	INIT CREDIT	MKT AT EXPIR	PROFIT EXPIR	EXPIR CPRM	EXPIR PPRM	SPRD VALUE	ANNUAL RETURN
EXPIR: 15/6/90															
OEX	22/5/90	340.09	5	9.72	350	335	1.94	1.94	$2.391	346.42	$2.391	0.00	0.00	$0	57.4%
NYA	22/5/90	195.28	9	5.81	200	193	1.00	1.00	$2.348	198.50	$2.348	0.00	0.00	$0	56.4%
XMI	22/5/90	567.30	3	18.43	585	560	4.75	2.38	$2.095	583.75	$2.095	0.00	0.00	$0	50.3%
EXPIR: 20/7/90															
OEX	18/6/90	346.47	5	9.72	355	340	1.63	1.63	$3.249	346.20	$3.249	0.00	0.00	$0	78.0%
NYA	18/6/90	197.86	8	5.81	205	195	0.50	0.50	$3.003	197.20	$2.581	0.00	0.50	$421	62.0%
XMI	18/6/90	586.14	3	18.43	600	580	2.75	2.75	$3.734	595.88	$3.734	0.00	0.00	$0	89.6%

SHORT SPREADS: NARROWER THAN +/- 2 SIGMA :BEARISH
: BASED ON MKT AT CLOSE DAY BEFORE TRADE

	EXEC DTE	MKT VAL	NO. OPT	2SIG	SHRT CALL	SHRT PUT	SPRD CPRM	SPRD PPRM	INIT CREDIT	MKT AT EXPIR	PROFIT EXPIR	EXPIR CPRM	EXPIR PPRM	SPRD VALUE	ANNUAL RETURN
EXPIR: 15/6/90															
OEX	22/5/90	340.09	5	9.72	345	330	3.63	1.94	$2.728	346.42	$2.031	1.42	0.00	$696	48.8%
NYA	22/5/90	195.28	9	5.81	190	190	3.00	1.00	$1.708	198.50	$1.708	0.00	0.00	$0	41.0%
XMI	22/5/90	567.30	3	18.43	575	550	5.63	1.63	$2.131	583.75	($441)	8.75	0.00	$2.572	-10.6%
EXPIR: 20/7/90															
OEX	18/6/90	346.47	5	9.72	350	335	3.00	3.50	$3.129	346.20	$1.834	2.69	0.00	$1.295	44.0%
NYA	18/6/90	197.86	8	5.81	200	190	1.50	1.44	$2.476	197.20	($2.160)	5.50	0.00	$4.636	-51.8%
XMI	18/6/90	586.14	3	18.43	595	570	4.00	6.25	$2.916	595.88	$2.916	0.00	0.00	$0	70.0%

The information in Tables 4.4, 4.5, 4.6, and 4.7 is integrated in Table 4.8, which should provide a handy reference for these OEX, NYA, and XMI examples. In addition, Table 4.8 gives the premium values for the puts and calls when the spreads were first executed and when they expired. For short spreads you hope that at expiration all your premiums are zero — then you get to keep all your initial credit. If not, you'll have to give money back, in some cases more than you got in the first place.

The whole object of the short spread strategy is to select spread widths so that you get to keep all your initial credit. My statistics clearly indicate the most prudent spread width is ±2 sigma. Remember, if the market fluctuates wildly it can end up at expiration outside your original safe limits. This is the fundamental risk of short spread trading.

WHAT IS THE BEST INDEX OPTION TO USE FOR SHORT SPREADS?

I have been using the S&P 100 stock index for some time now and recommend it as the best stock index option to use as of mid-1990. At one time I used the NYA, but the trading became too thin (open interest too low) to be safe. I've tried the XMI, but feel it is too volatile and subject to manipulation because of the small number of stocks (20) comprising the index.

HOW MUCH MONEY COULD YOU HAVE MADE IF YOU USED OEX FOR YOUR SHORT SPREAD STRATEGY FOR THE 13 TRADING MONTHS FROM JULY 1989 TO JULY 1990?

I will answer that question and at the same time show you some lessons I learned along the way. In the future I will make more money than in the past because of these lessons learned.

83

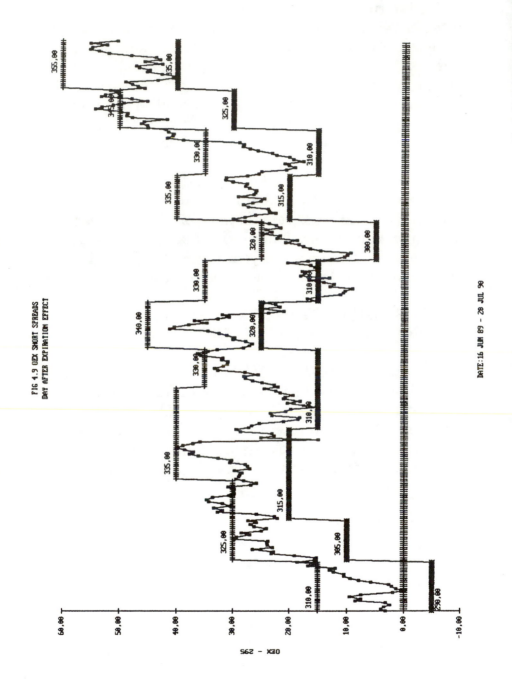

FIG 4.9 OEX SHORT SPREADS
DAY AFTER EXPIRATION EFFECT

DATE:16 JUN 89 - 20 JUL 90

The fluctuations in the S&P 100 (OEX) Index are portrayed in Figure 4.9. *Can we really make money using the short spread strategy in spite of the violent fluctuations?* The answer is a definite yes, but it requires careful selection of the ±2 sigma strike prices and, on occasion, protective changes in the spread during an option month when the put or call side of the spread is threatened.

The ±2 sigma short spreads are shown graphically as horizontal bars for each trading month (July 1989 through July 1990) in Figure 4.9. From 4.9 you can easily visualize the call strike price (upper bar) and the put strike price (lower bar). The expiration market value ended within the safe limits for each month except Jul 89, Jan 90, Mar 90, and Jun 90. Only Jul 89 and May 90 had net monthly trading losses.

Threats to the call strike price occurred in Aug 89, Sep 89, Oct 89, Dec 89 and Jan 90 and then dropped back below the call strike price. The market finished at expiration above the call strike price in Jul 89, Mar 90, May 90, and Jun 90 — the penetration occurred so late in the option month there was no time for protective action, except in May 90.

Threats to the put strike price occurred in Oct 89, Nov 89, Jan 90, Feb 90, Mar 90, Apr 90, May 90 and Jul 90, but subsequently the market rose again, removing the threat (except in Jan 90 when at expiration the market value was slightly below the put strike price).

Table 4.10 summarizes the details of short spread trading results for these 13 months (Jul 89 - Jul 90) in which no protective action was taken against either the call or put. In this case the trading profit on the initial $50,000 collateral capital was $32,593. This is an annual return of some 60% and a final capital of $82,593.

Figure 4.11 shows the cumulative before-tax trading profits for these 13 months of short spread trading in the OEX stock index.

TABLE 4.10.: S&P 100 INDEX OPTIONS: JUL 89 TO JUL 90 SHORT SPREADS
NO PROTECTIVE ACTION TAKEN: ACTUAL TRADING RESULTS
INITIAL CAPITAL: $50,000 BASED ON MKT AT EXPIRATION
FILENAME: OEXOPT.W MARGIN:30%
OEX SHORT SPREADS
REMARKS:EXEC DTE

OEX SHORT SPREADS	EXEC DTE	EXP DTE	MKT VAL	NO. OPTS	2SIG	SHRT SPRD CALL	SHRT SPRD PUT	CPRM	PPRM	INIT CREDIT	MKT AT EXPIR	PROFIT EXPIR	CUM PROFIT	EXPIR CPRM	PRM PPRM	EXPIR SPRD VALUE	ANNUAL RETURN
OPEN JUL	19/6/89	21/7/89	298.24	6	9.72	310	290	1.25	1.63	$1.507	313.46	($428)	($428)	3.46	0.00	$1.935	-10.3%
OPEN AUG	24/7/89	18/8/89	313.46	5	9.72	325	305	2.50	2.88	$2.740	322.25	$2.740	$2.312	0.00	0.00	$0	65.8%
OPEN SEP	21/8/89	15/9/89	322.25	5	9.72	330	315	1.13	4.38	$2.880	323.04	$2.880	$5.193	0.00	0.00	$0	69.1%
OPEN OCT	18/9/89	20/10/89	323.04	6	9.72	335	315	2.13	2.00	$2.248	324.35	$2.248	$7.441	0.00	0.00	$0	54.0%
OPEN NOV	23/10/89	17/11/89	324.35	6	9.72	335	315	1.44	4.38	$3.327	319.40	$3.327	$10.768	0.00	0.00	$0	79.8%
OPEN DEC	20/11/89	15/12/89	319.40	6	9.72	330	310	1.00	3.13	$2.503	329.12	$2.503	$13.271	0.00	0.00	$0	60.1%
OPEN JAN	18/12/89	19/1/90	329.12	6	9.72	340	320	1.06	5.25	$3.932	319.62	$3.688	$16.960	0.00	0.38	$244	88.5%
OPEN FEB	22/1/90	16/2/90	319.62	7	9.72	330	310	1.00	8.00	$6.163	311.68	$6.163	$23.122	0.00	0.00	$0	147.9%
OPEN MAR	20/2/90	22/5/90	311.68	8	9.72	320	300	1.69	4.00	$4.310	322.93	$2.017	$25.139	2.93	0.00	$2.293	48.4%
OPEN APR	19/3/90	20/4/90	322.93	8	9.72	330	315	1.94	2.56	$3.353	319.97	$3.353	$28.492	0.00	0.00	$0	80.5%
OPEN MAY	23/4/90	18/5/90	319.97	8	9.72	330	310	1.13	4.13	$4.148	336.95	($1.538)	$26.954	6.95	0.00	$5.686	-36.9%
OPEN JUN	21/5/90	15/6/90	336.95	8	9.72	345	325	3.25	1.31	$3.338	346.90	$1.891	$28.844	1.90	0.00	$1.447	45.4%
OPEN JUL	18/6/90	20/7/90	346.90	8	9.72	355	335	1.63	3.50	$3.749	349.53	$3.749	$32.593	0.00	0.00	$0	90.0%

TOTAL PROFIT   = $32.593
ANNUAL RETURN = 60.17%
FINAL CAPITAL = $82.593

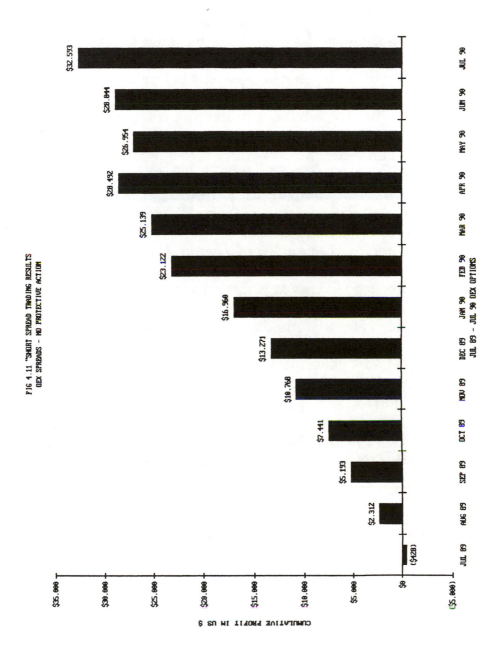

FIG 4.11 "SHORT SPREAD TRADING RESULTS
OEX SPREADS - NO PROTECTIVE ACTION

87

If you had panicked and made protective changes to your short spread each time your call or put was threatened, then the amount of profit would have been considerably reduced.

Lesson 1: don't make a protective change to your spread when there is a false threat to your put or call. A false threat is one in which the market penetrates your put or call threshold for only one day before pulling back.

Lesson 2: don't make a protective change unless the penetration of your threatened put or call is greater than 60% of the total premium of your spread. For example, the total premium for the Feb 90 spread was 9.0 for the spread of C330/P310. The call penetration would have to be 335.4, (the put penetration would have to be 304.6) before a protective action needed to be taken.

If you applied Lesson 1 and Lesson 2 to the 13 trading months Jul 89 - Jul 90, during which months would you make protective changes to your spread?

Nov 89 had a penetration of the put greater than 60% of the premium for only one day, Nov 6, 1989. No protective action needed.

Feb 90 had a penetration of the put greater than 60% of the premium for only one day, Jan 30, 1990. No protective action needed.

May 90 had a penetration of the call greater than 60% of the premium on May 9, 1990, and it persisted until expiration on May 18. Protective action should have been taken on May 15. The protective action: change from C330/P310 to C335/P325.

In other words, only during May 90 would a protective change have been made, at the close on the 15th.

The premium cost of this protective change was:
    C335 = +3.375
    C330 = -7.375
    P325 = +0.375
    P310 = -0.0625

Net premium = -3.6875

Dollar cost = 3.6875 x 800 + premium = $2950 + 288 (prem) = $3238

At expiration the OEX closed at 336.95, or 1.95 above the new CSP of 335.

Expiration dollar cost = 1.95 x 800 + prem = $1560 + 72 (prem) = $1632

The net profit for May = initial credit - (change cost + expiration cost)

$$= \$4148 - (3238 + 1632)$$
$$= -\$722 \text{ (a loss)}$$

This compares with a net loss without protective action or the May spread of $1538 — or an improvement of $816.

	Without protective action	With protective action
Total profit	$32,593	$33,409
Annual return	60.17%	61.68%
Final capital	$82,593	$83,409

I must confess: I didn't make the May 90 protective change. As you can see, in this example it didn't make much difference.

Chapter 5

Common Stock Options

Trading in common stock options entails greater risks than index options because an individual stock is subject to fluctuations affecting that stock which are distinct from the broader market. You should use stocks with a wide spread of strike prices, so that a safe spread width can be selected. Look for a stock whose prices generally follow the broad market trends. You may see by examining the Listed US Options section of the Wall Street Journal that there are many stocks in five markets: CBOE (Chicago Board of Options Exchange), AMEX (American Exchange), PHIL (Philadelphia Exchange), PACEX (Pacific Exchange), and NYSE (New York Stock Exchange).

I have selected eight stock options with the desired characteristics for short spread option positions — two on the CBOE, two on the AMEX, one on the PHIL, and three on the PACEX. The trading results for these stock options are presented in Table 5.1. These eight stocks are all suitable candidates for the short spread trading strategy. It is not always possible in a given month to select a given stock with

TABLE 5.1: STOCK OPTIONS SUITABLE FOR SHORT SPREAD STRATEGY:
SHORT SPREADS
INITIAL CAPITAL:$50,000
MARGIN: 30%
FILENAME: STKOPT.WKS

	EX DTE	EXP DTE	MKT VL	NO. OPT	2SIG	SHRT CLL	SRD PUT	INIT PREM CPRM	INIT PREM PPRM	INIT CREDIT	MKT VA EXP	EXPIR CPRM	PREM PPRM	PROFIT EXP	ANNUAL RETURN
COMMON STOCK OPTIONS:															
UAL	22/5/90	15/6/90	151.50	11	10.49	160	140	2.50	2.38	$5.363	157.75	0.00	0.00	$5.363	128.7%
IBM	22/5/90	15/6/90	117.13	14	4.70	120	110	1.00	0.25	$1.779	120.38	0.38	0.00	$1.245	29.9%
DISNEY	22/5/90	15/6/90	118.75	14	12.72	125	105	0.88	0.13	$1.404	131.75	6.72	0.00	($8.070)	-193.7%
APPLE	22/5/90	15/6/90	41.25	40	4.60	45	35	0.38	0.13	$2.020	39.50	0.00	0.00	$2.020	48.5%
TIME	22/5/90	15/6/90	100.25	17	10.80	110	90	0.69	0.50	$1.974	106.50	0.00	0.00	$1.974	47.4%
COMPAQ	22/5/90	15/6/90	118.75	14	14.04	135	105	0.38	0.63	$1.404	128.00	0.00	0.00	$1.404	33.7%
MICRSFT	22/5/90	15/6/90	70.25	24	6.29	75	65	2.00	1.19	$7.562	76.00	1.00	0.00	$5.190	124.6%
NIKE	22/5/90	15/6/90	76.25	22	9.81	85	65	0.63	0.63	$2.732	79.00	0.00	0.00	$2.732	65.6%
UAL	18/6/90	20/7/90	157.75	12	10.49	165	145	1.75	3.00	$5.557	161.13	0.00	0.00	$5.557	133.4%
IBM	18/6/90	20/7/90	120.38	14	4.70	125	115	0.94	0.75	$2.395	117.63	0.00	0.00	$2.395	57.5%
DISNEY	18/6/90	20/7/90	131.75	11	12.72	145	120	0.50	1.38	$1.989	126.50	0.00	0.00	$1.989	47.7%
APPLE	18/6/90	20/7/90	39.50	44	4.60	45	35	0.25	0.38	$2.744	41.50	0.00	0.00	$2.744	65.8%
TIME	18/6/90	20/7/90	106.50	16	10.80	115	95	0.63	0.88	$2.440	94.88	0.00	0.13	$2.237	53.7%
COMPAQ	18/6/90	20/7/90	128.00	13	14.04	135	115	1.63	2.13	$5.020	120.50	0.00	0.00	$5.020	120.5%
MICRSFT	18/6/90	20/7/90	76.00	24	6.29	80	70	2.00	1.63	$8.775	74.25	0.00	0.00	$8.775	210.6%
NIKE	18/6/90	20/7/90	78.75	22	9.81	90	70	0.38	0.94	$2.930	91.50	1.50	0.00	($3.419)	-10.0%

a safe ±2 sigma spread. You may have to choose a narrower (and riskier) spread or pass up that stock in favor of another in order to have a ±2 sigma spread.

In general, there are more opportunities for higher profits in Common Stock spreads than in Index Option spreads — but with more risk. For example, a buyout can cause sudden unexpected jumps and/or drops in a particular common stock price. This risk doesn't exist in the broader market of the index options.

Table 5.1 is a two month *snapshot* in 1990 of these 8 stock options that met the criteria for suitable short spreads: strike prices widely spread *plus* good premiums. If you should examine the stock option tables 2 years earlier or 2 years later, you would probably obtain a different list. Certain stock options are in vogue for a while and then disappear as market conditions for the stock change. IBM seems to be an exception. This huge capitalization stock has provided a good vehicle for stock option trading for many years because of the continued investor interest in *Big Blue*. The table shows the initial credit received for executing the short spread — varying from $1053 for the June Disney spread to $8775 for the July Microsoft spread — more than an 8 to 1 ratio. The short spread put and call strike prices, together with the market value at expiration, tell you if you get to keep your initial credit. If the MKT VAL EXP is between the PSP and CSP the final spread value is worthless and you get to keep the initial credit as your month's profit. If the MKT VAL EXP is outside the spread PSP to CSP, then you have to give back money and your monthly profit is diminished or you may even suffer a loss. For three June options (IBM, Disney, and Microsoft) the MKT VAL EXP was greater than the CSP, meaning the premiums (actually inherent values) at expiration were positive for the call strike price. Only Disney's value was great enough to cause a June loss.

The annual return column shows that three stock options

for this *2 month snapshot* exceeded 100%: UAL, Compaq, and Microsoft. Let me emphasize this is a snapshot — your sustained annual return won't be this high — else we could all become multi-millionaires very quickly.

Table 5.2 summarizes the June - July 1990 trading results for these 8 stock options. The top 3 performers were Microsoft, Compaq, and UAL — all with 2 month profits greater than $10,000. Not bad for an initial capital of $50,000.

TABLE 5.2: COMPARISON OF STOCK OPTION TRADING RESULTS
JUN & JUL 90 SHORT SPREAD +/-2 Sigma Variations
INITIAL CAPITAL: $50,000

	JUN PRFT	JUL PRFT	TOT PRFT	ANN RET
UAL	$5,363	$5,557	$10,920	$131.04%
IBM	$1,245	$2,395	$3,640	43.68%
DISNEY	($8,070)	$1,989	($6,081)	-72.97%
APPLE	$2,020	$2,744	$4,764	57.17%
TIME	$1,974	$2,237	$4,211	50.53%
COMPAQ	$1,404	$5,020	$6,423	77.08%
MICRSFT	$5,190	$8,775	$13,964	167.57%
NIKE	$2,732	($419)	$2,314	27.76%

The two month trading results are shown graphically in Figure 5.3 (again UAL, Compaq, and Microsoft are standouts). The annual return for these three varies from 131% for UAL to 167% for Microsoft (see Table 5.2). This all sounds too good to be true. Later we'll examine longer term trading in two of these stocks, UAL and IBM, to see what the risks and profits or losses can be for common stock options. UAL is a unique case because of huge fluctuations in market value caused by an employee buyout initiative that began in August 1989.

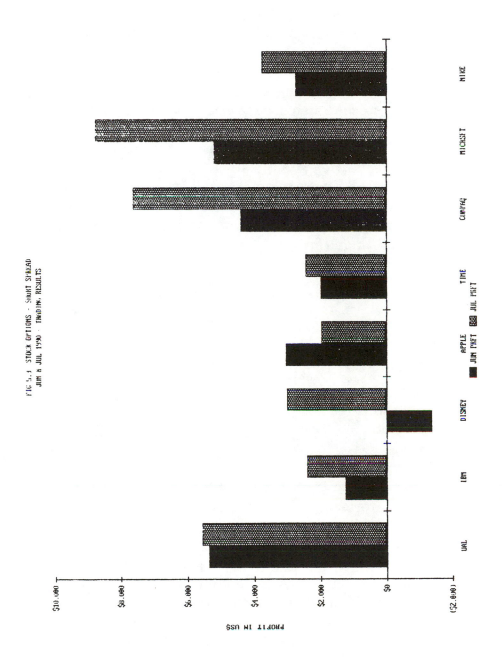

FIG 5.3 STOCK OPTIONS - SHORT SPREAD
JUN & JUL 1990 - TRADING RESULTS

HOW ABOUT TRADING VOLUME AND OPEN INTEREST IN THE FIVE STOCK OPTION MARKETS?

The *Listed US Options* table in the *Wall Street Journal* doesn't report the open interest on individual stocks, but only for all the stocks listed in each of the five markets. Table 5.4 lists the trading volume and open interest for the five markets. CBOE was the largest market and NEW YORK was the smallest. The example stock option short spreads selected for Table 5.1 were taken from all four of the markets except New York. Also listed in Table 5.4 are the number of different stock options in each market and the average open interest per stock option.

TABLE 5.4: COMMON STOCK OPTION MARKET SIZE
Reference Date: May 22, 1990

STK OPT MKT	TRADING PUT	VOLUME CALL	RATIO P/C	OPEN INTEREST PUT	CALL	RATIO P/C	NO. OPTs	AVG OI/OP
CBOE	132,532	221,286	0.60	1,438,298	2,633,912	0.55	193	21,100
AMEX	27,773	89,401	0.31	604,286	1,556,421	0.39	189	11,432
PHIL	26,995	66,382	0.41	488,157	853,151	0.57	126	10,645
PACEX	8,862	31,927	0.28	206,993	637,648	0.32	112	7,541
NY	2,680	7,160	0.37	41,061	122,780	0.33	39	4,201
TOTAL	198,842	416,156	0.39	2,778,795	5,803,912	0.43	659	10,984

The open interest is shown graphically in Figure 5.5.

The open interest ratio between puts and calls averages 0.43 — meaning *most* people who trade in common stock options are buying *call* options rather than the underlying stock because they believe the stock is going *up* and options give more leverage on the option traders' capital. This ratio can be considered bullish, since most traders (the ones who bought call options) are betting the market is going up.

The Expiration Date for the common stock options is the

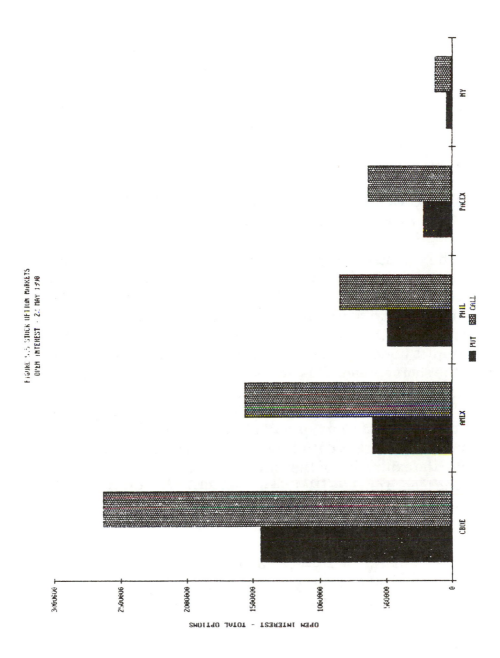

FIGURE 4.5 STOCK OPTION MARKETS
OPEN INTEREST - 22 MAY 1990

third Friday of each month. The stocks in each market are divided into two or three groups. All stocks in a given group have the same three expiration months — the two nearest months and one out-month. For example, in the CBOE the out-months for the three groups are August, September, and October. The nearest expiration months are June and July. This variation in the far out expiration date allows stock option traders to take positions several months in the future. My short spread trading strategy uses only the nearest expiration month.

HOW TO COMPUTE SAFE COMMON STOCK SHORT SPREAD POSITIONS

The safe strike prices for the stock options are computed in the same manner as for index options: take the market price, add 2 sigma (2σ) for the Call strike price, subtract 2σ for the Put strike price, rounding off to the nearest strike price. Table 5.1 shows the results for the June and July 1990 examples under the columns for Put and Call Strike Prices for the short spread. This procedure will be illustrated using July 1990 IBM stock options in Table 5.1.

First, compute the safe *Call* and *Put strike prices*. We will execute the *IBM short spread* at open on Monday, June 18, 1990, using market data from the close on Friday, June 15, 1990, the expiration of the June options. The options will be for the month of *July*. IBM closed at 120 3/8 on June 15, 1990.

The computations are summarized:

2σ (IBM) = 4.70

No.OPTS (30% margin) = 14

CSP = market + 2σ = 120.375 + 4.70 = 125.03
    round off to 125

PSP = market - 2σ = 120.375 - 4.70 = 115.67
    round off to 115

Safe strike prices: CSP = 125
                        PSP = 115

Second, compute the value of the spread at the open, SPRDVAL

The call and put premiums are obtained from the CBOE listed US Options for IBM on June 18, 1990:

CPRM = 0.9375, PPRM = 0.750

Total Premium (TPRM) = CPRM + PPRM = 1.6875

Ignoring commission

Initial Credit = (No.OPTS) x 100 x TRPM = $2395

CAN WE MAKE MONEY IN COMMON STOCK OPTION SHORT SPREADS OVER A LONG PERIOD OF TIME?

We will examine two stock options, UAL and IBM, to see what risks and profit opportunities there are in stock option short spreads. Table 5.6 displays UAL short spread trading results for the period from February 1989 through July 1990 with a gap for the option months Jan 90 through July 90. This is a total of 14 option months, beginning with the February 89 trade executed on January 23, 1989. We assume an initial capital of $50,000, a collateral margin requirement of 30% and that no protective action is taken. (Remember that in the case of OEX options, which covered approximately the same period, a good profit was made without protective action.)

The first five option months (Feb 89 - Jun 89) go relatively well, ending up with a cumulative profit of $15,060. Then during the July option month, the market value of UAL jumps from 139.50 to 170.75 — a 22% jump or a +3 sigma change. This is too much for our 2 sigma spread. The monthly loss is $18,635 — all of our cumulative profit and then some. The next month is even worse, a jump from 170.75 to 277.88, 177 points, a 104% increase in a month. Sorry, 2 sigma short spreads can't handle such astounding changes. The monthly loss is $48,371. We have now lost a

< no>
TABLE 5.6: UAL STOCK OPTIONS USING SHORT SPREAD STRATEGY:
NO PROJECT ACTION TAKEN : FEB 89 - JUL 90
INITIAL CAPITAL: $50.000
MARGIN: 30%

FILENAME: STKOPT

EXEC DTE	EXP DTE	WKS	MKT VAL OPT	2SIG	CLL	PUT	INIT PREM CPRM	PPRM	INITIAL CREDIT	MKT VAL EXP	EXPIR VAL CFRM	PPRM	PREM PPRM	PROFIT EXP	ANNUAL RETURN	CUM PROFIT
COMMON STOCK OPTIONS:																
UAL 23/1/89	17/2/89	15	112.75	10.49	125	100	0.94	0.38	$1.940	125.88	0.88	0.00	0.00	$647	15.5%	$647
UAL 20/2/89	17/3/89	13	125.88	10.49	135	115	1.50	0.69	$2.934	119.50	0.00	0.00	0.00	$2.934	70.4%	$3.581
UAL 20/3/89	21/4/89	15	119.50	10.49	130	115	1.38	2.13	$5.168	127.00	0.00	0.00	0.00	$5.168	124.0%	$8.748
UAL 24/4/89	19/5/89	14	127.00	10.49	135	115	1.69	0.69	$3.439	127.88	0.00	0.00	0.00	$3.439	82.5%	$12.187
UAL 22/5/89	16/6/89	14	127.88	10.49	140	120	1.06	1.00	$2.873	139.50	0.00	0.00	0.00	$2.873	69.0%	$15.060
UAL 30/6/89	21/7/89	13	139.50	10.49	150	130	4.00	2.00	$7.580	170.75	20.75	0.00	0.00	($18.635)	-447.2%	($3.575)
UAL 24/7/89	18/8/89	6	170.75	10.49	180	160	6.50	4.50	$6.735	270.00	90.00	0.00	0.00	($48.371)	-1160.9%	($51.946)
UAL 25/8/89	15/9/89	6	277.88	10.49	290	260	2.88	4.50	$4.423	279.75	0.00	0.00	0.00	$4.423	106.2%	($47.523)
UAL 18/9/89	20/10/89	6	279.75	10.49	290	270	3.38	6.25	$6.242	168.25	0.00	0.00	101.75	($59.741)	-1433.8%	($107.264)
UAL 27/10/89	17/11/89	10	171.00	10.49	180	160	7.50	6.00	$13.158	180.38	0.38	0.00	0.00	$12.792	307.0%	($94.471)
UAL 20/11/89	15/12/89	12	180.38	10.49	190	170	7.38	8.13	$17.986	176.79	0.00	0.00	0.00	$17.986	431.7%	($76.485)
UAL 30/4/90	18/5/90	15	150.50	10.49	160	140	1.88	2.75	$6.964	154.75	0.00	0.00	0.00	$6.964	167.1%	($69.521)
UAL 21/5/90	15/6/90	12	154.75	10.49	165	145	2.00	3.50	$6.749	157.50	0.00	0.00	0.00	$6.749	162.0%	($62.772)
UAL 18/6/90	20/7/90	12	157.50	10.49	165	145	2.75	2.50	$6.305	162.25	0.00	0.00	0.00	$6.305	151.3%	($56.467)

CUM LOSS = ($56.467)
EMPLOYEE BUY OUT CAUSED HUGE SWINGS
YOU WOULD HAVE LOST DISASTROUS AMOUNTS IN AUG 89 & OCT 89

total of $51,946 — a real financial disaster!

What happened? A buyout bid by the UAL employees caused this huge increase in value. **Why?** *Because the market believed the buyout bid made the stock worth that much.* You are now left with a *very* empty money bag. Do you want to keep trading? If so, add another $50,000 capital and keep going.

September 89 worked OK, you made $4,423 with your short spread C290/C260.

October 1989 — another disaster for UAL option short spread. The price of UAL collapsed to 171 (most of the drop on Friday the 13th), back to the same value before the huge August 89 jump. (Later the analysts said the huge drop in the overall market on Friday the 13th of October was caused by the banks' rejection of the UAL employee buyout effort.) *Could protective action have helped during either the August jump or the October collapse? Very little, it happened too fast.* So you lose another $59,741 in October 1989 — a total loss to date of $107,264 after 9 months of trading!

Give up or keep trying? Let's assume you decide to keep trying and add capital to bring your collateral back up to $50,000. The next five option months go smoothly. You reduce your loss at the end to $56,467 — a loss greater than the capital you started with in the first place.

UAL is a very extreme case, but illustrative of the risks you entail in single stock option trading. Dear reader, that's why I use *index option short spreads*. You still have risks from sudden broad market jumps or drops, but they are much less than the risks that accompany a single stock option short spread.

Before you give up completely on individual stock options, let's look at *Big Blue*, IBM. It's so big you'll (probably) never have to worry about a buyout or takeover such as occurred with UAL. Table 5.7 illustrates short spread trading in IBM stock options for the same option months as for

UAL. No protective action is taken for this example either.

The results are mediocre because of significant (but not disastrous) losses in Mar 89, Oct 89 and May 90. Trading provided a total cumulative profit of $7,567 for an annualized return of 12.97%. *Why use common stock option short spread trading* when you make over 13% in Eurosterling bonds with a lot less risk?

Before giving up, let's examine the IBM stock options using *protective action* in March 89 and May 90, illustrated in Table 5.8. (The October 89 collapse was so sudden and so near the expiration that protective action for IBM would not have worked. Unfortunately, IBM didn't recover like the broader market did and ended up with a loss, whereas the OEX short spread for Oct 89 recovered to make a profit.)

The protective action taken on the March 89 option spreads consisted of buying back the original C130/P120 and selling new calls and puts for a spread C120/P115. This protective action reduced the March 89 loss from $8577 (Table 5.7) to only $3976 (Table 5.8), a loss reduction of some $4,601. Similarly, the May 90 protective action reduced the May 90 loss from $4799 (Table 5.7) to only $645 (Table 5.8), a loss reduction of some $4154.

Sorry, we had to "eat" the October 89 loss of $6385 — same for Table 5.7 and Table 5.8. Nevertheless, the bottom line was significantly improved by taking the two protective actions: $19,326 compared with $7,567, an annualized return of 33% (some 2 1/2 times the return on Eurosterling bonds). As already explained, you could *still* buy Eurosterling bonds and use them as collateral for your short spread trading (if you have a London broker). The IBM cumulative profit with and without protective action is shown graphically in Figure 5.9.

TABLE 5.7: IBM STOCK OPTIONS USING SHORT SPREAD STRATEGY:
NO PROTECT ACTION TAKE: FEB 89 - JUL 90
INIT CAPITAL:$50.000

FILENAME: STKOPT.WKS   MARG 30%

	EXEC DTE	EXP DTE	WKS DTE	MKT VAL	NO. OPT	2SIG	CLL	PUT	INIT PREM CPRM	PPRM	INITIAL CREDIT	MKT EXP	EXT PREM CPRM	PPRM	PROFIT EXP	ANNUAL RETURN	CUM PROFIT
COMMON STOCK OPTIONS:																	
IBM	23/1/89	17/2/89		123.75	13	4.71	130	120	0.44	1.19	$2.189	125.50	0.00	0.00	$2.189	52.5%	$2.189
IBM	20/2/89	17/3/89		125.50	14	4.71	130	120	0.94	0.50	$1.993	112.38	0.00	7.63	($8.577)	-205.8%	($6.388)
IBM	20/3/89	21/4/89		112.38	12	4.71	115	110	2.25	1.50	$4.608	113.50	0.00	0.00	$4.608	110.6%	($1.781)
IBM	24/4/89	19/5/89		113.50	16	4.71	120	110	0.44	1.31	$2.807	111.75	0.00	0.00	$2.807	67.4%	$1.026
IBM	22/5/89	16/6/89		111.75	16	4.71	115	105	1.25	0.38	$2.560	109.50	0.00	0.00	$2.560	61.4%	$3.586
IBM	30/6/89	21/7/89		109.50	16	4.71	115	105	0.94	0.75	$2.700	114.38	0.00	0.00	$2.700	64.8%	$6.286
IBM	24/7/89	18/8/89		114.38	15	4.71	120	110	0.56	0.94	$2.304	115.13	0.00	0.00	$2.304	55.3%	$8.589
IBM	21/8/89	15/9/89		115.13	14	4.71	120	110	0.94	0.56	$2.172	115.75	0.00	0.00	$2.172	52.1%	$10.761
IBM	18/9/89	20/10/89		115.75	15	4.71	120	110	1.06	0.44	$2.254	104.25	0.00	5.75	($6.385)	-153.2%	$4.376
IBM	27/10/89	17/11/89		104.25	16	4.71	110	100	0.81	1.31	$3.397	99.13	0.00	0.88	$1.998	48.0%	$6.374
IBM	20/11/89	15/12/89		99.13	17	4.71	105	95	0.69	0.81	$2.623	97.29	0.00	0.00	$2.623	62.9%	$8.997
IBM	30/4/90	18/5/90		107.38	16	4.71	110	105	0.75	1.69	$3.982	115.38	5.38	0.00	($4.799)	-115.2%	$4.198
IBM	21/5/90	15/6/90		115.38	13	4.71	120	110	0.56	0.38	$1.224	120.38	0.38	0.00	$735	17.6%	$4.933
IBM	18/6/90	20/7/90		120.38	14	4.71	125	115	1.19	0.69	$2.634	117.17	0.00	0.00	$2.634	63.2%	$7.567

CUMULATIVE PROFIT = $7.567
FINAL CAPITAL = $57.567
ANN RETURN =   12.97%

103

TABLE 5.8: IBM STOCK OPTIONS USING SHORT SPREAD STRATEGY:
PROTECTIVE ACTION TAKEN   : FEB 89 - JUL 90
INIT CAPITAL: $50,000

FILENAME: STKOPT.WKS   MARG   30%
                        NO.

COMMON STOCK OPTIONS:

EXEC DTE	EXP DTE	MKT VAL	NO. OPT	2SIG	CLL	PUT	INIT PREM CPRM	PPRM	INITIAL CREDIT	MKT EXP	EXP PREM CPRM	PPRM	PROFIT EXP	ANNUAL RETURN	CUM PROFIT
IBM 23/1/89	17/2/89	123.75	13	4.71	130	120	0.44	1.19	$2.189	125.50	0.00	0.00	$2.189	52.5%	$2.189
IBM 20/2/89	17/3/89	125.50	13	4.71	130	120	0.94	0.50	$1.909	118.25	0.00	0.00	$1.909	45.8%	$1.909
IBM 10/3/89	17/3/89	118.25	15	4.71	120	115	0.50	-1.88	($2.023)	112.38	0.00	2.63	($5.885)	-141.2%	($3.696)
IBM 20/3/89	21/4/89	112.38	13	4.71	115	110	2.25	1.50	$4.907	112.38	0.00	0.00	$4.907	117.6%	$1.211
IBM 24/4/89	19/5/89	112.38	16	4.71	115	110	0.44	1.31	$2.850	111.75	0.00	0.00	$2.850	68.4%	$4.061
IBM 22/5/89	16/6/89	111.75	16	4.71	115	105	1.25	0.38	$2.562	109.50	0.00	0.00	$2.562	61.5%	$6.623
IBM 30/6/89	21/7/89	109.50	15	4.71	115	105	0.94	0.75	$2.700	114.38	0.00	0.00	$2.700	64.8%	$9.323
IBM 24/7/89	18/8/89	114.38	14	4.71	120	110	0.56	0.94	$2.304	115.13	0.00	0.00	$2.304	55.3%	$11.627
IBM 21/8/89	15/9/89	115.13	15	4.71	120	110	0.94	0.56	$2.172	115.75	0.00	0.00	$2.172	52.1%	$13.799
IBM 18/9/89	20/10/89	115.75	16	4.71	120	110	1.06	0.44	$2.254	104.25	0.00	5.75	($6.385)	-153.2%	$7.413
IBM 27/10/89	17/11/89	104.25	17	4.71	110	100	0.81	1.31	$3.397	99.13	0.00	0.88	$1.998	48.0%	$9.412
IBM 20/11/89	15/12/89	99.13	15	4.71	105	95	0.69	0.81	$2.623	97.29	0.00	0.00	$2.623	62.9%	$12.035
IBM 30/4/90	18/5/90	113.50	16	4.71	110	105	0.75	1.69	$3.767	114.25	0.00	0.00	$3.767	90.4%	$15.802
IBM 30/4/90	18/5/90	114.25	16	4.71	115	110	-3.31	0.50	($4.412)	115.38	0.38	0.00	($5.000)	-120.0%	$10.801
IBM 21/5/90	15/6/90	114.25	16	4.71	120	110	0.56	0.38	$1.471	120.38	0.38	0.00	$882	21.2%	$16.684
IBM 18/6/90	20/7/90	120.38	14	4.71	125	115	1.19	0.69	$2.642	120.38	0.00	0.00	$2.642	63.4%	$19.326

PROTECTIVE ACTION TAKEN: MAR 89
                         : MAY 90

CUMULATIVE PROFIT = $19.326
FINAL CAPITAL   = $69.326
ANN RETURN   =   33.13%

WHY DID IBM OPTION SHORT SPREADS WORK SO MUCH BETTER THAN UAL SHORT SPREADS?

The fluctuations of IBM and UAL stock are portrayed graphically in Figure 5.10 for the same periods as the stock options of Tables 5.7 and 5.8. At a glance you can see why UAL option short spreads didn't work. The pathological fluctuations of UAL stock in August 89 and October 89 were such that nothing short of inside information could have worked, and that's illegal. The IBM fluctuations were much more normal. Sure, there was a big drop in October 89, but not enough to wipe out all your capital the way the UAL trading did. **Twice.**

TO SUMMARIZE: There are a number of stocks that have options with adequately wide strike prices to permit use of the short spread trading strategy. Eight of these stock options, for a two month window (Jun 90 and Jul 90), are listed in Table 5.1 with their short spread trading results. Safe short spreads for common stock options can be used, but it is impossible to protect yourself from the enormous jumps that may occur in an individual stock like UAL. A frequent problem with stock options is that the safe ±2 sigma strike prices do not always exist. This problem rarely occurs for stock index option spreads. My advice is to stick with index options over the long haul and only use stock options when you feel adventurous enough to try to make an occasional large profit. But you should be well aware of the risk of huge losses that can happen when a convulsive vacillation in an individual stock occurs, like UAL in August and October 89.

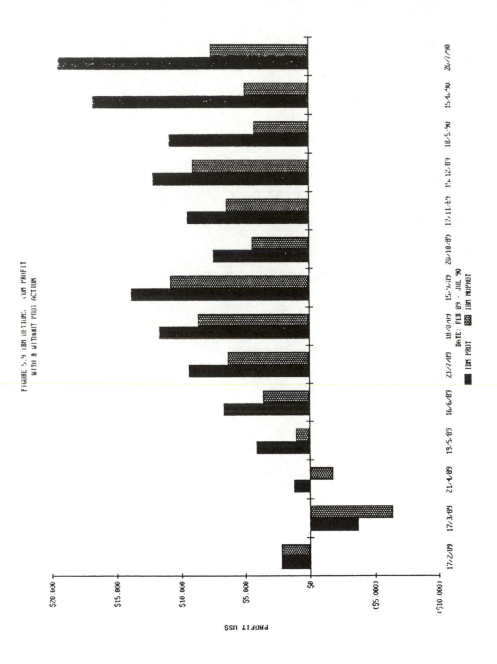

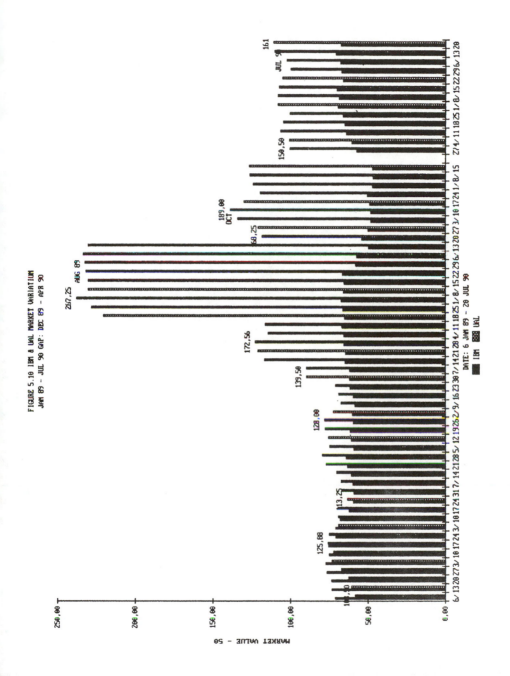

FIGURE 5.10 IBM & UAL MARKET VARIATION
JAN 89 - JUL 90 GAP: DEC 89 - APR 90

Chapter 6

Currency Option Trading

Currency Options are based upon the exchange rate of various currencies relative to the US dollar. There are a number of currency option markets, but all the examples in this chapter are based upon the Philadelphia Exchange currency options. The PE has options for:

- £12,500   British Pounds   values in .01$/£
- DM62,500   Deutsche Marks   values in .01$/DM
- SF62,500   Swiss Francs   values in .01$/SF
- ¥6,250,000   Japanese Yen   values in .0001$/¥
- $50,000   Australian Dollars   values in .01$/A$
- C$50,000   Canadian Dollars   values in .01$/C$

A single currency option is for the amounts given in the first column above.

Jun 90 - Jul 90 Currency Option Trading Results are presented in Table 6.1 for the six currency options listed on the Philadelphia Exchange using ±2 sigma short spreads. In each case except the Yen, the market value of the currency is expressed in US cents (.01$) per unit of the currency. For

TABLE 6.1: CURRENCY OPTIONS SUITABLE FOR SHORT SPREAD STRATEGY:
SHORT : for +/- 2 Sigma Variations about Original Position
INITIAL CAPITAL: $50.000
MARGIN: 30%
FILENAME: CURROPT.WKS NO. 30%

	EXEC DTE	EXP DTE	MKT VAL	OPT	2SIG	SHRT CALL	SPRD PUT	INIT PREM CPRM	PPRM	INIT CREDIT	MKT EXP	EXP PREM CPRM	PPRM	PROFIT EXP	ANNUAL RETURN
CURRENCY OPTIONS:															
AUS$	22/5/90	15/6/90	76.66	4	2.06	79.0	75.0	0.06	0.22	$609	77.94	0.00	0.00	$609	14.6%
BR LB	22/5/90	15/6/90	169.26	3	8.58	177.5	160.0	0.11	0.10	$207	171.3b	0.00	0.00	$207	5.0%
CAN$	22/5/90	15/6/90	84.35	4	1.08	85.5	83.5	0.10	0.45	$1.087	85.14	0.00	0.00	$1.087	26.1%
DM	22/5/90	15/6/90	59.85	4	2.07	62.0	58.0	0.08	0.17	$473	59.64	0.00	0.00	$473	11.4%
YEN	22/5/90	15/6/90	66.10	4	2.19	68.5	64.0	0.10	0.09	$479	65.03	0.00	0.00	$479	11.5%
SF	22/5/90	15/6/90	70.54	4	2.27	73.0	68.5	0.12	0.12	$567	70.66	0.00	0.00	$567	13.6%
AUS$	18/6/90	20/7/90	77.94	4	2.06	80.0	75.0	0.07	0.09	$342	78.58	0.00	0.00	$342	8.2%
BR LB	18/6/90	20/7/90	171.35	3	8.58	180.0	162.5	0.07	0.12	$185	181.34	1.34	0.00	($1.119)	-26.8%
CAN$	18/6/90	20/7/90	85.14	4	1.08	86.0	84.0	0.22	0.18	$783	86.68	0.68	0.00	($548)	-13.2%
DM	18/6/90	20/7/90	59.64	4	2.07	61.5	58.0	0.12	0.11	$643	60.92	0.00	0.00	$643	15.4%
YEN	18/6/90	20/7/90	65.03	4	2.19	67.0	64.0	0.10	0.18	$718	67.10	0.10	0.00	$461	11.1%
SF	18/6/90	20/7/90	70.66	4	2.27	72.0	69.0	0.31	0.23	$1.274	71.11	0.00	0.00	$1.274	30.6%

the Yen: .0001$/Yen. The short spread is opened at the beginning of the new option month (the first Monday after the third Friday of the month) using the short spread call and put prices shown in the table. The number of currency option short spreads opened are based on an initial capital of $50,000 and a 30% margin.

Market Values for currency options are reported in the financial section of many leading newspapers. The initial call and put premium values for the short spread (see CPRM and PPRM column in Table 6.1) are taken from newspaper tables. (I used the *Wall Street Journal* and the *International Herald Tribune,* both available worldwide, which report the **Philadelphia Exchange** currency options daily).

If an option market value at a particular strike price is not listed (denoted by an "r" in newspaper tables) it is possible to estimate the value by a process of interpolation or extrapolation. But this is dangerous to do in practice, because it means the option is thinly traded and you may not be close to the real price. A blank in the table is denoted by an "s" and means an option at that strike price does not exist. It's best to avoid the thinly traded options with lots of *r*'s and *s*'s — you often cannot find a safe short spread.

Currency Option Short Spreads presented in Table 6.1 have the execution and expiration dates shown under the columns EXEC DTE and EXP DTE. The dollar amount credited to your account for the executed option is shown under the column INIT/CREDIT. You get to keep all those dollars if the market value at expiration (column MKT EXP) is between your put and call strike prices. All the June 90 currency options finished within the limits, but only the DM, AUS$, and SF finished within the limits for the July 90 options. The expiration premiums (actually inherent values) are shown under the columns EXP PREM/CPRM PPRM. For those that finished outside the spread limits, the amount of loss might have been reduced by protective action.

A special risk for Currency Options is that some options are so thinly traded that no protective action is possible. The desired strike prices may simply not exist or not be available. *Appropriate protective action examples* are described for SFR and DM later in this chapter.

Currency Option Short Spread Trading Results for June - July 90 are given in Table 6.2. The results are slightly optimistic, since the commissions were ignored. The table shows clearly that for this two month window, Deutsche Marks (DM) and Swiss Francs (SFRNC) are the clear winners. Later in this chapter, tables covering some 13 months of short spread currency trading will show the DM and SF are the best currency options to use. CAN$ options (which had a good month for June 90) are too thinly traded to give good long term results in short spread trading.

TABLE 6.2: CURRENCY OPTIONS TRADING RESULTS:
JUN & JUL 90 SHORT SPREAD: +/-2 Sigma Spread Width
NO PROT ACTION: INITIAL CAPITAL: $50,000

	JUN PRFT	JUL PRFT	TOT PRFT		ANRET
AUS$	$609	$342	$951	AUS$	11.41%
BRIT LB	$207	($1,119)	($912)	BRIT LB	-10.94%
CAN$	$1,087	($548)	$539	CAN$	6.46%
DM	$473	$643	$1,116	DM	13.39%
YEN	$479	$461	$940	YEN	11.28%
SFRNC	$567	$1,274	$1,841	SFRNC	22.09%

The profit results and annualized return for June - July 90 currency trading are given graphically in Figures 6.3 and 6.4, respectively. You may see from the bar charts that DM and SFRNC were the best options for this time period.

I've included Table 6.5 to make a comment on the currency option market size. As of the 22nd of May, 1990, the largest US currency market PHIL had a total open interest of some 600,000 and a daily trading volume of about 60,000 options — **not a big market.**

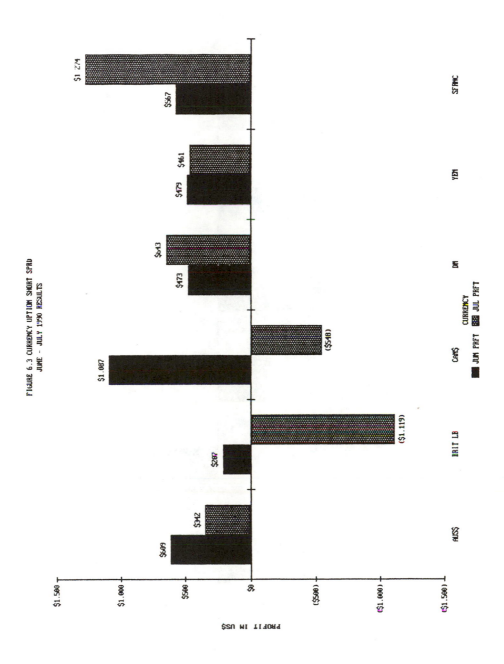

FIGURE 6.3 CURRENCY OPTION SHORT SPRED
JUNE - JULY 1990 RESULTS

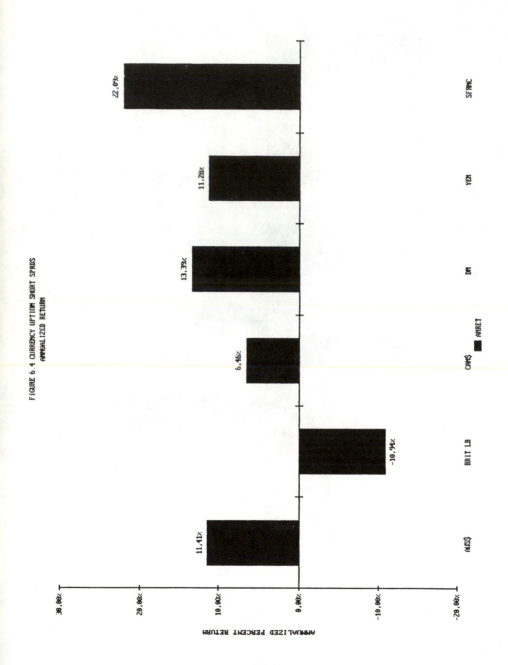

FIGURE 6.4 CURRENCY OPTION SHORT SPRDS
ANNUALIZED RETURN

TABLE 6.5: CURRENCY OPTION MARKET SIZE
Reference Date: May 22, 1990

STK MKT	OPT TRADING VOLUME PUT	CALL	RATIO P/C	OPEN PUT	INTERST CALL	RATIO P/C
PHIL	18604	42004	0.44	321180	307150	1.05

A 13 Month Examination for Currency Option Short Spreads is presented in the next four tables (6.6 through 6.9). First we look at Swiss Francs *without protective action* from July 89 to July 90 using ±2 sigma short spreads when available (Table 6.6). We find the market value at expiration is outside the limits of the short spread 3 out of the 13 months, resulting in an unimpressive cumulative profit of $4,318 for an annualized return of 8.64%. You could do just as well with high quality corporate bonds at less risk. On the other hand, the total initial credit is an impressive $16,388 (annual return of 32.78%). This figure gives hope that a significant improvement could be made by using protective strategies when the call or put side of the short spread is threatened. In all cases, it was the call side which was exceeded; the Swiss Franc was strengthening relative to the US Dollar during this period.

Protective Action Significantly Improves the Swiss Franc Option Short Spread Profit, as demonstrated in Table 6.7. Protective action was taken only for the May 90 spread. The criteria for changing the threatened spread was when the market value of the Swiss Franc exceeded the call price plus 60% of the initial total premium. Remember, in order to change a short spread position: *buy back* the original put and call options and *sell* new put and call options. For the May 90 threatened calls, we increased both the call and put strike prices. We lost money on the call, but offset the call loss with a put profit. The net change in the call and put premiums is given on the line marked SFR (Protec-

TABLE 6.6.: SWISS FRANC CURRENCY OPTIONS USING SHORT SPREAD STRATEGY:
NO PROT ACTION: JUN 89 - JUL PHILADELPIA
INITIAL CAPITAL: $50,000
MARGIN: 30%
FILENAME: CURROPT.WKS

	EXEC DTE	CURROPT.WKS EXP DTE	MKT V	NO. OPT	2SIG	SHRT CALL	SPRD PUT	INIT CPRM	PREM PPRM	INIT CREDIT	MKT EXP	EXPIR CPRM	PREMIU PPRM	ANNUAL RETURN	CUM PROFIT	PROFIT EXP
CURRENCY OPTIONS:																
SFR	19/6/89	21/7/89	58.46	5	2.27	61.0	56.0	0.25	0.32	$1.625	60.70	-0.30	0.00	59.5%	$2.480	$2.480
SFR	24/7/89	18/8/89	60.70	5	2.27	63.0	58.0	0.16	0.09	$720	59.32	0.00	0.00	17.3%	$3.201	$720
SFR	21/8/89	15/9/89	59.32	5	2.27	62.0	57.0	0.15	0.21	$1.061	59.26	0.00	0.00	25.5%	$4.262	$1.061
SFR	18/9/89	20/10/89	59.26	5	2.27	62.0	57.0	0.15	0.18	$1.007	61.45	-0.55	0.00	64.5%	$6.948	$2.686
SFR	23/10/89	17/11/89	61.45	5	2.27	64.0	59.0	0.17	0.10	$834	61.23	0.00	0.00	20.0%	$7.782	$834
SFR	20/11/89	15/12/89	61.23	5	2.27	64.0	59.0	0.13	0.06	$598	63.94	-0.06	0.00	18.9%	$8.568	$786
SFR	18/12/89	19/1/90	63.94	5	2.27	66.0	62.0	0.31	0.11	$1.282	65.74	0.00	0.00	30.8%	$9.851	$1.282
SFR	22/1/90	16/2/90	65.74	5	2.27	68.0	63.0	0.30	0.16	$1.396	66.48	0.00	0.00	33.5%	$11.247	$1.396
SFR	20/2/90	16/3/90	66.48	5	2.27	69.0	64.0	0.32	0.05	$1.136	65.85	0.00	0.00	27.3%	$12.383	$1.136
SFR	19/3/90	20/4/90	65.85	5	2.27	67.5	63.5	0.35	0.09	$1.389	67.34	0.00	0.00	33.3%	$13.773	$1.389
SFR/	24/4/90	18/5/90	67.34	5	2.27	69.0	65.0	0.08	0.07	$474	71.09	2.09	0.00	-147.0%	$7.648	($6.124)
SFR	22/5/90	15/6/90	71.09	4	2.27	73.5	69.0	0.11	0.28	$1.054	69.73	0.00	0.00	25.3%	$8.703	$1.054
SFR	18/6/90	20/7/90	69.73	4	2.27	72.0	68.0	0.31	0.10	$1.151	71.08	0.00	0.00	27.6%	$9.853	$1.151

NPA: NEEDS PROTECTIVE ACTION
CUM $9.853
ANN   18.19%

TABLE 6.7: SWISS FRANC CURRENCY OPTIONS USING SHORT SPREAD STRATEGY:
PROTECTIVE ACTION: MAY 90
INITIAL CAPITAL: $50,000
MARGIN: 30%
FILENAME: CURROPT.WKS NO.
EXEC DTE EXP DTE MKT VAL OPT 2SIG

	EXEC DTE	EXP DTE	MKT VAL	2SIG	SHRT CALL	SPRD PUT	INIT CPRM	PREMIUM PPRM	INITIAL CREDIT	MKT VAL EXP	VALXPIR CPRM	PREMIU PPRM	ANNUAL RETURN	CUM PROFIT	PROFIT EXP
CURRENCY OPTIONS:															
SFR	19/6/89	21/7/89	58.46	5 2.27	61.0	56.0	0.25	0.32	$1,625	60.70	0.30	0.00	59.5%	$2,400	$2,400
SFR	24/7/89	18/8/89	60.70	5 2.27	63.0	58.0	0.16	0.09	$720	59.32	0.00	0.00	17.3%	$3,201	$720
SFR	21/8/89	15/9/89	59.32	5 2.27	62.0	57.0	0.15	0.21	$1,061	59.26	0.00	0.00	25.5%	$4,262	$1,061
SFR	18/9/89	20/10/89	59.26	5 2.27	62.0	57.0	0.15	0.18	$1,007	61.45	-0.55	0.00	64.5%	$6,948	$2,686
SFR	23/10/89	17/11/89	61.45	5 2.27	64.0	59.0	0.17	0.10	$834	61.23	0.00	0.00	20.0%	$7,782	$834
SFR	20/11/89	15/12/89	61.23	5 2.27	64.0	59.0	0.13	0.06	$598	63.94	-0.06	0.00	18.9%	$8,568	$786
SFR	18/12/89	19/1/90	63.94	5 2.27	66.0	62.0	0.31	0.11	$1,282	65.74	0.00	0.00	30.8%	$9,851	$1,282
SFR	22/1/90	16/2/90	65.74	5 2.27	68.0	63.0	0.30	0.16	$1,396	66.48	0.00	0.00	33.5%	$11,247	$1,396
SFR	20/2/90	16/3/90	66.48	5 2.27	69.0	64.0	0.32	0.05	$1,136	65.85	0.00	0.00	27.3%	$12,383	$1,136
SFR	20/3/90	20/4/90	65.85	5 2.27	67.5	63.5	0.35	0.09	$1,389	67.34	0.00	0.00	33.3%	$13,773	$1,389
SFR	24/4/90	18/5/90	67.34	5 2.27	69.0	65.0	0.08	0.07	$474	69.34	0.34	0.00	-14.4%	$13,173	($600)
SFR/	4/5/90	18/5/90	69.34	5 2.27	72.5	67.0	-0.33	0.05	($850)	71.09	0.00	0.00	-20.4%	$12,322	($850)
SFR	22/5/90	15/6/90	71.09	5 2.27	73.5	69.0	0.11	0.28	$1,140	69.73	0.00	0.00	27.4%	$13,462	$1,140
SFR	18/6/90	20/7/90	69.73	5 2.27	72.0	68.0	0.31	0.10	$1,244	71.08	0.00	0.00	29.9%	$14,706	$1,244

CUMU $14,706
FINA $64,706
ANN 27,15%

117

tive action taken) under the CPRM/PPRM columns under INIT PREMIUMS. Now our bottom line is much better than before:

A cumulative profit of $14,706

A final capital of $64,706

An annualized return of $27.15%

More than 3 times better than 1990 yields on high grade US$ corporate bonds.

How about Canadian Dollar Option Short Spreads over the long haul? Table 6.8, covering the period July 89 to July 90, provides the disappointing answer to this question. It became obvious to me in generating this table that Canadian dollar options are just too thinly traded to allow safe short spreads to be executed. The lack of trading volume also would prevent you from executing protective strategies for the threatened puts and calls. My conclusion is CAN$ options should not be used for short spreads. Of course, if the open interest picks up in the future, then CAN$ options may become a good vehicle for short spreads.

The Deutsche Mark Currency Option Short Spreads Appear Attractive, as may be seen by examining Table 6.9, which shows DM short spreads for the 13 months July 89 - July 90. The bottom line is: a cumulative profit of $11,293 and a respectable annual return of 20.85%. Only one protective action was required, in December 1989, and one slight overshoot of the call occurred in May 1990. The large trading volume and open interest of the DM options allowed safe short spreads to be executed each month — you'll notice these are *very few blanks in the option tables.*

Figure 6.10 shows you the healthy growth in cumulative profits for the DM and SF short spreads from July 89 through July 90. The May loss in SF caused a slight setback towards the end of the time period. Occasional setbacks can be expected in all option short spread trading.

The profits for Currency Option Short Spreads are

TABLE 6.8: CAN$ CURRENCY OPTIONS USING SHORT SPREAD STRATEGY:
NO PROTECT ACTION: FEB 89 - JUL 90
INITIAL CAPITAL: $50.000
MARGIN: 30%
FILENAME: CURROPT.WKS

	EXEC DTE	EXP DTE	MKT VAL	NO. OPT	2SIG	SHRT CALL	SPRD PUT	INIT PREM CPRM	PPRM	INIT CREDIT	MKT EXP	EXP PREM CPRM	PPRM	PROFIT EXP	ANNUAL RETURN	CUM PROFIT
CURRENCY OPTIONS:																
CAN$	19/6/89	21/7/89	83.52	4	1.08	84.0	82.5	0.15	0.15	$599	84.17	0.17	0.00	$259	6.2%	$259
CAN$	26/7/89	18/8/89	84.17	4	1.08	84.5	83.0	0.10	0.00	$198	84.92	0.42	0.00	($634)	-15.2%	($374)
CAN$	21/8/89	15/9/89	84.92	4	1.08	85.0	84.0	0.39	0.00	$765	84.36	0.00	0.00	$765	18.4%	$391
CAN$	18/9/89	20/10/89	84.36	4	1.08	84.5	83.5	0.26	0.14	$790	85.16	0.66	0.00	($514)	-12.3%	($122)
CAN$	23/10/89	17/11/89	85.16	4	1.08	86.0	84.5	0.09	0.22	$607	85.49	0.00	0.00	$607	14.6%	$484
CAN$	20/11/89	15/12/89	85.49	4	1.08	86.0	84.5	0.26	0.03	$565	86.08	0.08	0.00	$409	9.8%	$894
CAN$	18/12/89	19/1/90	86.08	4	1.08	86.5	84.5	0.26	0.36	$561	84.50	0.00	0.98	$561	13.5%	$1,455
CAN$	22/1/90	16/2/90	84.50	4	1.08	84.0	82.0	0.12	0.36	$947	83.02	0.00	0.00	($986)	-23.7%	$469
CAN$	20/2/90	16/3/90	83.02	4	1.08	84.0	82.0	0.17	0.19	$723	84.68	0.68	0.00	($642)	-15.4%	($173)
CAN$	20/3/90	20/4/90	84.68	4	1.08	85.5	83.5	0.15	0.19	$657	86.25	1.25	0.00	($1,791)	-43.0%	($1,965)
CAN$	24/4/90	18/5/90	86.25	4	1.08	86.5	84.0	0.15	0.19	$669	85.05	0.00	0.45	($213)	-5.1%	($2,177)
CAN$	22/5/90	15/6/90	85.05	4	1.08	86.0	84.0	0.04	0.62	$1.293	85.33	0.00	0.00	$1,293	31.0%	($884)
CAN$	18/6/90	20/7/90	85.33	4	1.08	86.0	84.5	0.00	0.41	$801	86.70	0.00	0.00	$801	19.2%	($83)

NOTE: CAN$ OPTIONS TOO THINLY TRADED FOR SAFE SHORT SPREADS

CUM PROFIT   = ($83)
FINAL CAPIT = $49.917
ANN RETURN = -0.15%

TABLE 6.9: DEUTSCHE MARK CURRENCY OPTIONS USING SHORT SPREAD STRATEGY:
WITH PROT ACTION:JUN 89 - JUL 90   PHILADELPIA

INITIAL CAPITAL: $50.000
MARGIN: 30%

FILENAME: CURROPT.WKS

	EXEC DTE	EXP DTE	MAT VAL	NO. OPT	2SIG	SHRT CALL	SPRD PUT	INIT PREM CPRM	PPRM	INIT CREDIT	MAT EXP	EXP PREM CPRM	PPRM	PROFIT EXP	ANNUAL RETURN	CUM PROFIT
CURRENCY OPTIONS:																
DM	19/6/89	21/7/89	50.49	5	2.07	53.0	48.0	0.14	0.12	$858	52.41	0.00	0.00	$858	20.6%	$858
DM	24/7/89	18/8/89	52.41	5	2.07	54.0	50.0	0.18	0.05	$744	51.13	0.00	0.00	$744	17.9%	$1.602
DM	21/8/89	15/9/89	51.13	5	2.07	53.0	49.0	0.15	0.10	$841	51.19	0.00	0.00	$841	20.2%	$2.443
DM	18/9/89	20/10/89	51.19	5	2.07	53.0	49.0	0.24	0.15	$1.332	53.86	0.00	0.00	$1.332	32.0%	$3.775
DM	23/10/89	17/11/89	53.86	5	2.07	56.0	52.0	0.11	0.08	$632	54.27	0.00	0.00	$632	15.2%	$4.407
DM/NFA	20/11/89	15/12/89	54.27	5	2.07	56.0	52.0	0.15	0.05	$668	57.67	0.00	0.00	$668	16.0%	$5.076
DM/PRA	28/11/89	15/12/89	56.31	5	2.07	58.0	54.0	-0.65	0.48	($554)	57.67	0.00	0.00	($554)	-13.3%	$4.522
DM	18/12/89	19/1/90	57.67	5	2.07	60.0	56.0	0.16	0.12	$891	58.48	0.00	0.00	$891	21.4%	$5.967
DM	22/1/90	16/2/90	58.48	5	2.07	61.0	56.0	0.08	0.16	$766	59.10	0.00	0.00	$766	18.4%	$6.733
DM	20/2/90	16/3/90	59.10	5	2.07	61.0	57.0	0.25	0.06	$992	58.87	0.00	0.00	$992	23.8%	$7.725
DM	19/3/90	20/4/90	58.87	5	2.07	61.0	57.0	0.23	0.09	$1.046	59.26	0.00	0.00	$1.046	25.1%	$8.771
DM	24/4/90	18/5/90	59.26	5	2.07	60.5	57.0	0.10	0.07	$562	60.57	0.07	0.00	$331	7.9%	$9.101
DM	21/5/90	15/6/90	60.57	5	2.07	62.0	59.0	0.12	0.20	$1.041	59.22	0.00	0.00	$1.041	25.0%	$10.142
DM	18/6/90	20/7/90	59.22	5	2.07	61.0	57.0	0.20	0.14	$1.151	60.86	0.00	0.00	$1.151	27.0%	$11.293

NPA: NEEDS PROTECTIVE ACTION

CUM PROFIT = $11.293
FINAL CAPIT = $61.293
ANN RETURN = 20.85%

not as great as for either index options or common stock options. Nevertheless, these currency options are available for you, the option trader. The short spread strategy works well, at least for SF and DM. The premiums for the 2 sigma currency option short spreads are, of course, smaller than for index or stock options. The 13 month profits and annual returns for the best currency options are considerably less than for the best index option (OEX) or the best common stock options (IBM, UAL, Microsoft, etc.)

Special Risks of Currency Options depend on the many factors that can cause the exchange rates relative to the US Dollar to fluctuate. For example, political or economic policies of either the US government or of the country of the currency involved can cause short term fluctuations in the exchange rate that may adversely affect your option position. Some examples follow, showing how government policies or actions can cause currency exchange rate fluctuations.

The US Dollar was supported strongly by large Japanese companies during the month of March 1988 because of a unique Japanese law that required a company to report currency exchange losses in its Profit/Loss Statement if the *Yen* dropped below 126 Yen/Dollar before the end of the fiscal year ending March 31, 1988. A few days before the end of the month of March the required average exchange rate was achieved, so that reporting of the losses was no longer needed. At that point, the Japanese companies *stopped* supporting the Dollar and it dropped sharply relative to the Yen. If you had had a short spread in Yen, then your call strike price would have been threatened or exceeded by the sudden strengthening of the Yen relative to the Dollar. Protective action for the call would probably have been required.

Another example was caused by a military action by one country against another country, neither of whose currencies were involved in any of the currency options. In 1983,

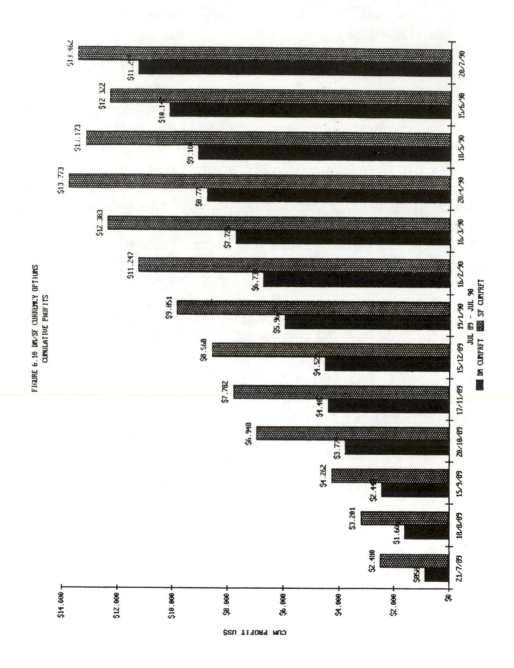

FIGURE 6.10 DM/SF CURRENCY OPTIONS
CUMULATIVE PROFITS

when the Israeli Air Force bombed the Iraqi nuclear reactor near Baghdad, the US Dollar dropped sharply relative to the DM and other European currencies. Why? It is said by the experts that traders move to the US Dollar during times of world crisis. Such news items can affect the currency markets and perhaps threaten your currency put or call position.

Government action (artificially interfering with free market forces to support their currency or to cause it to drop) is another hazard which may adversely affect your currency short spread. For example, the US government decided in the fall of 1985 that the Dollar was *too* strong and should be dropped because of the view that a fall in the US Dollar would improve the US trade deficit. Since 1985, the Dollar has dropped precipitously relative to the currencies for which options are available (and yet the US trade deficit remains high).

In March 1988, the British government became concerned about the sudden surge in strength of the Pound Sterling relative to the Dollar and the DM. The Prime Minister was concerned that the sterling strength would adversely affect British export industries. Public announcements by top UK politicians about the strength of the pound sterling affected the market, causing it to fluctuate abnormally.

Since settlement of currency options must occur in the country issuing the currency, a trader with a short currency call position that finishes *in-the-money* may have to deliver the underlying currency, through his broker, to close out his short call option. This is called *Early Assignment* and requires settlement in cash in US Dollars. Fees, taxes, or changes associated with such a forced delivery have to be born by the trader. Index options have no such problem.

Early Assignment is a problem for any short call position that ends up *in-the-money* before the expiration date. The OCC (Options Clearing Corporation) has the power to close out such a short call whether you, the option trader, want this done or not. In such an assignment case, you must — through your broker — furnish the amount of the underlying currency to the OCC within four days after assignment is taken. This action is rarely taken, but you need to be aware that it can happen.

TO SUMMARIZE: Currency options are another trading vehicle for the short spread strategy. These currency option short spreads have special problems and characteristics quite different from the other types of options. The ±2 sigma wide short spread trading results for the SF and DM depicted in Figure 6.10 show good profit potential, but less than for index or stock options. During 13 currency trading months protective action was required once each for DM and SF.

Chapter 7

Summary of Option Markets

HOW TO MINIMIZE RISKS OF OPTION SHORT SPREAD TRADING

By now I hope I have convinced you that *Option Trading* using the ±2 *sigma short spread strategy* is a safe way to multiply your capital. There are risks in short spread option trading. Sometimes the market acts wildly, like October 87, October 89, May 90, and July 90. The ±2 sigma spread width, plus at times protective action, will protect you from these wild market swings. It is important not to panic when a market move threatens your put or call position. Sometimes I think the boys and their computer programs who play the stock index futures arbitrage game try to make you panic. They want to scare you into leaving your potential profit in their money bag. To quote the Wall Street Journal, July 20-21, 1990: Traders said the buy programs focused on the Chicago Board of Trade's Major Market Index futures, a target of program trading earlier in the week as well. The MMI (the index used for XMI options), when active, has a major impact on the Dow Jones Industrials (DJIA) because it includes 17 of the average's 30 stocks.

In other words, the program traders can manipulate the market by buying or selling the 20 stocks that make up the MMI. They sell or buy billions of dollars worth in a matter of minutes, or even seconds, because their computers are connected directly to the exchanges. They don't have the time delay of going through brokers. Program trading is responsible for many of the markets' exuberant jumps and falls which typically occur during the last 30 minutes of the trading day.

To reduce your risk of loss during these manipulated and short term fluctuations, remember my golden rules:
- Wait until the market exceeds your limit for more than one day,
- Set your limit for taking protective action at:
    Put strike price minus 60% of your initial spread premium,
    Call strike price plus 60% of your ISP,
- When your limit is exceeded for more than one day:
    Buy back your threatened put or call and sell the next higher call or lower put,
    Buy back your safe put or call and sell the next higher put or lower call (if the difference is greater than 1/4),
- Don't be greedy. Don't try to squeeze your short spread position. Keep ±2 sigma or greater width.

If you follow these golden rules, your ±2 sigma option short spreads should earn you a handsome return on your capital — month after month.

WHAT ARE THE BEST OPTIONS FOR MONTH-AFTER-MONTH PROFITS?

There are really only three option markets that are suitable for long term trading if your objective is to generate a monthly income with an annual return greater than 20%. These are summarized in Table 7.1, which ranks the three types: Index Options, Stock Options, and Currency Options, in that order. For the 13 months of option trading covered in the previous examples, the S&P 100 Index Option (OEX) was the best — yielding a 65% return and a profit of $32,593 on your assumed beginning capital of $50,000. A minimum of corrective action was required, if you followed the *golden rules* set forth above.

TABLE 7.1: COMPARISON OF BEST OPTION SHORT SPREADS
INITIAL CAPITAL $50,000
13 MONTHS OF TRADING   MARGIN: 30%
FILENAME: OPTMKTS1.WKS

OPTION TYPE	OPTION	RANK	CUM PRFT	FINCAP	ANN RET
INDEX	OEX	1	$32,593	$82,593	65.19%
STOCK	IBM	2	$19,326	$69,326	33.13%
CURRENCY	DM	3	$11,293	$61,293	22.59%

The results for these three best options are displayed graphically in Figure 7.2 for the cumulative profits, annual return, and final capital for 13 months of trading.

The other three option types covered in Chapter 3 are not suitable for month-after-month trading, primarily because there are not monthly expirations for these options. I believe it is too risky to leave options open for more than one month. To summarize the problems connected with these other three options:

Commodity Futures Options do not have monthly expirations. If you wait to enter the market until one month before the option expiration date, the premiums are too low to make a reasonable profit. *Don't use.*

Precious Metal Options (Gold & Silver) have monthly expirations (except during January) but you must switch between markets to find a monthly expiration. So you lose your ability to specialize in a given market. *Don't use.*

Treasury Issue Options have quarterly, not monthly, options and the annualized return from short spreads is too low. *Don't use.*

HOW DO YOU SELECT AN OPTION SHORT SPREAD?

WHAT'S AVAILABLE AND WHAT'S BEST? This is answered by Table 7.3, which is separated into the six option types: Stock Index Options, Common Stock Options, Currency Options, Precious Metal Options, Commodity Futures Options, and Treasury Issue Options. This evaluation was made using Thursday, July 19, 1990 closing data — the day before the July option expirations. This table assumes that you have $50,000 capital to risk, that your broker requires a 30% margin for the short spreads, and that the short spread will be executed at the close on Monday, July 23, 1990, for the options expiring the third Friday of August (August 18, 1990).

The spreadsheet table shows the computed ±2 sigma short spread put and call strike prices. The initial premiums were taken using the Thursday, July 19, 1990, option table data for the call and put strike prices. The initial credit was reduced by a linear correction factor for the expected decrease in premiums for the four day delay between Thursday's evaluation and Monday's execution.

The table also computes the expected spread market values for a +2 sigma and -2 sigma change in the underlying market at expiration. For example:

OEX Market Value = 345.32

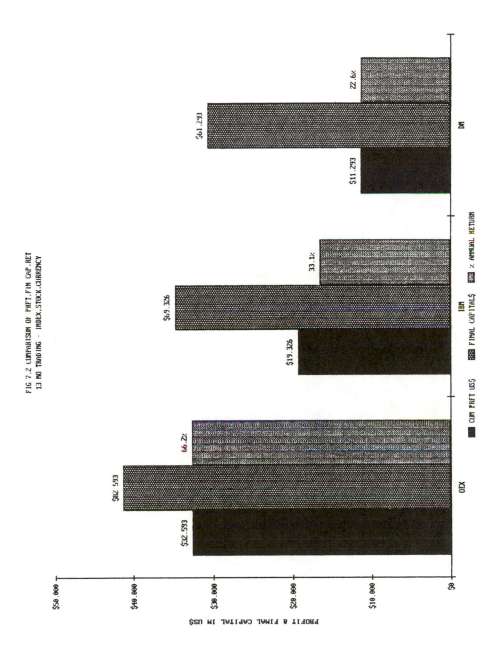

FIG 7.2 COMPARISON OF PROFIT,FIN CAP.RET
13 MO TRADING - INDEX,STOCK,CURRENCY

TABLE 7.3 OPTIONS EVALUATION FOR AUGUST 90 SHORT SPREADS:
WHAT'S AVAILABLE & WHAT'S BEST?   DJIA =2961
    INITIAL CAPITAL:$50,000
         MARGIN: 30.00%
    EVALUATION DATE:19/7/90
    NO. DAYS TIL EXP   30
FILENAME: OPTIEMKTS1.WKS

EXEC EXPIR	MKT V	NO. OPT	2SIG	SHRT CALL	SPRD PUT	INIT CPRM	PREMII PPRM	INIT CREDIT	MAT V PROFIT +2SIG	MAT V PROFIT +2SIG	MAT V PROFIT -2SIG	MAT V PROFIT -2SIG	ANNUAL RETURN

STOCK INDEX OPTIONS:

OEX	23/7/90 18/8/90	345.32	5	9.72	355	335	2.00	2.75	$1.987	0.04	$1.988	0.00	$1.987	47.7%
NYA	23/7/90 18/8/90	197.20	8	5.81	200.0	192.5	2.75	1.50	$3.113	3.01	$588	1.11	$2.175	74.2%
XMI	23/7/90 18/8/90	595.88	3	18.43	615	575	4.50	3.50	$1.939	0.00	$1.939	0.00	$1.939	46.5%

COMMON STOCK OPTIONS:

UAL	23/7/90 18/8/90	161.125	10	10.49	170	150	4.00	3.75	$6.948	1.62	$5.277	0.00	$6.948	166.7%
IBM	23/7/90 18/8/90	117.625	14	4.70	120	115	2.19	0.94	$3.830	2.33	$543	2.08	$897	92.1%
MSFT	23/7/90 18/8/90	75.250	22	6.29	85	65	1.00	0.75	$3.359	0.00	$3.359	0.00	$3.359	80.6%
APPLE	23/7/90 18/8/90	41.500	40	9.97	50	35	0.25	0.25	$1.740	1.47	($4.160)	3.47	($12.195)	41.8%
TIME	23/7/90 18/8/90	94.875	18	9.97	105	90	1.25	0.63	$2.855	0.00	$2.855	5.10	($6.096)	68.5%
COMPAQ	23/7/90 18/8/90	60.250	28	6.29	70.0	55.0	1.13	0.81	$4.645	0.00	$4.645	1.04	$1.768	111.5%
MSFT	23/7/90 18/8/90	73.250	23	6.52	85	65	1.38	1.25	$5.176	0.00	$5.176	0.00	$5.176	124.3%
NIKE	23/7/90 18/8/90	91.500	18	6.29	100	85	1.06	6.75	$12.333	0.00	$12.333	0.00	$12.333	296.0%

CURRENCY OPTIONS:

AUS$	23/7/90 18/8/90	78.58	4	1.00	80.0	78.0	0.00	0.61	$1.121	0.00	$1.121	0.42	$230	26.9%
BR LB	23/7/90 18/8/90	181.34	3	4.00	185.0	177.5	0.63	0.79	$1.131	0.34	$819	0.16	$584	27.1%
CAN$	23/7/90 18/8/90	86.68	4	1.00	87.5	85.5	0.08	0.12	$333	0.18	($13)	0.00	$333	8.0%
DM	23/7/90 18/8/90	60.92	4	2.07	63.0	59.0	0.09	0.23	$759	0.00	$759	0.15	$510	18.-8%
YEN	23/7/90 18/8/90	67.10	4	1.50	68.5	65.5	0.28	0.08	$775	0.10	$527	0.00	$775	18.6%
SF	23/7/90 18/8/90	71.11	4	1.00	72.0	70.0	0.35	0.37	$1.463	0.11	$1.205	0.00	$1.463	35.1%

PRECIOUS METAL OPTIONS:

| GOLD | 23/7/90 18/8/90 | 362.30 | 46 | 20.00 | 380.0 | 340.0 | 1.60 | 0.90 | $997 | 2.30 | $986 | 0.00 | $997 | 23.9% |

COMMODITY FUTURES OPTIONS:

| S/B | 23/7/90 18/8/90 | 602.50 | 6 | 52.70 | 650.0 | 550.0 | 0.13 | 0.13 | $60 | 5.20 | ($1.579) | 0.20 | $5 | 1.4% |

TREASURY ISSUE OPTIONS:
NONE EXPIRING IN AUGUST

OEX MKT VAL + 2 sigma = 345.32 + 9.72 = 355.04

This exceeds the 355 strike price by 0.04.

In the table you see the MKT VAL ±2 SIG = 0.04

A similar computation shows that:

OEX MKT VAL - 2 SIG = 345.32 - 9.72 = 335.60,

This value is greater than the put strike price of 335. Therefore, the MKT VAL - 2 SIG = 0

From these ±2 sigma market values the profits for a +2 sigma and -2 sigma change at expiration in the market value are given under the columns marked PROFIT/+2SIG and PROFIT/-2SIG. The annual return is computed based upon the INITIAL CREDIT column, rather than the profit after a + or - 2 sigma change, since we don't know how the August market ended.

THE BEST STOCK INDEX OPTION was the OEX, since your profit potential for a ±2 sigma fluctuation in the OEX is $1968, greater than for the NYA or XMI. I avoid using NYA index options because they are too thinly traded (open interest is too low). The XMI, as pointed out in the *Wall Street Journal* quotation earlier, is subject to manipulation by the futures arbitrage program traders, so that raises the risk in XMI trading. Table 7.4 summarizes the evaluation of the OEX for August 1990 short spreads. I use a form like this for my monthly decision making. If I wished to consider a wider or narrow spread, I would use the same type of form, so I could compare the profit and risk alternatives side-by-side.

FIGURE 7.4: EVALUATE OPTION SPREAD:
S&P 100 OPTION INDEX. OE
Today's DATE: 19/7/90

2 SIG = 9.72	OEX =	345.32	DJIA = 2961.14	
	CALL SAFE for OEX =	355.04	PUT SAFE for OEX =	335.60
	for DJIA =	3044.49	for DJIA =	2878
MRKT DATA DATE: 20/7/90	EXEC DTE: 23/7/90		NO. DAYS:	3

OPTION EXPIRATION DATE: 18/8/90   NO. DAYS TIL EXPIR: 26

	OPTION MONTH:	8/90	NO SPRDS:	5
CALL = 355	CALL MKT VALUE = 2.0000		CALL MARGIN =	-0.04
PUT = 335	PUT MKT VALUE = 2.7500		PUT MARGIN =	0.60

INITIAL CREDIT = $1,987
PRFT FOR +2SIG = $1,968
PRFT FOR -2SIG = $1,987

THE BEST COMMON STOCK OPTION for August 1990 appeared to be NIKE, but I shied away from using this stock option because it had been very volatile relative to its 2 sigma value in recent months. The next best common stock option was UAL, but recent newspaper articles revealed the deadline for an on-again-off-again employee buy-out was August 9, 1990, which might cause unpredictable fluctuations. **Too risky.**

The best stock option for August 90 was MICROSOFT, which is traded on both the AMEX and PACEX option exchanges. I would have used the PACEX because here MSFT (Microsoft) had a wider selection of strike prices than AMEX. The MSFT spread C85/P65 was wider than ±2 sigma, because the August option month has historically been a volatile month. You may remember that the DJ fell over 100 points on July 23, 1990, the first day of the August option month, but recovered for a net drop of 57 points. Pretty wild! The Evaluation Sheet for the MSFT option spread, presented in Table 7.5, shows a predicted $5176 profit for August for a healthy annual return of 124%.

**FIGURE 7.5: EVALUATE OPTION SPREAD:
MICROSFT STCK OPTION, MS**
Today's DATE: 19/7/90

2 SIG = 6.52	MSFT =	73.25	DJIA = 2961.14	
CALL SAFE for MSFT =		79.77	PUT SAFE for MSFT =	66.73
for DJIA =		3224.71	for DJIA =	2698
MRKT DATA DATE: 20/7/90 EXEC DTE: 23/7/90			NO. DAYS:	3

OPTION EXPIRATION DATE: 18/8/90   NO. DAYS TIL EXPIR: 26

	OPTION MONTH:	8/90	NO SPRDS:	23
CALL = 85	CALL MKT VALUE = 1.3750		CALL MARGIN =	5.23
PUT = 65	PUT MKT VALUE = 1.2500		PUT MARGIN =	1.73

INITIAL CREDIT = $5,176
PRFT FOR +2SIG = $5,176
PRFT FOR -2SIG = $5,176

The biggest risk in common stock options is that some event may trigger a big drop (or rise) in the stock price that wouldn't be seen in the broader markets like OEX. You need to know the history of the stock option you're considering using. The sudden huge jump in UAL stock in August 1989 made protective action impossible. If you had been holding UAL short spreads you would have lost a huge pile of money. In the raging bull market that took-off in May 1990, if one *stock* in a high technology group reported low earnings, the short term traders sold off *all* the stocks in that group — causing their values to be pounded down.

If you want to take a one month risk and make a big one-month profit, you might try one of the stock options with big premiums like MSFT. **But remember,** you could lose disastrously, like UAL stock option **short spreads** did in August and October 1989. Once again, I believe that for *month-after-month profits, you should use stock index options.* Index options spread your risk over a large number of stocks. Then you only have to worry about overall market trends, not the fluctuations of individual stocks.

THE BEST CURRENCY OPTION for August 1990 was Swiss Francs. The Evaluation Sheet in Table 7.6 yields a profit of $1205 for a ±2 sigma change in the SF exchange rate, giving a respectable return of over 30%. Currency option spreads characteristically have lower yields than either index or stock option spreads. But if you want to specialize in currency options, you can probably earn about 20% per annum on your capital.

FIGURE 7.6: EVALUATE OPTION SPREAD: SF CURRENCY OPTION, SF

Today's DATE: 19/7/90

2 SIG = 1.00	SF =	71.11	DJIA = 2961.00	
CALL SAFE for SF =		72.11	PUT SAFE for SF =	70.11
for DJIA =		3002.64	for DJIA =	2919
MRKT DATA DATE: 20/7/90 EXEC DTE: 23/7/90			NO. DAYS:	3

OPTION EXPIRATION DATE: 18/8/90   NO. DAYS TIL EXPIR: 26

	OPTION MONTH:	8/90	NO SPRDS:	4
CALL = 72	CALL MKT VALUE = 0.3500		CALL MARGIN =	-0.11
PUT = 70	PUT MKT VALUE = 0.3700		PUT MARGIN =	0.11

INITIAL CREDIT = $1,463
PRFT FOR +2SIG = $1,205
PRFT FOR -2SIG = $1,463

THE ONLY PRECIOUS METAL OPTION available for August 1990 was gold (EOE). Table 7.7 evaluates gold (EOE) short spreads. *I wouldn't touch this option* because the EOE trading volume and open interest are too small. For example, on Thursday, July 19, 1990, only 10 options were traded. Your 46 short spreads would be almost 5 times the Thursday trading volume! Your trade would impact the market adversely. Too risky.

FIGURE 7.7:   EVALUATE OPTION SPREAD: GOLD OPTION, EOI
Today's DATE: 19/7/90

2 SIG = 20.00	GOLD = 362.30	DJIA = 2961.00
	CALL SAFE for GOLD = 382.30	PUT SAFE for GOLD = 342.30
	for DJIA = 3124.46	for DJIA = 2798
MRKT DATA DATE: 20/7/90 EXEC DTE: 23/7/90		NO. DAYS: 3

OPTION EXPIRATION DATE: 18/8/90   NO. DAYS TIL EXPIR: 26

	OPTION MONTH: 8/90	NO SPRDS: 46
CALL = 380	CALL MKT VALUE = 1.6000	CALL MARGIN = -2.30
PUT = 335	PUT MKT VALUE = 0.9000	PUT MARGIN = 2.30

INITIAL CREDIT = $997
PRFT FOR +2SIG = $986
PRFT FOR -2SIG = $997

Figure 7.8 compares graphically the profits and annual returns for those short spreads with a return greater than 20% for August 1990. As previously pointed out, the only commodity futures option with an August expiration was *soybeans* and the profit potential was too low to execute a short spread. The gold (EOE) short spread would be too risky to execute because of the very low trading volume and open interest.

IN SUMMARY

As you may see, common stock options are potentially the most profitable, but the risks for individual stock options are greater than for the stock index options. For stock index options you never have to worry about taking delivery or furnishing the underlying financial instrument at option expiration. All transactions are settled in cash. This avoids embarrassing and costly problems should your index option finish in-the-money or should you suffer an early assign-

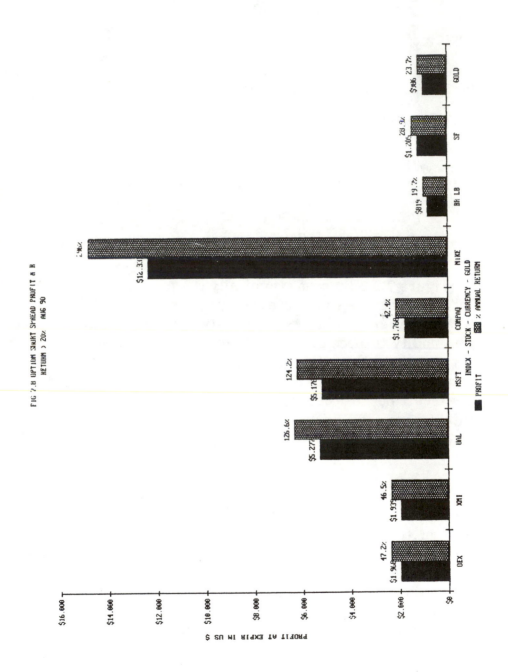

FIG 7.8 OPTION SHORT SPREAD PROFIT & R
RETURN > 20% AUG 90

ment. However, if you feel adventurous, you may select one of the high profit stock option spreads like Microsoft to augment your annual profit and capital return—from time-to-time. Currency options have less profit potential than either stock or stock index options. Gold and silver options require shifting from one option to another to find monthly expirations, and are too thinly traded. Neither commodity futures options nor Treasury Issue options have monthly expirations. Besides, the profit potential is too low for Treasury Issue option short spreads.

I recommend the use of Index Options as your best trading vehicle. The S&P 100 (OEX) is clearly the best index option to use for reasons already explained.

PART 3

MODELING OPTION MARKET PRICES FOR STOCK INDEX OPTIONS

Chapter 8

Option Premium Valuation Model (OPVAM)

In this chapter, I will develop a mathematical model which predicts option premiums for stock index options, stock options, and currency options as a function of the strike price. The model is called OPVAM (Option Premium Valuation Model). OPVAM predicts, with reasonable accuracy, the *out-of-the-money* put and call premiums.

OPVAM is handy for predicting the premium values when you only know the value of the option's underlying financial instrument — the OEX index, stock price, currency exchange rate, etc. By using a spreadsheet model or a BASIC program, the out-of-the-money strike prices are predicted with reasonable accuracy if you don't have the actual market values. It is particularly useful for predicting the value of your short spread when you only know the underlying market value.

The generic form of this mathematical model is:

Option Premium Value = $K_0 t e^{-K|M-SP|/2\sigma(30)}$

where K_0, K_1 = coefficients, usually valid for at least one month

t = time in days until option expiration

M = market value of option

SP = strike price of put or call

$\sigma(30)$ = the 30 day standard deviation (sigma) for the option

K_0 and K_1 have different values for the put and call options. These coefficients can be determined simply, by a graphical technique using the put and call premiums from a given day for which you have the data. Then the model can be used later to estimate the put and call premium values on particular days of the month, given the market values for the index, stock, or currency option for that day. I will show you how to compute the model parameters and how to use them. But first, I will present you a classical option valuation model.

BLACK-SCHOLES OPTION VALUATION MODEL

This model was first published in 1973 and is intended to compute the option price as a function of the market price of the stock or stock index, the strike price of the put or call, the market volatility as measured by the standard deviation (s), interest rates, and the time until expiration. The Black-Scholes model is given by:

Theoretical option price = $Me^{-d_1^2} - SPe^{-rt/365}e^{-d_2^2}$

$$\text{where } d_1 = \frac{\ln \dfrac{M}{SP} + (r + \dfrac{\sigma^2}{2}) \; \dfrac{t}{365}}{\sigma \, (t/365)^{1/2}}$$

$$d_2 = d_1 - \sigma \, (t/365)^{1/2}$$

t	=	number of days until option expires
M	=	market price of option index
SP	=	strike price of put or call
r	=	prime interest rate
σ	=	standard deviation for t
ln	=	natural logarithm

I used this model to predict the value of the NYA put at strike price 140 (P140) and call at strike price 155 (C155) on Friday, March 25, 1988, for April 1988 options. On this day:

t	=	21 days
r	=	6 1/4% = .0625
M	=	146.58

The model predicted that

P140	=	3 1/4
C155	=	12

The model proved to be very inaccurate, since the *Wall Street Journal* tables showed P140 = 2 1/8; C155 = 1/2 for that date.

It is apparent from this one example that a more accurate model is needed.

RATIONALE FOR THE OPVAM

I developed the OPVAM (Option Premium VAluation Model) to predict the strike price premiums when I only know the market value of the index, stock, or currency. This allows me to predict the Initial Credit of a future OEX spread when, for example, I only know the market value for the OEX. The OPVAM Model includes the following factors that affect the option premium prices:

Difference between Strike Price and Market Price: The premiums for the put and call options decrease based on a decaying exponential, as the *out-of-the-money* distance of the strike price from the market price increases.

Time to Expiration: The premium diminishes almost linearly as the time to expiration runs out. This effect is modeled by multiplying the premium value by the number of days until expiration.

Market Sentiment: The OPVAM uses different parameters for puts and calls to account for the difference between the put and call premiums for the same distance from the market price — caused by market sentiment. Put premiums are higher than call premiums for a bearish sentiment. For a bullish sentiment, call premiums are higher then put premiums.

Market Volatility: The premiums are greater during times of increased market volatility and vice versa. The market volatility effect is included in the model parameters K_0 and K_1.

Interest Rate: There is a small effect of the long US bond interest rates on the value of option premiums. The OPVAM model includes any interest rate impact in the values of the coefficients of the model, rather than having an explicit expression for interest rates such as is included in the Black-Scholes model.

OPVAM FOR INDEX OPTIONS, OEX

Originally, I developed the OPVAM model by plotting the put and call premiums versus the absolute value of the difference between the market value **M** of the NYA index option and the strike price **SP** for the *out-of-the-money* puts and calls. These plots, or curves, were made to determine the coefficients of OPVAM. It became apparent, when examining the plots for the puts and the calls, that the premium values decreased exponentially from the strike price nearest to the market value to the strike prices further away (higher for calls and lower for puts). Table 8.1 is a spreadsheet that presents the put and call premiums for the August 90 OEX options as a function of strike price for July 20, 1990. The premiums for the calls were from SP345 to SP365; the puts were from SP300 to SP345 — the out-of-the-money values. The in-the-money premiums were arbitrarily set to zero, since they are not of interest in short spread option trading. The absolute value of the difference between the strike price and the OEX, ABS/SP - OEX column, were calculated by the spreadsheet. Next the call and put premiums were tabulated for ABS/SP-OEX from 0 to 25, carefully including the 2 sigma value of 9.72 as one value. These last three columns are plotted in Figure 8.2, to be used for computing the OPVAM parameters K_{0c}, K_{1c}, K_{0p} and K_{1p}. You may observe from the shape of the put and call curves that they do decay exponentially, thus confirming the form of the OPVAM model.

TABLE 8.1: AUGUST 90 PREMIUM DATA FOR OPVAM MODEL

EVALUATION DATE: 20/7/90 FILENOPTMODEL
EXPIRATION DATE: 18/8/90

NDTE, t = 29   KOC = 0.2123 K1C = 1.1301

OEX = 345.33 2 SIG = 9.72 KOP = 0.1814 K1P = 0.6156

OEX	SK PR	CPRM	PPRM	ABS SP-OX	ABS SP-OX	CPRM	PPRM	OPVAM CPRM	OPVAM PPRM
OEX PUT	300	0.00	0.50	45.33	0.00	6.16	5.26	0.00	0.25
OEX PUT	305	0.00	0.50	40.33	5.00	3.52	3.68	0.00	0.38
OEX PUT	310	0.00	0.56	35.33	9.72	1.99	2.84	0.00	0.50
OEX PUT	315	0.00	1.00	30.33	15.00	0.90	2.04	0.00	0.75
OEX PUT	320	0.00	1.25	25.33	20.00	0.41	1.45	0.00	1.00
OEX PUT	325	0.00	1.44	20.33	25.00		1.27	0.00	1.44
OEX PUT	330	0.00	2.00	15.33				0.00	1.94
OEX PUT	335	0.00	2.75	10.33				0.00	2.69
OEX PUT	340	0.00	3.63	5.33				0.00	3.75
OEX P/C	345	6.00	5.38	0.33				5.88	5.13
OEX CALL	350	3.63	0.00	4.67				3.56	0.00
OEX CALL	355	2.00	0.00	9.67				2.00	0.00
OEX CALL	360	0.94	0.00	14.67				1.06	0.00
OEX CALL	365	0.44	0.00	19.67				0.63	0.00

The coefficient K_{ot} is the intersection of the y-axis, the premium value for $|SP-M| = 0$, since $e^0 = 1$.

K_{oct} = 6.1250

t   = 29 days

K_{oc} = 6.1250/29 = 0.2123

Similarly, Kop can be computed:

K_{opt} = 5.2630

The coefficient $K1$ is determined form the value for which $|M-SP| = 2\sigma = 9.72$.

for the call: $|M-SP| (2\sigma) = 2.0371$

for the put: $|M-SP| (2\sigma) = 0.9045$

Using numbers shown on Figure 8.2 for an x-axis value of 9.72, it can be easily shown that:

$K1$ = -ln $|M-SP|/K_{ot}$

where ln is the natural logarithm

Using the above equation the coefficients $K1c$ and $K1p$ can be computed as:

K_{1C} = -ln 2.0371/6.1250 = 1.1301 and

K_{1P} = -ln 0.9045/5.2630 = 0.6156, the numbers, of course, obtained from Figure 8.2

HOW WELL DOES OPVAM PREDICT PREMIUM VALUES?

The answer, depicted in Figure 8.3, is fairly well. The put premiums are to the left of Strike Price 345 and the call premiums are to the right. The Actual Put Premiums (ACT PPRM) are compared with the OPVAM Put Premiums (OPVAM PPRM) at the left and the Actual Call Premiums (ACT CPRM) are compared with the OPVAM Call Premiums (OPVAM CPRM) on the right. You can see that OPVAM predicts the actual premiums quite well on this one day — July 20, 1990. Later, we will see how well OPVAM predicts the premiums for the complete option month.

HOW TO USE OPVAM TO GENERATE OPTION PREMIUMS is displayed graphically in Figure 8.4, a bar graph showing the premiums above each bar. A spreadsheet (similar to that of Table 8.1) was used to generate the out-of-the-money PUT/CALL premiums for the OEX strike prices from 300 to 365. This is shown in Figure 8.4, based upon an estimated value of 342.14 for OEX for July 25, 1990. This example shows how you may use OPVAM to generate an option table or chart when all you know is the value of the OEX on that date. For example, a spread of call 355 and put 330 would have OPVAM estimated premiums of 1.125 and 2.000, respectively. (Later, I found out that on July 25, 1990, C355 and P330 had actual premiums of 0.75 and 2.6875 for a total of 3.4375 compared with an OPVAM estimated total of 3.125 — not too bad). The total OPVAM predicted premium was 9% lower than actual, so you would have made more money.

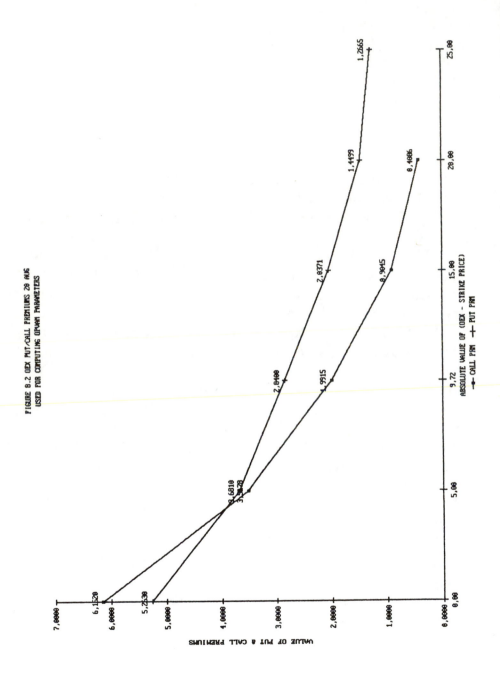

FIGURE 8.2 OEX PUT/CALL PREMIUMS 28 AUG
USED FOR COMPUTING OPXAM PARAMETERS

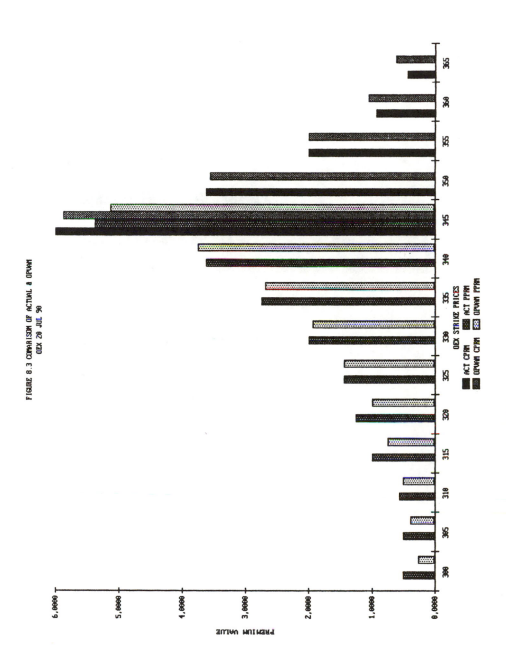

FIGURE 8.3 COMPARISON OF ACTUAL & OPVAN
OEX 20 JUL 90

The Insider's Automatic Options Strategy

149

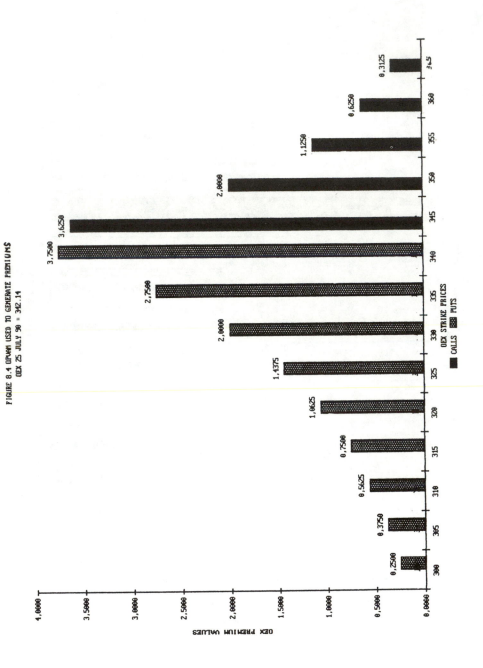

FIGURE 8.4 OPVWH USED TO GENERATE PREMIUMS
OEX 25 JULY 90 = 342.14

APPLICATION OF OPVAM FOR COMPUTING MSFT PREMIUMS is presented in Table 8.5 using the same format as the OEX Table 8.1. The OPVAM computed parameters for Microsoft Stock Options are given in the table for K_{OC}, K_{1C}, K_{OP} and K_{1P}. The Table 8.5 spread sheet computes the four OPVAM parameters for MSFT using the same generic equations used for the corresponding OEX parameters. The OPVAM generated call and put premiums are listed in the table.

TABLE 8.5: AUGUST 90 PREMIUM DATA FOR OPVAM MODE - MSFT

EVALUATION DATE: 20/7/90 FILENOPTMODEL

EXPIRATION DATE: 18/8/90

NDTE, t = 29 K_{OC} = 0.1550 K_{1C} = 0.9036

MSFT = 73.25   2 SIG = 6.29 K_{OP} = 0.1373 K_{1P} = 0.9160

MSFT	SK PR	CPRM	PPRM	ABS SP-MS	ABS SP-MS	CPRM	PPRM	OPVAM CPRM	OPVAM PPRM
MSFT PUT	65	0.00	1.25	8.25	0.00	4.49	3.98	0.00	1.13
MSFT PUT	70	0.00	2.13	3.25	1.75	3.75	3.50	0.00	2.38
MSFT P/C	75	3.75	3.50	1.75	3.25	2.13	2.13	3.38	3.00
MSFT CALL	80	1.63	0.00	6.75	6.29	1.82	1.59	1.63	0.00
MSFT CALL	85	1.38	0.00	11.75	8.25	1.55	1.25	0.75	0.00
					11.75	1.38	0.64		

The plot of MSFT premiums versus the absolute value of (MSFT - STRIKE PRICE) is presented in Figure 8.6. The actual versus OPVAM predicted premiums are displayed in the bar chart of Figure 8.7. The OPVAM model is used to predict MSFT premiums for July 25, 1990, shown in another bar chart (Figure 8.8).

I think you would agree that OPVAM does a good job of predicting premium values for MSFT common stock options.

HOW ABOUT USING OPVAM FOR CURRENCY OPTIONS?

OPVAM works equally well for currency options as shown in Table 8.9 for DM options — the same generic form as Table

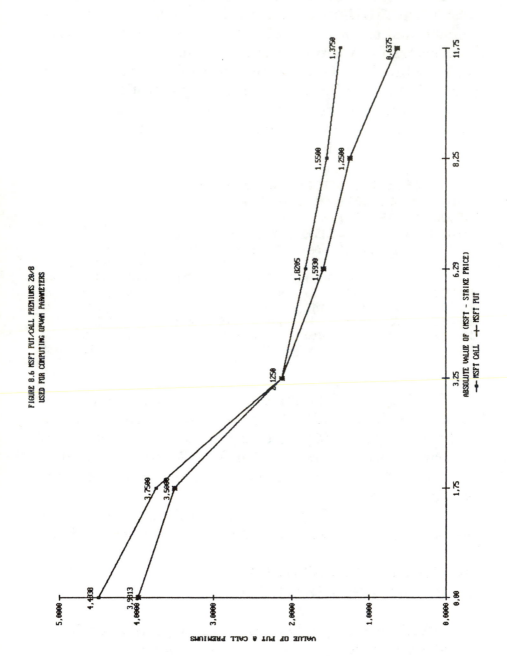

FIGURE 8.6 MSFT PUT/CALL PREMIUMS 20/8
USED FOR COMPUTING OPTION PARAMETERS

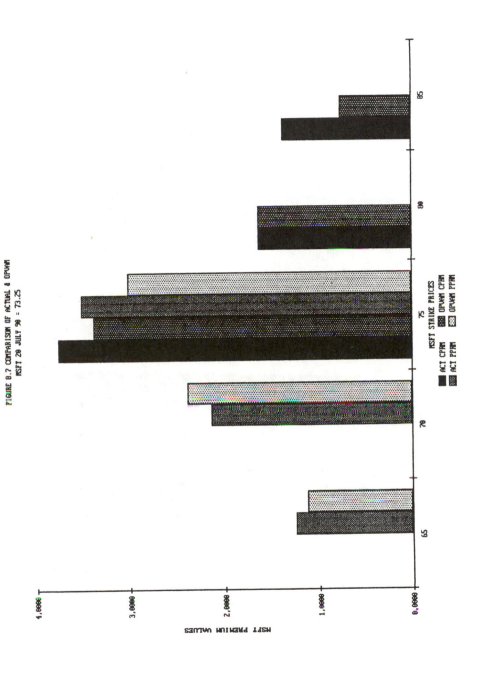

FIGURE 8.7 COMPARISON OF ACTUAL & OPWAM
MSFT 20 JULY 90 = 73.25

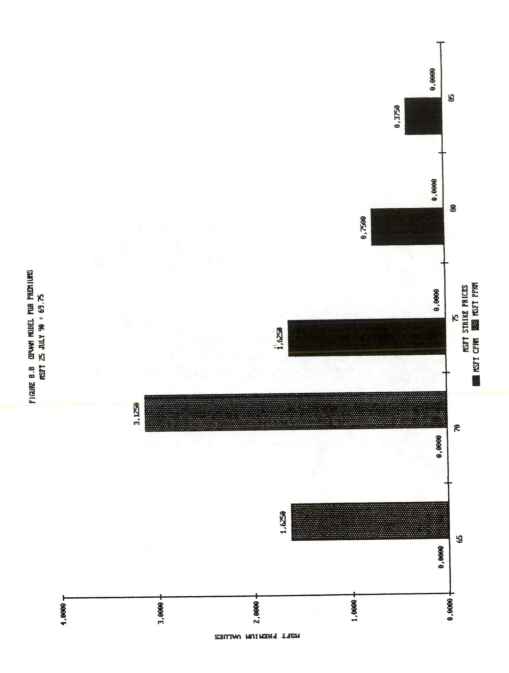

FIGURE 8.8 OPTION MODEL FOR PREMIUMS
MSFT 25 JULY 90 = 69.75

8.1 (OEX Index Options) and Table 8.5 (MSFT Common Stock Options). The table's spreadsheet computes the OPVAM parameters K_{OC}, K_{1C}, K_{OP} and K_{1P} for DM options, as well as the OPVAM put and call premiums.

TABLE 8.9: AUGUST 90 PREMIUM DATA FOR OPVAM MODEL

EVALUATION DATE: 20/7/90 FILENOPTMODEL
EXPIRATION DATE: 18/8/90

NDTE, t = 29 K_{OC} = 0.175 K_{1C} = 2.3185
DM = t = 29 K_{OC} = 0.0175 K_{1C} = 2.3185
DM = 60.96   2 SIG = 2.07 K_{OP} = 0.0184 K_{1P} = 1.8183

DM	SK PR	CPRM	PPRM	ABS SP-MS	ABS SP-MS	CPRM	PPRM	OPVAM CPRM	OPVAM PPRM
DM PUT	58	0.00	0.02	2.96	0.00	0.51	0.53	0.00	0.03
DM PUT	58.5	0.00	0.04	2.46	0.54	0.40	0.36	0.00	0.06
DM PUT	59	0.00	0.10	1.96	1.04	0.17	0.17	0.00	0.09
DM PUT	59.5	0.00	0.14	1.46	1.54	0.10	0.13	0.00	0.14
DM PUT	60	0.00	0.18	0.96	2.07	0.05	0.09	0.00	0.23
DM PUT	60.5	0.00	0.36	0.46	2.46	0.03	0.04	0.00	0.35
DM P/C	61	0.50	0.55	0.04	2.96	0.01	0.02	0.48	0.51
DM CALL	61.5	0.40	0.00	0.54				0.27	0.00
DM CALL	62	0.17	0.00	1.04				0.15	0.00
DM CALL	62.5	0.10	0.00	1.54				0.09	0.00
DM CALL	63	0.05	0.00	2.04				0.05	0.00

The plot of DM put and call premiums (DM PPRM and DM CPRM) is presented in Figure 8.10. The absolute value of (DM - STRIKE PRICE), the x-axis, at values of 2.07 (2 sigma) and zero give the figures needed to compute the OPVAM parameters for DM options. The results are given in the above table.

The comparison of the actual versus OPVAM values for DM option premiums as a function of strike price is given in Figure 8.11 — a bar graph for DM premiums on July 20, 1990, when the market value for DM was 60.96 US cents per DM. Again you may see that OPVAM predicts the premium values reasonably closely. The bar chart of Figure 8.12 predicts the DM premiums on July 27, when we knew only

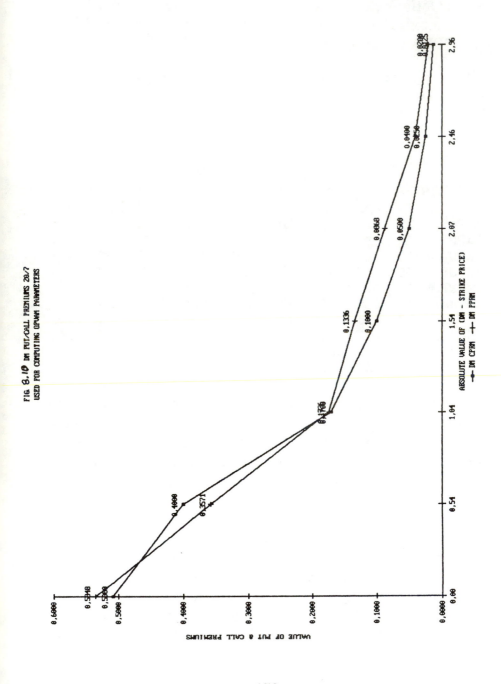

FIG 8.10 DM PUT/CALL PREMIUMS 20/7
USED FOR COMPUTING QPVAR PARAMETERS

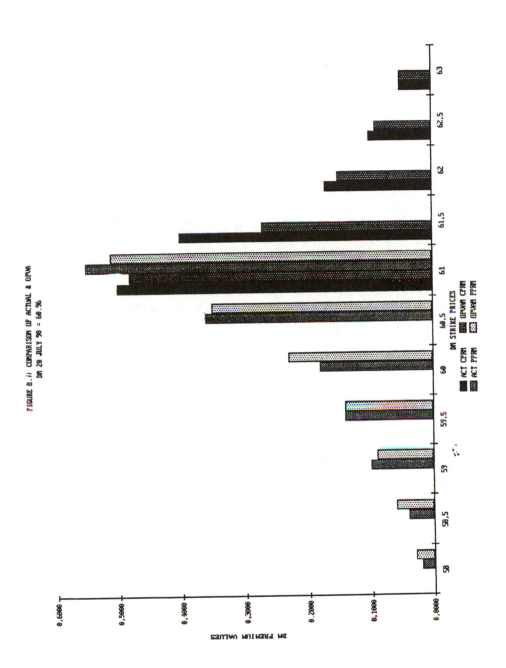

FIGURE 8.1: COMPARISON OF ACTUAL & OPVM
DM 20 JULY 90 = 60.96

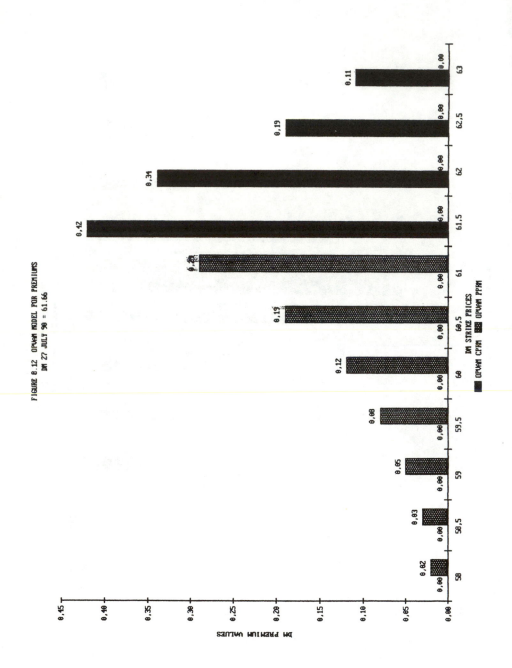

FIGURE 8.12 OPVAN MODEL FOR PREMIUMS
DM 27 JULY 90 = 61.66

the DM exchange rate (61.66 US cents per DM).

HOW WELL DOES OPVAM PREDICT THE PREMIUMS DURING A COMPLETE OPTION MONTH?

The April 1990 OEX option short spread with call strike price 335 and put strike price 310 (C335/P310) was used to answer this question. Figure 8.13 compares the actual and OPVAM computed P310 and C335 premiums as a function of the number of days until the option expiration. As you may conclude studying the chart, OPVAM does a good, but not perfect, job in predicting the premium values during a complete option month.

OPVAM does a better job of predicting the total premium (put premium + call premium), as shown in the bar chart of Figure 8.14 — again for the April 1990 OEX short spread C335/P310. For reasons unknown to me, market enthusiasm pushed the actual premiums higher than the OPVAM premiums during the first few days of the option month — and later during the middle of the option month. Otherwise, OPVAM does a credible job of predicting the inevitable decay of out-of-the-money spread premiums as the option month runs out — *the evaporation of hope.*

TO SUMMARIZE: I have developed a model for estimating the premium values for put and call options. The model is called OPVAM and has the form of a decaying exponential as a function of distance of strike price from option market price. The premium levels decay linearly with time as the option month runs out. OPVAM was shown to be valid for three types of options: the OEX index option, the MSFT stock option, and the DM currency option. OPVAM is a valuable tool for analyzing the premium values of index options when only the market value of the index is known. My OPVAM model appears to do a better job of predicting premium values than the earlier Black-Scholes model.

OPVAM can also be used to evaluate the cost of protective trading strategies when one side of a short spread is threatened, but the actual premiums are unknown. This is clearly another valuable tool in your toolbox for option trading analysis.

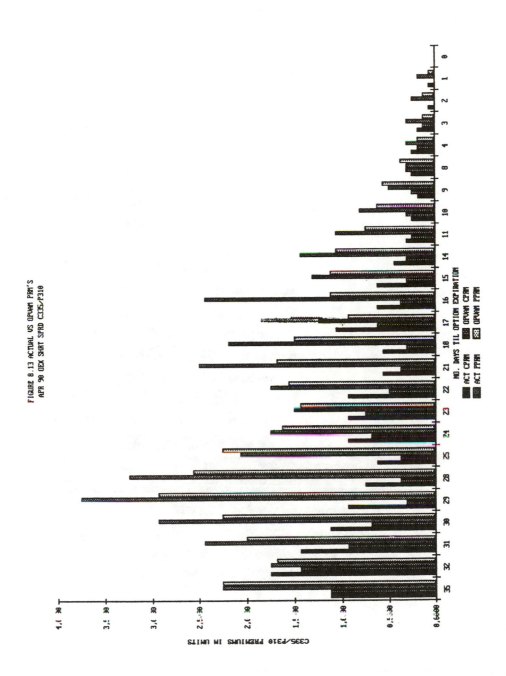

FIGURE 8.13 ACTUAL VS OPXAM PRM'S
APR 90 OEX SHRT SPRD C335/P310

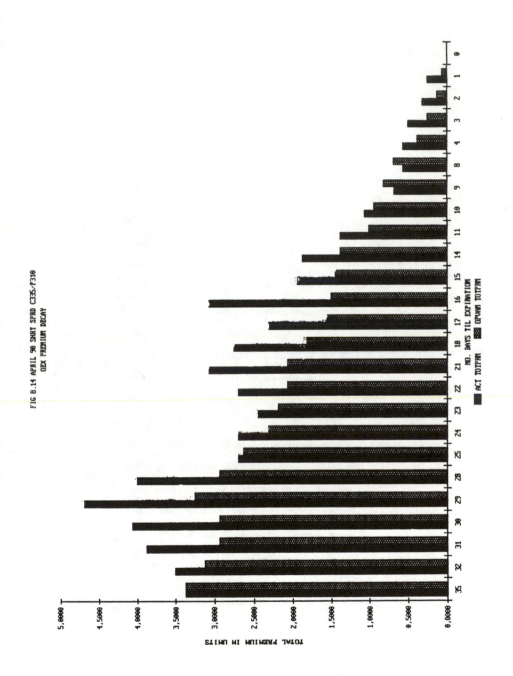

Chapter 9

Statistical Fluctuations Of Option Prices

The stock and currency markets fluctuate in a random fashion — sometimes they go up, sometimes they go down. Statisticians use the term *random walk* to describe the fluctuations of a process when it is impossible to predict at a given time which direction the process will move. We never know for sure on a given day whether the market will move up or down. Just because the market went up yesterday, doesn't mean it will go up today. Even if the market has moved up for, say, 5 days in a row, today is a new ballgame. The market is just as likely to do down as to go up.

In option trading you are most interested in predicting statistically how much the market may move up or down during the time period your short spread option position is open. Statisticians use the term standard deviation, or sigma, for measurements of variations. Option market volatility varies from time to time — meaning the statistics will change over a period of time. The sigma (σ) is a measure

163

of these statistical fluctuations. As you have learned from this book up to now: the option short spread width (difference between call strike price and put strike price) is normally ±2 sigma, rounded off to the nearest available strike price. I will show you in this chapter how to compute both the 30 day sigma and the 1 day sigma — the latter being a measure of how much the market may move in one trading day. I will also show you how to use these two sigmas to evaluate the profit potential of an open spread on a statistical basis.

I use the market value at the close on the third Friday of each month for at least 13 months as the basis for computing the 30 day sigmas, called $\sigma(30)$ or SIG (30) in the charts. The 1 day sigma, $\sigma(1)$ or SIG (1), uses at least 21 consecutive trading days from a recent trading month.

S&P 100 INDEX SIGMAS

Table 9.1 lists the numbers needed to compute the sigmas for the S&P 100 Index (OEX), using my PC spread sheet for doing all the computations.

TABLE 9.1: S&P 100 SIGMA COMPUTATIONS

OEX: 30 DAY SIGMA, SIG (30) = 5.09   JUN 89 - JUL 90
OEX: 1 DAY SIGMA, SIG (1) = 1.64   JUN 90 - JUL 90

30DA DLTA	ABS DLTA (30)	1DA DLTA	ABS DLTA (1)	SQR DLT30-M	SQR DLT1-M
-15.22	15.22	6.01	6.01	56.50	11.89
-8.79	8.79	-1.26	1.26	1.18	1.69
-0.79	0.79	-0.92	0.92	47.79	2.69
-1.31	1.31	-1.24	1.24	40.87	1.74
4.95	4.95	5.61	5.61	7.58	9.31
-8.26	8.26	2.66	2.66	0.31	0.01
8.06	8.06	0.71	0.71	0.13	3.42
7.92	7.92	-2.67	2.67	0.05	0.01
-11.25	11.25	-2.67	2.67	0.05	0.01
0.46	0.46	0.44	0.44	52.46	4.49
-14.48	14.48	-1.80	1.80	45.93	0.58
-9.66	9.66	-0.55	0.55	3.82	4.04
1.29	1.29	4.52	4.52	41.17	3.85
		-3.02	3.02		0.21
		2.60	2.60		0.00
		-0.59	0.59		3.86
30 DAY:		-4.39	4.39		3.35
MEAN. M = 7.70		-3.90	3.90		1.80
VAR. V = 25.86		-1.69	1.69		0.75
$\sigma(30) = 5.09$		-1.52	1.52		1.08
		0.36	0.36		4.83
1 DAY:		2.55	2.55		0.00
MEAN. m = 2.56		-2.78	2.78		0.05
VAR. V = 2.68		4.69	4.69		4.54
$\sigma(1) = 1.64$		2.40	2.40		0.03

The first column of the table (30 DA DLTA) lists the differences (the deltas) in the market value from one month's option expiration date to the next month's expiration. This is beginning with the 3rd Friday in June 1989 and ending with the 3rd Friday of July 1990 — 14 months or 13 deltas (Δ's). The next column computes the absolute value of the Δ's — in other words, ignores the sign of the differences. Only the magnitude of the changes is used. The third column lists the Δ's between consecutive trading days — 24 days beginning with June 15, 1990, the June 90 option expiration date, and ending on July 20, 1990, the July 90 option expiration date. The 30 day deltas, Δ (30), were used to compute the σ (30), and Δ (1)'s to compute the σ (1). The equations for computing these sigmas are:

$$m = \frac{\Sigma \Delta}{n} \qquad V = \frac{\sum\limits_{i=1}^{n} (\Delta_i - m)^2}{n} \qquad \sigma = V^{1/2}$$

where $\quad \Delta$ = difference
$\quad\quad\quad$ n = number of samples
$\quad\quad\quad$ m = arithmetic mean
$\quad\quad\quad$ V = variance
$\quad\quad\quad$ σ = standard deviation

The spread sheet of Table 9.1 performs the computations defined in the above equation for both SIG (30) and SIG (1) and the results are given in the table. The bottom line is SIG (30) = 5.09 and SIG (1) = 1.64 for OEX.

I will present similar tables for IBM stock and DM currency options and then will tabulate the sigmas in a graph.

IBM STOCK SIGMAS

Table 9.2 shows the numbers I collected in order to compute the σ (30) and σ (1) for IBM stock, and also the results of those computations.

TABLE 9. 2 IBM SIGMA COMPUTATIONS

IBM: 30 DAY SIGMA, SIG (30) = 1.86   JUNE 89 - JUL 90
IBM: 1 DAY SIGMA, SIG (1) = 1.50   APRIL 90
FILENAME: STKOPT. WKS

30 DA DLT	ABS DLT (30)	ABS DLT (1)	SQR DL30-M	SQR DL1-M
-4.875	4.875	1.19	3.54	0.11
-0.750	0.750	0.50	5.03	0.13
-0.625	0.625	0.49	5.61	0.14
				0.75
5.125	5.125	1.38	4.54	0.26
1.830	1.830	1.63	1.35	0.58
-5.000	5.000	1.00	4.03	0.02
2.750	2.750	0.63	0.06	0.06
30 DAY:				
MEAN. m =	2.99	2.38		2.28
VAR. V =	3.45	0.13		0.55
SIG (30) =	1.86	0.25		0.38
2SIG (30) =	3.72	0.50		0.13
		1.13		0.07
		1.13		0.07
1 DAY:		0.75		0.01
MEAN. m	0.86	1.25		0.15
VAR. V =	2.25	0.00		0.75
SIG (1) =	1.50	0.63		0.06
		0.88		0.00

DM CURRENCY SIGMAS

Table 9.3 presents the spread sheet and results for computing the Deutsche Mark currency sigmas using exactly the same equations as for the OEX Index (Table 9.1) and for IBM stock (Table 9.2).

TABLE 9. 3 DM SIGMA COMPUTATIONS

FILENAME: DJOEXDAT.WKS

DM: 30 DAY SIGMA, SIG (30) = 1.05   JUNE 89 - JUL 90

DM: 1 DAY SIGMA, SIG (1) = 0.71   JUNE 90 - JUL 90

30 DA DLTA	ABS DLTA (30)	ABS 30 DA DLTA	ABS DLT (1)	SQR DL30-M	SQR DL1-M
-1.97	1.97	0.00	0.00	0.17	0.11
1.29	1.29	0.00	0.00	0.07	0.11
0.24	0.24	0.00	0.00	1.75	0.11
-3.16	3.16	0.00	0.00	2.57	0.11
-0.25	0.25	0.00	0.00	1.72	0.11
-3.50	3.50	0.00	0.00	3.76	0.11
-0.01	0.01	0.00	0.00	2.40	0.11
-1.87	1.87	0.00	0.00	0.10	0.11
1.25	1.25	0.00	0.00	0.10	0.11
-0.82	0.82	0.00	0.00	0.54	0.11
-1.31	1.31	0.00	0.00	0.06	0.11
1.35	1.35	-0.55	0.55	0.04	0.05
-1.70	1.70	-2.10	2.10	0.02	3.17
30 DAY:		-0.99	0.99		0.45
MEAN, m = 1.56		1.20	1.20		0.76
VAR. V = 1.11		2.69	2.69		5.61
σ (30) = 1.05		-0.24	0.24		0.01
		0.00	0.00		0.11
		0.00	0.00		0.11
		0.00	0.00		0.11
		0.00	0.00		0.11
1 DAY:		0.00	0.00		0.11
MEAN, m = 0.32		0.00	0.00		0.11
VAR. V = 0.50		0.00	0.00		0.11
σ (1) = 0.71		0.00	0.00		0.11

INDEX OPTION SIGMAS — PRESENTED IN BAR CHART FORM

The sigmas computed for all the stock index options suitable for the short spread strategy are presented in Figure 9.4 — a bar chart with the 2 sigma values denoted numerically above the bar. The 30 day sigmas used the same time period as Table 9.1: the differences in values between option expirations from June 16, 1989 through July 20, 1990. The one day sigmas were computed using the differences between the trading days from the June 90 expiration (June 18, 1990) to the July 90 expiration (July 20, 1990). The computations were the same as the spread sheet computations of Table 9.1. The S&P 500 index option is included, as well as the OEX (S&P 100) index. Both of these S&P indices have large open interest, but the daily trading volume of the OEX is greater than for the S&P 500. The sigmas for the Dow Jones Industrial Average (DJIA) are provided for reference, even though no index option is available for it. However, as previously mentioned, the XMI includes 17 of the DJIA's 30 stocks, so the XMI is a good emulation of the DJIA and therefore tends to correlate closely with it. The ratio of about 5:1 holds between DJIA and XMI (i.e. XMI almost equals DJIA/5).

COMMON STOCK SIGMAS — PRESENTED IN BAR CHART FORM

The common stock sigmas are pictured in Figure 9.5, with the one day and 30 day 2 sigmas imprinted above the bars. The two wild months for UAL (August 1989 and October 1989) were expunged to avoid undue influence on the sigmas computed for this stock. These sigmas were usable for evaluating stock option short spreads. The same data base was used as for the index options (June 89 through July 90 for the 30 day sigmas, and the option month June 15, 1990, through July 20, 1990, for the one day sigmas). The UAL sigmas should be recomputed after the employee buyout perturbation dies out. This buyout caused major disturbances in the UAL stock price during August 89, October 90, and August 90.

These 30 day 2 sigmas are suitable for computing safe ±2 sigma short spreads (in 1990) for the 8 stocks included on the

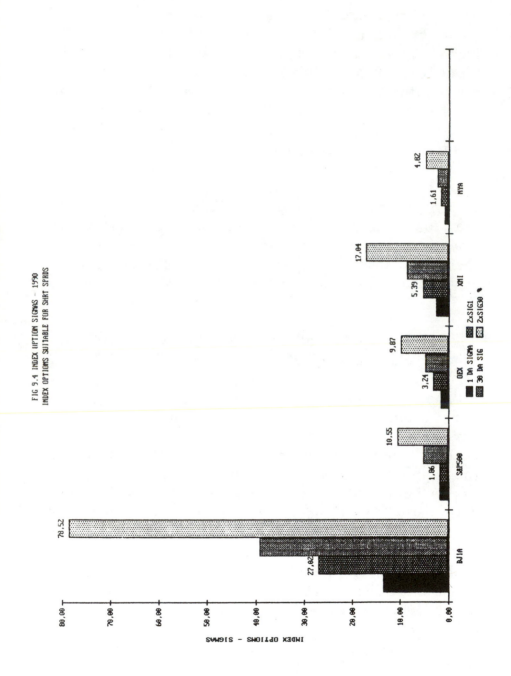

FIG 9.4 INDEX OPTION SIGNAS - 1990
INDEX OPTIONS SUITABLE FOR SHRT SPRDS

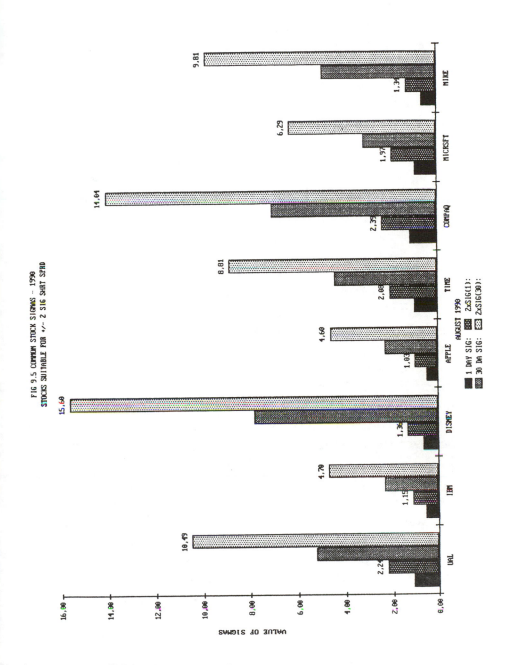

FIG 9.5 COMMON STOCK SIGMAS - 1990
STOCKS SUITABLE FOR +/- 2 SIG SHRT SPRD

AUGUST 1990

1 DAY SIG: 2xSIG(1):
30 DA SIG: 2xSIG(30):

VALUE OF SIGMAS

chart (with the UAL reservations).

CURRENCY EXCHANGE SIGMAS — PRESENTED IN BAR CHART FORM

The currency sigmas are depicted in Figure 9.6 for the six options listed on the Philadelphia currency option exchange — with the one and 30 day 2σ's printed above the corresponding bars. These sigmas used the same time period as the index and stock sigma charts. The sigmas can be used to compute safe short spreads for the currency options. Remember my warning: *if a ±2σ short spread is not available on the currency index tables, don't open a position.* **It will be unsafe.**

HOW TO USE THE SIGMA VALUES TO PROTECT YOUR PROFIT

The three charts in this section evaluate the August 1990 short spreads theoretically opened on Monday, July 23, 1990. These short spreads were defined in Table 7.4 of Chapter 7 and include index options, stock options, and currency options. The *Wall Street Journal* dated August 1, 1990, stated that the Dow Jones Industrial Average had dropped over 88.81 points, more than 2 sigma (30 day), since July 19, 1990 (the day on which the market values for Table 7.4 were used to compute the August short spreads).

The profit projections in the three charts are based on further changes above and below the market values on the evaluation date of July 31, 1990. The *center value* (NO CHNGE) is the profit (or loss) of the spread *if no further changes in market value occur.* The values on the *right* of *NO CHNGE* give the profit (or loss) for *progressive increases* in the market value of +1 sigma (1 day), +1 sigma (30 days), and finally +2 sigma (30 days). On the *left* of *NO CHNGE* the

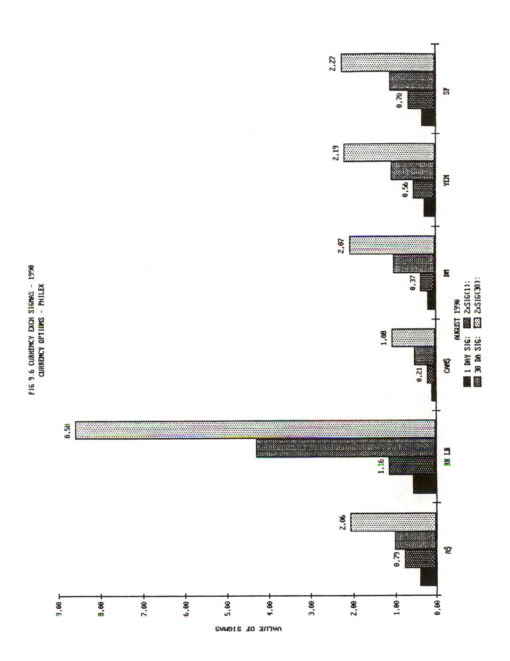

FIG 9.6 CURRENCY EXCH SIGNALS - 1990
CURRENCY OPTIONS - PHILEX

values of profit (or loss) are given for *progressive decreases in the market value of -1 sigma (1 day), -2 sigma (1 day), -1 sigma (30 days), and -2 sigma (30 days).*

If the profit is negative (a loss) for *NO CHNGE,* then a corrective action is needed.

Remember the rule: if your short spread put or call is exceeded by more than 60% of the total premium received for that short spread for more than one day, *then take corrective action:*

If the *call is threatened,* **raise** your put and call.

If the *put is threatened,* **lower** your put and call.

Index Option Short Spread Profit Projections are charted in Figure 9.7 for **no change,** ±1 sigma (1 day), ±2 sigma (1 day), ±1 sigma (30 day), and ±2 sigma (30 day). As may be seen in the graph, an additional 2 sigma (30 day) drop will cause a small loss in both OEX and XMI and a reduction in profit for NYA. This chart shows clearly that no protective action in the index short spreads is required at this time.

Stock Option Short Spread Profit Projections are depicted in Figure 9.8 for the same x-axis values as the index options chart (Figure 9.7). The most important item to notice from this chart is that *corrective action is needed for both UAL and IBM. Both stocks are currently in-the-money.* (The market dropped on this day because of rumors that the UAL employee buyout had collapsed.) Take the *Protective Action* to **lower** your spread call and put positions:

UAL market value 41

Buy back 9 C170/P150 Cost: 5/8 + 12 1/4 = 12 7/8

Sell 9 C150/P135 Credit: 5 1/4 + 7 = 12 1/4

Net change (cost) = (12 7/8 - 12 1/4) x 100 x 9 = - $562

Remaining Credit = (7288 - 562) = $6726

IBM market value 112 1/2

Buy back 13 C120/P115 Cost: 1/4 + 4 = 4 1/4

Sell 13 C115/P110 Credit: 1 + 1 1/4 = 2 1/4

Net change (cost) = (4 1/4 - 2 1/4) x 100 x 13 = -$2600

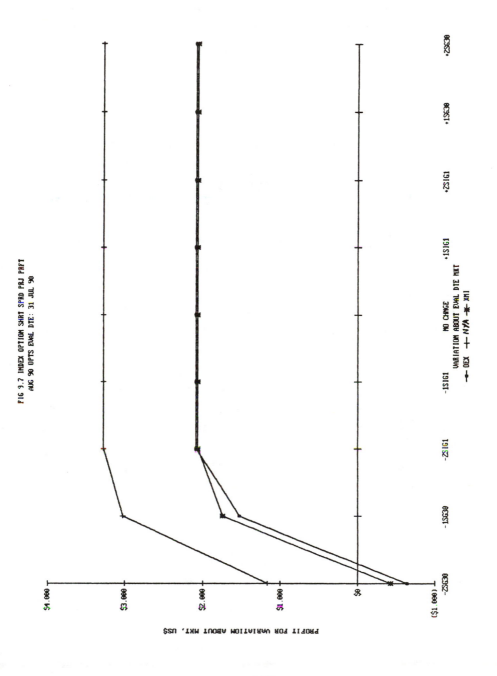

FIG 9.7 INDEX OPTION SHRT SPRD PRJ PRFT
AUG 90 OPTS EVAL DTE: 31 JUL 90

Remaining Credit = (4025 - 2600) = \$1425

You gave up some of your initial credit in making these two protective changes to your UAL and IBM short spreads, but now you have a much safer position.

The other four stocks are currently safe, but all except NIKE are projected to lose if there is an additional 2 sigma (30) drop in their market values.

Currency Option Short Spread Profit Projections are presented in Figure 9.9 for the same values as the index and stock options (Figures 9.7 & 9.8). You will note that the Swiss Franc (SF) spread is in danger because of a rise in the SF relative to the dollar. *The call is threatened* and needs protective action.

Take *Protective Action* to raise your spread put and call positions:

SF market value = 74.34

Buy back 3 C73/P69   Cost: 1.42 + 0.01 = 1.43

Sell 3 C76/P72 Credit: 0.25 + 0.07 = 0.32

Net change (cost) = (1.45 - 0.32) x 3 x 62500/100 = \$2119

Remaining Credit (loss) = (863 - 2119) = -\$1256

A significant loss, but now you have a safer spread to protect you against additional market fluctuations.

You will see from the chart that all the spreads except AUS\$ and CAN\$ will lose money for additional rises in the currencies (or a fall in the dollar). The Iraqi invasion of Kuwait the next day gave a temporary reversing boost in the fall of the dollar. This stemmed, for at least a short time, the threat to the currency calls.

So you see, in spite of our careful selection of safe short spreads for August 1990, world and market events caused some of those positions to be threatened. When your short spread is threatened **take corrective action. Don't procrastinate.**

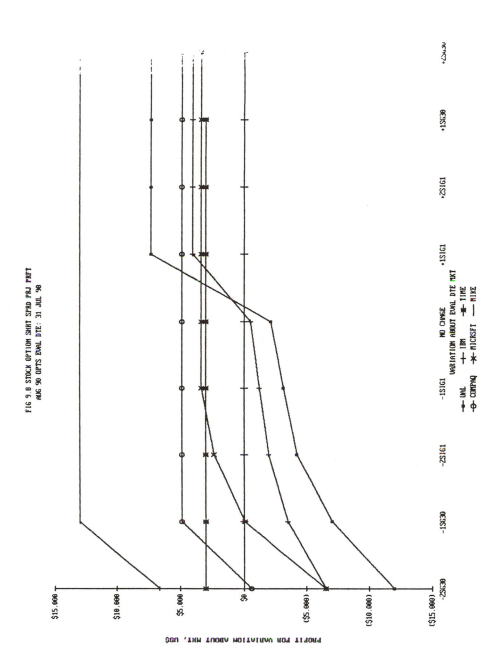

FIG 9.8 STOCK OPTION SHRT SPRD PRJ PRFT
AUG 90 OPTS EVAL DTE: 31 JUL 90

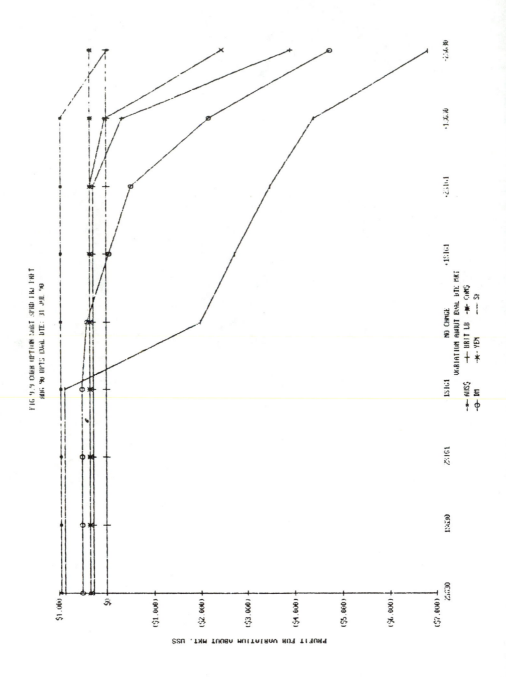

TABLE 9.10 OPTIONS EVALUATION FOR SHORT SPREAD STRATEGY:

SHORT SPREADS: +/- 2 SIGMA
INIT CAPITAL: $50,000
MARGIN: 33.00%
EVAL DATE: 31/7/90
EXPIR DATE: 17/8/90
DAYS TIL EXP: 17
FILENAME: OPTEVAL.WKS

	NO. OPTS	1 DA 2SIG	30DA 2SIG	SHRT CALL	SPRD PUT	MKT V EVL DT	INITIAL $CREDIT	-2SG30 $SSVAL	-1SG30 $SSVAL	-2SIG1 $SSVAL	-1SIG1 $SSVAL	NO CHNGE $SSVAL	+1SIG1 $SSVAL	+2SIG1 $SSVAL	+1SG30 $SSVAL	+2SG30 $SSVAL
STOCK INDEX OPTIONS:																
OEX	4	3.24	9.87	355	335	338.68	$2.084	($631)	$1.534	$2.084	$2.084	$2.084	$2.084	$2.084	$2.084	$2.084
NYA	8	1.61	4.82	200.0	192.5	194.59	$3.265	$1.168	$3.019	$3.265	$3.265	$3.265	$3.265	$3.265	$3.265	$3.265
XMI	3	5.39	17.04	615	580	587.26	$2.066	($421)	$1.746	$2.066	$2.066	$2.066	$2.066	$2.066	$2.066	$2.066
COMMON STOCK OPTIONS:																
UAL	9	2.24	10.49	170	150	140.00	$7.288	($11.980)	($7.048)	($4.222)	($3.169)	($2.116)	$7.288	$7.288	$7.288	$7.288
IBM	13	1.15	4.70	120	115	111.50	$4.025	($6.537)	($3.510)	($1.964)	($1.224)	($483)	$4.025	$4.025	$4.025	$4.025
DISNEY	12	1.36	15.60	145	115	117.63	$1.105	($14.193)	($4.996)	$1.105	$1.105	$1.105	$1.105	$1.105	$1.105	$1.105
APPLE	37	1.03	4.60	45	35	42.00	$3.651	$3.651	$3.651	$3.651	$3.651	$3.651	$3.651	$3.651	$3.651	$3.651
TIME	16	2.08	8.81	105	85	91.38	$2.994	($894)	$2.994	$2.994	$2.994	$2.994	$2.994	$2.994	$2.994	$2.994
COMPAQ	25	2.39	14.04	75	45.0	56.88	$4.872	($572)	$4.872	$4.872	$4.872	$4.872	$4.872	$4.872	$4.872	$4.872
MSFT	21	1.97	6.29	80	65	66.50	$3.361	($6.547)	($41)	$2.389	$3.361	$3.361	$3.361	$3.361	$3.361	$3.361
NIKE	17	1.34	9.81	100	80	86.00	$12.937	$6.628	$12.937	$12.937	$12.937	$12.937	$12.937	$12.937	$12.937	$12.937
CURRENCY OPTIONS:																
AUS$	4	0.79	2.06	81.0	77.0	79.44	$945	$945	$945	$945	$945	$945	$945	$945	$945	($19)
BR LB	3	1.16	8.58	190.0	172.5	186.44	$280	$280	$280	$280	$280	$280	$280	$280	($330)	($3.914)
CAN$	3	0.21	1.08	88.0	85.5	86.80	$350	$350	$350	$350	$350	$350	$350	$350	$350	$350
DM	4	0.37	2.07	63.0	59.0	63.04	$510	$510	$510	$510	$510	$410	($50)	($510)	($2.164)	($4.738)
YEN	4	0.56	2.19	69.5	65.0	68.55	$350	$350	$350	$350	$350	$350	$350	$350	$23	($2.450)
SF	3	0.70	2.27	73.0	69.0	74.34	$863	$863	$863	$863	$863	($1.992)	($2.738)	($3.484)	($4.411)	($6.829)

HOW DO YOU MAKE ALL THE COMPUTATIONS NEEDED TO EVALUATE YOUR EXISTING SHORT SPREADS?

If you have an IBM-compatible Personal Computer (PC), there is an easy way: I have developed an extensive and logically clever spreadsheet for generating the curves of Figures 9.7 through 9.9. This spreadsheet (Table 9.10) provided the data for the curves for evaluating the August short spreads discussed in this chapter. Its equations are listed in Appendix B.

TO SUMMARIZE: In this chapter you have seen my methods for computing the needed sigmas from collected market data. More importantly, I have provided three valuable reference charts, Figures 9.4, 9.5, and 9.6, which display values of one day and 30 day sigmas for index options, stock options and currency options through 1990. Examples of using the sigmas to evaluate short spreads for August 1990 are also given.

You can use these 30 day 2 sigmas to compute the safe $\pm2\sigma$ strike prices for option short spreads in these 3 option markets. You can also use the sigmas for evaluating an open short spread *within* an option month (Figures 9.7, 9.8, and 9.9).

You should update your sigmas about once per year. They do change slowly over the years. Be sure and collect the market data you will need for the updating.

The sigmas are an extremely important tool in your option trading tool kit. In the next chapter we will examine tools to make your option trading easier, a computer program and PC spread sheets.

PART 4

COMPUTER PROGRAM & PC SPREAD SHEETS FOR SAFE OPTION TRADING

Chapter 10

Option Trading Computer Program

INTRODUCTION: The examples I have presented so far could all have been made with a small and inexpensive handheld electronic calculator. The arithmetic for evaluating spreads is simple. **Making a mistake is also simple.** The OPVAM model can be used for computing stock index tables, but a more sophisticated calculator is required. I used the Hewlett Packard Model 15C, which has the necessary mathematical functions: logarithms to base 10 and base e, exponents (including e^x), square, and square root.

In short, the job of selecting the best short spreads, and of evaluating short spreads during the option month, can be done with a hand-held calculator, but it is tedious and subject to human error, **which could cost you money.** Shortly after I began to do serious short spread option trading, I wrote a computer program in the programming language BASIC to make my job of selecting the best, safe short spread easier and quicker. It now takes less than ten minutes to select the best short spread using the computer program.

One of the problems I wanted to solve with the computer program was to be able to generate estimated market values when my newspaper omitted the Option Tables — or the Option Strike Price I was interested in — on the very day I needed to use the information. If you are connected to one of the Telex or computer market information services, this would only be a problem if you wanted to predict the call or put market values in the future.

Because of this problem of lack of current put and call market information, I modified my original program so that it would generate a complete Index Option Market Table, in the format given in a newspaper such as the *Wall Street Journal.* The OPVAM model provides the mathematical tool needed to accomplish this most useful modification.

An Overview of the Computer Program, OPTEVAL is presented in Figure 10.1. Since I have concluded that the *short spread strategy* is the best and most robust strategy, the computer program is dedicated to this strategy. It is set up so you can select the best new short spread and then evaluate the existing short spread during the option month. The program also uses OPVAM to generate option tables or to generate individual put and call market values needed in an evaluation, when appropriate. The program is an **Interactive Program** in that it asks the user to input information needed.

The Main Menu is shown in the figure. For Main Menu selections 1 and 3 the computer screen asks you to select the desired index option (the UAL common stock option is also included). The three index options are the *NYSE Index (NYA), the S&P 100 Index (OEX), and the AMEX Major Market Index (XMI).*

If you have the market data for the day you wish to *execute* your options, then you can go directly to Menu

FIGURE 10.1 OPTEVAL OVERVIEW

INDEX OPTIONS SHORT SPREAD EVALUATION

```
     +--------------+      +------------+      +------------+      +----------+
     |MENU 1        |      |SELECT      |      |COMPUTE     |      |PRINT     |
     |1.NEW SPREAD  | 1    |INDEX OPTION| 1    |SPREAD VALUE|      |EVALUATION|
RUN→|2.OLD SPREAD   |---→|1.NYA        |--→|1.AT OPEN     |--→|RESULTS    |
     |3.OPTION TABLE| 2    |2.OEX       |      |2.AT EXPIR- |      |FOR NEW   |
     |              |--+   |3.XMI       |      |   ATION    |      |SPREAD    |
     |              | 3|   |4.UAL STOCK | 3    |            |      |          |
     |              |---→|              |-+   |            |      |          |
     +--------------+  |  +------------+  |  +------------+      +----------+
                       ↓                  ↓
                       |                  |
                  +-+------+--------+
                  | |
                  | |
                  | |  +------------+      +------------+      +----------+
                  | |  |EVALUATE    |      |IF SPREAD   |      |PRINT     |
                  | +→|EXISTING     |--→|THREATENED,    |--→|EVALUATION|
                  |    |SPREAD AT   |      |EVALUATE    |      |RESULTS   |
                  |    |EXPIRATION  |      |COST OF     |      |FOR OLD   |
                  |    |            |      |PROTECTION  |      |SPREAD    |
                  |    +------------+      +------------+      +----------+
                  ↓
                  |
                  |
                  |
                  |    +------------+      +------------+      +----------+
                  |    |USE OPVAM   |      |USE OPVAM   |      |PRINT     |
                  +--→|TO GENERATE  |--→|TO GENERATE  |--→|OPTION    |
                       |PUT MARKET  |      |CALL MARKET |      |TABLES    |
                       |VALUES(PMKT)|      |VALUES(CMKT)|      |          |
                       +------------+      +------------+      +----------+
```

TOP LEVEL MENU

Main Menu for INDEX OPTION SHORT SPREAD EVALUATION

1. Evaluate New Short Spread
2. Evaluate Existing Short Spread
3. Generate INDEX OPTION Market Table
4. END EVALUATION, Leave Program
Select 1 through 4 and push intro

selection 1 to evaluate the best short spread to open. The program allows you to use slightly stale market data — up to three days old.

The program prompts you to enter the current value of your selected index, or the Dow Jones Industrial Average, in which case the index is estimated from the DJIA. The program computes the SAFE 2 SIGMA put and call strike prices, and then asks you to enter the put and call market prices. This is a conservative spread with positive margins; i.e., greater than ±2 sigma wide.

The program then allows you to interactively evaluate other positions which are riskier but which give higher initial profit. In just a few minutes you can evaluate the three or four sensible spreads available at the time and then select the one you wish to execute. The program will print out each of your evaluations on the line printer so you can have the copy in front of you when you call your broker.

Main Menu Selection 2 allows you to evaluate your **existing short spread** as the option month progresses. *It is important* to use this feature during the month, particularly if there is a sharp market rise threatening your short call or a sharp market drop threatening your short put. The information concerning your option is stored in a data file. This data file must be updated any time you change your short spread position — at the beginning of the option month or when you make a protective change to your existing spread.

The evaluation of the existing spread only requires the input of the date and the current index market value (or the DJIA, if you don't have the index value). The program uses OPVAM to evaluate (1) the current value of the spread, (2) the amount of profit (or loss) if you close out the spread on the day of the evaluation, and (3) the value of the spread for a ±2 sigma change in the index value at expiration.

The existing spread evaluation provides another important feature. If the index value gets close to either your call or put position, then the program:

(1) tells you what protective action to take including the strike prices to buy and sell, and

(2) tells you the net cost of the protective action.

The periodic evaluation and the taking of any required *protective action* are absolutely mandatory for safe short spread trading. Remember, take the required protective action. Don't procrastinate.

The program gives you the option of *printing out* the evaluation of the existing spread, including any required protective action.

Another important use for the Menu 2 program is the ability to *simulate* what may happen to your existing spread in the future, should the DJIA rise or fall to a given level. To employ this powerful simulation feature, you merely enter the **date in the future** and DJIA index for which you wish an evaluation. This way you can predict what would happen to your spread. In other words, you can ask the question **What if —?** and get an immediate, accurate answer.

Main Menu Selection 3 allows you to generate a reasonably accurate Index Option Market Table, similar to the one printed in your newspaper, for any one of the three index options (NYA, OEX, or XMI) or for UAL stock options. The program uses OPVAM to generate put and call market prices at specified strike prices.

The table will be generated for today's date. You can also use other dates if you wish. For example, if you would like an option table for a future date, simply enter the *future date* as *today's date* when you start up the OPTEVAL program. The program asks you to specify the option month for which you want the table. Then you may select any one of the four options: NYA, OEX, XMI or UAL. You must enter the index value or the DJIA if you don't know the index value. The program will ask you to enter how many strike prices you wish to include in the table. Then you enter the put and call strike prices as *pairs* for the *number* of strike prices you select.

Next the option table is printed on the screen. The program asks you if you want a printout of the option table on the line printer. You may re-enter the program to print out as many option tables as you need.

This Option Table Generation Subroutine uses data files to store the OPVAM coefficients for each of the four option types. It is necessary to change these coefficients from time to time: for example, if the market changes from a bear market to a bull market. The procedure for evaluating these coefficients was explained in Chapter 8.

You will find it handy to use the Option Generation Table to obtain put and call market values when they are unavailable in your local newspaper. These tables can then be used to select the best new short spread for a given date using Menu 1.

TO SUMMARIZE: the OPTEVAL program provides a computer-aided tool to allow you to select the best, safe short spread at the beginning of an option month. After your spread position is executed, OPTEVAL permits you to quickly evaluate your position as the market fluctuates during the month. This includes advice on protective changes to a threatened put or call. The program also allows you to generate a table of market values using a mathematical model called OPVAM — in case your newspaper has omitted the option tables you need, or if you would like to predict what the market values might be in the future. *The program listing for the OPTEVAL program is provided in Appendix A so you can enter the program in your own PC.*

COMPUTER PROGRAM TRADING USING OPTEVAL

Selection of the Best Short Spread is accomplished by

selecting: *(1) Evaluate New Short Spread Position* from the Main Menu of the computer program **OPTEVAL**. The computer program informs you that a safe short spread is:

Sell Calls at 2 Sigma above Market, and

Sell Puts at 2 Sigma below Market.

The program also reminds you that if the market gets close to your **put** strike price or **call** strike price during the month your spread is open, then you must take *corrective action.* Now select Main Menu Item (2). *Evaluate Existing Short Spread,* which will tell you what protective action to take if your put or call position should be threatened.

Next the program requests that you enter the *date* that the option position will be executed.

Now the program requests that you enter the option month of the spread and the type of option (UAL, NYA, OEX, or XMI). The program stores in the data file the numerical parameters for that particular type of option in order to compute the necessary information to evaluate whichever short spread you may select.

Next the program requests that you enter the date of the latest market data that you have available to use in the evaluation. If your market data is not too stale (i.e., less than three days old) then the program allows you to continue. If the data is too old, the program will use OPVAM to estimate the current market values from the value of the index or from the DJIA.

Now the program requests that you enter the current value of the index for the type of option selected. Then the program tells you how many spreads you can execute using a data file that contains the amount of capital you have available for option trading. The computation of the number of spreads you can execute takes into account the margin requirements applicable to your account. You may, of course, choose to execute fewer spreads than the maximum allowed for the capital you have.

189

Next the program informs you the value of the *call safe strike price* and asks you to enter the *call market value* for this strike price. Then the program tells you the value of the *put safe strike price* and asks you to enter the corresponding put market value. Immediately, the results for this short spread position are displayed on the screen.

You may read the data on the screen and then decide if you wish to have a copy of the screen information printed out on the line printer. If so, you inform the program and a copy will be printed out for your reference.

Next the computer asks *What do you want to do next?* The options are:

1. Evaluate another spread with different put and call strike prices, but everything else the same.
2. Evaluate another spread with different types of index.
3. Return to Main Menu.
4. Exit program.

Typically, you would select (1). Evaluate another spread with different put and call strike price. You want to assure yourself that you have looked at all the reasonable combinations of put and call strike prices before deciding which ones to execute.

EXAMPLE OF SELECTING BEST OEX SHORT SPREAD FOR AUGUST 1990

Assume that on Friday, July 20, 1990, the final day of the July option month, you heard on the late news that the S&P 100 Index, OEX, closed at 345.32. You check your newspaper the next morning and the index option tables are missing, with a polite note from the editor saying the *index option data was unavailable at press time.* So you use Main Menu 3 of **OPTEVAL** to generate the August 1990 OEX index option tables for Monday, July 23, 1990 — the first day of the next option month and the day you wish to open your short spread — based on the index value of 345.32. The resulting option index table shown in Table 10.2 is generated.

TABLE 10.2

Option Index Table for S&P 100 Option Index, OEX for Aug Option 90
Generated By Model: OPVAM Sigma = 4.86
Date: 7/23/90   S&P 100 Option Index, OEX = 345.32

STRIKE PRICE	CALL	PUT
325		1.18975
330		1.6250
335		2.2500
340		3.000
350	2.8750	
355	1.6250	
360	0.8750	
365	0.5000	

Now you return to the *Main Menu* of the **OPTEVAL** program to *evaluate a new short spread position* using Main Menu Selection 1, going through the procedure described above in this chapter. The safe 2 sigma strike prices computed are:

Call Strike Price   C360
Put Strike Price   P335

The index option table (Table 10.2) is used to determine that:

C360 Market Value = 0.875
P335 Market Value = 2.250

Immediately after you enter the market values, the program generates the information in Table 10.3 for the safe 2 sigma short spread.

TABLE 10.3
EVALUATE OPTION SPREAD OF S&P 100 Option Index, OEX
Today's Date: 7/23/90

SIGMA = 4.86
S&P 100 Option Index, OEX = 345.32
CALL SAFE for +SIG: index <= 355.04 CALL SAFE for DJIA <= 3046
PUT SAFE for -SIG: index >= 335.60 PUT SAFE for DJIA >= 2879

Market Data Date 7/20/90

Date of Option Execution 7/23/90

No. of Days from market Data to Transaction is: 3

Option Expiration Date: 8/17/90
No. Days Til Option Expires = 24
Aug option   No. Sprds = 5 C-360   P-335
            Call Mkt Val = 0.8750 Put Mkt Val = 2.2250
            Call Margin = 4.96 Put Margin = 0.60
            Spread Val Today $1,374.
            Proj Sprd Prft @ Expir for +/- 2 sig $1,374.
            **** OK TO EXECUTE SPREAD ****

You print out the information from the screen using the line printer so you can have a copy in front of you while you try out other possible spreads. You tell the program you want to evaluate another spread with a different strike price. You note from the printout of the C360/P335 short spread that your profit (spread value at close) is $1374 and that the call margin is 4.96 and the put margin is 0.60. The call margin means that the strike price less the index value plus 2 sigma is 4.86; and the put margin means that the index value plus 2 sigma less the put strike price is 0.32. In other words, you have a spread that is wider than ±2 sigma. You can safely lower the call strike price from C360 to C355.

In response to the question on the screen, WHAT DO YOU WANT TO DO NEXT?, you should select 1, *Evaluate another spread with different PUT & CALL STRIKE PRICES.* Enter CALL of 355 with value of 1.6250 (from Table 10.1) and PUT of 335 with value of 2.250 (also from Table 10.1). This new OEX short spread C355/P335 is evaluated and printed on the screen. You select a print-out (see Table 10.4). Profit at expiration is $1714. SAFE and BETTER than C360/ P335.

TABLE 10.4
EVALUATE OPTION SPREAD OF S&P 100 Option Index, OEX
Today's Date: 7/23/90

SIGMA = 4.86
S&P 100 Option Index, OEX = 345.32
CALL THRT if index goes ABOVE 355.00 or DJIA goes ABOVE 3046
PUT SAFE for -SIG: index >= 335.60 PUT SAFE for DJIA >= 2879

Market Data Date 7/20/90

Date of Option Execution 7/23/90

No. of Days from market Data to Transaction is: 3

Option Expiration Date: 8/17/90
No. Days Til Option Expires = 24
Aug option   No. Sprds = 5 C-355   P-335
Call Mkt Val = 1.6250 Put Mkt Val = 2.2500
Call Margin = -0.04   Put Margin = 0.60
Spread Val Today $1,732.
Proj Sprd Prft @ Expir for +/- 2 sig $1,714.
**** OK TO EXECUTE SPREAD ****

EVALUATION OF OTHER SHORT SPREADS

Now you can evaluate other NYA, XMI and UAL short spreads for August to examine other possibilities, but you finally decide to execute the OEX short spread so you call your broker and tell him:

Sell 5 OEX August call options at strike price 355 and
Sell 5 OEX August put options at strike price 335
at open today, July 23, 1990.

Evaluate your August 90 OEX Short Spread on
Thursday, August 2, 1990, after a sharp market drop pro-
voked by Iraq's invasion of Kuwait. You select Main Menu
Item 2, *Evaluate Existing Short Spread Position.* The information concerning the existing short spread is stored in a
data file which must be updated anytime your existing
spread position is changed — either through protective
action or when you open a new position. First the program
asks you to enter today's value of the index, or if you don't
have the index value, you may enter the DJIA and the
program will compute the corresponding value of the index.
The program reminds you what type of index your existing
spread is and then prints out an evaluation of your existing
spread. An example printout for an evaluation of the August
90 OEX short spread C355/P335 is given in Table 10.5.

TABLE 10.5
Evaluation of EXISTING S&P 100 Option Index, OEX Spread

Today's DATE: 8/2/90

SIGMA = 4.86

S&P 100 Option Index, OEX = 334.33
CALL SAFE for +SIG: index <=344.05 CALL SAFE for DJIA <= 2952
PUT THRT if index goes BELOW 335.00 or DJIA goes BELOW 2874

Market Data Date 8/2/90

Date of Option Execution 8/17/90

No. of Days from Market Data to Transaction is: 0

Option Expiration Date: 8/17/90
No. Days Til Option Expires = 15
Aug option   No. Sprds = 5   C-355   P-335

Call Mkt Val = 0.2500 Put Mkt Val = 2.5000
Call Margin = 10.95   Put margin = %-10.39

Spread Val Today $1,310.

If Closed-out today Profit = $357
Proj Sprd Prft @ Expir for +/- 1 sig $-1,033.
Proj Sprd Prft @ Expir for +/- 2 sig $-3,463.

Note that the evaluation does not recommend any protective action at this time. In other words, wait and see if the market recovers before changing your spread to protect your threatened put at 335.

TO SUMMARIZE: This section has described in detail how to use the three principal features of the OPTEVAL computer program:

1. Selecting a new short spread
2. Evaluating an existing short spread, and
3. Generating the table of index values.

The examples used the program to select short spreads, to generate August 90 index option tables for OEX, and to evaluate your existing August 90 OEX short spread after a sudden market drop.

I have found this computer program handy for my option trading. You can use the BASIC program by entering it into your IBM-compatible PC using the listing in Appendix A. The program uses Microsoft GW BASIC version 3.2. If you have a different version of BASIC, consult your manual and make the necessary changes.

USE OF PC SPREADSHEETS AS OPTION TRADING TOOLS

Throughout the book I have used spreadsheets and associated graphics generated by my Microsoft Works. This integrated software package is resident on my IBM-compatible Personal Computer (includes a 80286 processor, 40 megabyte hard disk, and 1 megabyte of RAM working memory). The MS WORKS integrated package includes a spreadsheet, graphics, word processor, data base management, and communications programs. There are, of course, other integrated packages such as LOTUS SYMPHONY, and LOTUS 1-2-3 with graphics you could use instead. I *strongly recommend* you use **Spreadsheets** as a tool in your option trading toolkit. You may use the spreadsheet formats sprinkled throughout the book, *adapted to your own use.*

*A **Summary of those Spreadsheets*** in the book that I believe would be most useful to your short spread option trading are listed here:

Table 4.8 Stock Index Options Suitable for Short Spreads
Table 5.1 Stock Options Suitable for Short Spreads
Table 6.1 Currency Options Suitable for Short Spreads

Table 7.1 Comparison of Best Option Short Spreads

Table 7.3 What's Available & What's Best?

Tables 7.4, 7.5, 7.6 Evaluation Forms for Individual Options (tied to Table 7.3 and handy for generating evaluation forms similar to Table 10.2 of the BASIC Program OPEVAL)

Table 8.1 OEX Premium Data (Used for generating OPVAM parameters. This spreadsheet can be adapted to the type option you select for your short spread trading)

Table 9.1 S&P 100 Sigma Computations (This spreadsheet can be adapted to compute 1 and 30 day sigmas for whatever type option you select for short spreads)

Table 9.10 Options Evaluation for Short Spread Strategy.

The listings of the equations used in the most basic of these spread sheets are provided in Appendix B.

APPENDIX A

BASIC PROGRAM LISTING FOR EVALUATION OF OPTION SHORT SPREADS. This program is coded in Microsoft GWBASIC, version 3.2 Interpreter. Check your BASIC manual and make any changes necessary to this IBM PC-compatible program for a VGA color monitor.

```
10 SCREEN 9,4
20 CLS
30 COLOR 7,1
40 PRINT TAB(15);"EVALUATION OF STOCK INDEX OPTION SHORT SPREADS"
50 PRINT TAB(25);"Filename: OPTEVAL.APP"
60 PRINT: REM ** JON SCHILLER — COPYRIGHT 1990 ** Version 130890/0130
70 INPUT "Enter today's date as dd.mm.yy in numerals:  ",DD,MM,YY
80 PRINT
90 PRINT TAB(40);"TODAY'S DATE: ";DD;"-";MM;"-";YY
100 PRINT TAB(40);"============================="
110 PRINT TAB(5);"MAIN MENU for Index Option Spread Evaluation":PRINT
120 PRINT TAB(20);"1  Evaluate New Short Spread Position"
130 PRINT TAB(20);"2  Evaluate Existing Short Spread Position"
140 PRINT TAB(20);"3  Generate Table of Index Option Market Values"
150 PRINT TAB(20);"4  END EVALUATION, LEAVE PROGRAM":PRINT:PRINT
160 INPUT "Please make your selection, enter 1 thru 4: ",MEN1
170 IF MEN1=1 THEN GOTO 570
180 IF MEN1=2 THEN GOSUB 1890
190 IF MEN1=3 THEN GOSUB 3010
200 IF MEN1=4 THEN PRINT "THAT'S ALL FOLKS, HAVE A NICE DAY":PRINT :PRINT
210 END
220 REM COMPUTE NO. OF DAYS UNTIL OPTION EXPIRES
230 RESTORE 350:OPMO$="Jan option":GOTO 470
240 RESTORE 360:OPMO$="Feb option":GOTO 470
250 RESTORE 370:OPMO$="Mar option":GOTO 470
260 RESTORE 380:OPMO$="Apr option":GOTO 470
270 RESTORE 390:OPMO$="May option":GOTO 470
280 RESTORE 400:OPMO$="Jun option":GOTO 470
290 RESTORE 410:OPMO$="Jul option":GOTO 470
300 RESTORE 420:OPMO$="Aug option":GOTO 470
310 RESTORE 430:OPMO$="Sep option":GOTO 470
320 RESTORE 440:OPMO$="Oct option":GOTO 470
330 RESTORE 450:OPMO$="Nov option":GOTO 470
340 RESTORE 460:OPMO$="Dec option":GOTO 470
350 DATA 18,1,91
360 DATA 15,2,91
```

```
370 DATA 15,3,91
380 DATA 20,4,90
390 DATA 18,5,90
400 DATA 15,6,90
410 DATA 20,7,90
420 DATA 17,8,90
430 DATA 21,9,90
440 DATA 19,10,90
450 DATA 16,11,90
460 DATA 21,12,90
470 READ DOP,MOP,YOP
480 PRINT TAB(10);"Option Expiration Date: ";DOP;"-";MOP;"-";YOP
490 IF MEN1=3 GOTO 3040 ELSE 500
500 IF MEN1=2 THEN 2000
510 IF MEN1=1 THEN GOTO 520
520 IF MOP=MEX THEN OPDA=DOP-DEX
530 IF MEX>MOP OR MEX<MOP THEN OPDA=30-DEX+DOP
540 PRINT TAB(10);"No. Days Til Option Expires = ";OPDA
550 PRINT
560 RETURN
570 PRINT TAB(20);"EVALUATION OF NEW SAFE SHORT SPREAD POSITION":PRINT:PRINT
580 PRINT TAB(5);"A Safe Short Spread: Sell CALLs at 2 sigma above MKT";
590 PRINT TAB(32);"Sell PUTs at 2 sigma below MKT":PRINT
600 PRINT TAB(20);"You MUST take corrective action if the MKT gets close"
610 PRINT TAB(20);"to either your CALL or PUT Strike Price!"
620 PRINT
630 PRINT TAB(20);"USE2 on MAIN MENU to determine PROT ACTION for Exist SPRD"
640 PRINT:PRINT "EVALUATE NEW OPTION SPREAD"
650 GOSUB 1590
660 PRINT:INPUT "Month of Spread: ",OPMO
670 IF OPMO=1 THEN GOSUB 230:GOTO 790
680 IF OPMO=2 THEN GOSUB 240:GOTO 790
690 IF OPMO=3 THEN GOSUB 250:GOTO 790
700 IF OPMO=4 THEN GOSUB 260:GOTO 790
710 IF OPMO=5 THEN GOSUB 270:GOTO 790
720 IF OPMO=6 THEN GOSUB 280:GOTO 790
730 IF OPMO=7 THEN GOSUB 290:GOTO 790
740 IF OPMO=8 THEN GOSUB 300:GOTO 790
750 IF OPMO=9 THEN GOSUB 310:GOTO 790
760 IF OPMO=10 THEN GOSUB 320:GOTO 790
770 IF OPMO=11 THEN GOSUB 330:GOTO 790
780 IF OPMO=12 THEN GOSUB 340:GOTO 790
790 IF MEN1=2 GOTO 2000
800 IF MEN1=1 GOTO 820
810 IF MEN1=3 THEN GOTO 3040
820 INPUT "Type of Option: MSFT=1, NYA=2,OEX=3,XMI=4 Enter Number; ",TYPOP
830 IF TYPOP=1 THEN GOTO 910
840 IF TYPOP=2 THEN GOTO 920
850 IF TYPOP=3 THEN GOTO 930
860 IF TYPOP=4 THEN GOTO 940
870 DATA 0.1373,0.9160,0.1550,0.9036,3.14,44.4213,0.98,-0.98:REM MSFT
880 DATA .1523,0.7191,0.1465,0.9163,2.73,14.3475,1.00,0.20:REM NYA
890 DATA 0.1814,0.6156,0.2123,1.1301,4.86,8.5792,1.62,-1.80:REM OEX
900 DATA 0.3594,0.5900,0.4766,1,0904,8.8,4.9848,2.74,0.76:REM XMI
910 RESTORE 870:TYPOP$="MSFT Stock Option, MSFT":GOTO 950
920 RESTORE 880:TYPOP$="NYSE Option Index, NYA":GOTO 950
930 RESTORE 890:TYPOP$="S&P 100 Option Index, OEX":GOTO 950
940 RESTORE 900:TYPOP$="Amex Maj Mkt Index, XMI":GOTO 950
950 READ KOP,K1P,KOC,K1C,SIG,DJR,SIG1,DEL
960 SIG=SIG
970 PRINT "sig for ";OPDA;" = ";SIG
980 GOSUB 2640:REM *** SUBROUTINE FOR COMPUTING SPREAD PARAMETERS ***
990 REM **** SUBROUTINE FOR INTERACTIVE EVALUATION OF SHORT SPREAD ****
1000 REM ********** MAKE SURE index,nopt ARE DEFINED BEFORE CALLING **********
```

LABEL NOT DEFINED

```
1010 PRINT TAB(30);"INTERACTIVE EVALUATION OF SHORT SPREAD"
1020 PRINT:PRINT"Evaluate safe SHORT SPREAD for ";TYPOP$;" for ";OPMO$
1030 INPUT"Call Strike Price: ",CSTRK
1040 INPUT "Call Market Value: ",CMKT
1050 INPUT "Put Strike Price: ",PSTRK
1060 INPUT "Put Market Value: ",PMKT
1070 GOSUB 1090
1080 GOTO 1290
1090 SPRDVAL=100*NOPT*(CMKT+PMKT)-13*NOPT:REM *** SR for sprdval &spexval ***
1100 CMGN=CSTRK-(INDEX+2*SIG):PMGN=(INDEX-2*SIG)-PSTRK:PRINT "sig = ";SIG
1110 IF PMGN<0 GOTO 1160 ELSE 1170
1120 IF CMGN<0 GOTO 1130 ELSE 1150
1130 CTHRTI$="CALL THRT if index goes ABOVE ":CTHRTD$=" or DJIA goes ABOVE ":GOT
O 1180
1140 DJU%=(DJR*INDU):DJD%=(DJR*INDD)
1150 CTHRTI$="CALL SAFE for +SIG: index <= ":CTHRTD$="CALL SAFE for DJIA <= ":GO
TO 1180
1160 PTHRTI$="PUT THRT if index goes BELOW ":PTHRTD$=" or DJIA goes BELOW ":GOTO
1120
1170 PTHRTI$="PUT SAFE for -SIG: index >= ":PTHRTD$="PUT SAFE for DJIA >= ":GOTO
1120
1180 IF CMGN>0 AND PMGN>0 THEN SPEXVAL=SPRDVAL
1190 IF CMGN<0 THEN INDU=CSTRK ELSE INDU=CSTRK-CMGN
1200 IF PMGN<0 THEN INDD=PSTRK ELSE INDD=PSTRK+PMGN
1210 DJU%=(DJR*INDU):DJD%=(DJR*INDD)
1220 IF CMGN<0 AND PMGN>0 THEN SPEXVAL=SPRDVAL+100*CMGN*NOPT
1230 IF CMGN>0 AND PMGN<0 THEN SPEXVAL=SPRDVAL+100*PMGN*NOPT
1240 IF CMGN<0 AND PMGN<0 THEN GOTO 1250 ELSE GOTO 1280
1250 IF CMGN<PMGN THEN GOTO 1260 ELSE GOTO 1270
1260 SPEXVAL=SPRDVAL+100*NOPT*CMGN:GOTO 1280
1270 SPEXVAL=SPRDVAL+100*NOPT*PMGN
1280 RETURN
1290 PRINT;OPMO$;TAB(20);"No.Sprds=";NOPT%; TAB(40);"C-";CSTRK;TAB(50);"P-";PSTR
K
1300 PRINT"No.Days to Exp=";OPDA TAB(20);"Call Mkt Val=";USING'##.####";CMKT;
1310 PRINT TAB(42);"Put Mkt Val=";USING"##.####";PMKT;
1320 PRINT " SIGMA =";USING"##.##";SIG;
1330 PRINT TAB(20);TYPOP$;" - ";INDEX
1340 PRINT CTHRTI$;USING"###.##";INDU;
1350 PRINT TAB(40);CTHRTD$;USING"####.##";DJU%
1360 PRINT PTHRTI$;USING"##.##";INDD;
1370 PRINT TAB(40);PTHRTD$;USING"####.##";DJD%
1380 PRINT TAB(20);"CALL Margin=";USING"##.##";CMGN;
1390 PRINT TAB(50);"PUT Margin=";USING"##.##";PMGN
1400 PRINT TAB(5)"Spread Val Today";TAB(50)USING"$#######..";SPRDVAL
1410 IF MEN1=2 GOTO 2320 ELSE 1420
1420 PRINT TAB(5);"Proj Sprd Prft @ Expir for +/- 2 SIG";TAB(50)USING"$#######..
";SPEXVAL
1430 SDOK$="******OK TO EXECUTE SPREAD******"
1440 SDNG$="******TOO MUCH RISK TO EXECUTE SPREAD******"
1450 IF SPEXVAL>0 THEN PRINT SDOK$ ELSE PRINT SDNG$
1460 INPUT "Enter 1 If You Want Evaluation Printout, else enter 2: ",EVALPRT:PRI
NT
1470 IF EVALPRT=1 THEN GOSUB 1630
1480 PRINT TAB(20);"WHAT DO YOU WANT TO DO NEXT?":PRINT:PRINT
1490 PRINT "1  Evaluate another Spread with different CALL & PUT STRIKE PRICES"
1500 PRINT TAB(5) "BUT with SAME index, date of execution, and with known MKT va
lues"
1510 PRINT "2  Evaluate Another Sprd, with NEW INDEX but everything else SAME"
1520 PRINT "3  RETURN TO MAIN MENU"
1530 PRINT "4  Evaluations Competed, EXIT Program"
1540 INPUT "Make your selection please, 1 thru 4:  ",ANEVAL
1550 IF ANEVAL=1 THEN GOTO 990
1560 IF ANEVAL=2 THEN GOTO 790
```

```
1570 IF ANEVAL=3 THEN GOTO 90
1580 IF ANEVAL=4 THEN PRINT:PRINT"Your Evaluations are Completed! GOOD LUCK IN T
HE MKT":END
1590 PRINT:INPUT "Enter Date OPTION to be Executed AS dd,mm,yy: ",DEX,MEX,YEX
1600 PRINT:PRINT TAB(40);"Date of Option Execution";DEX;"-";MEX"-";YEX
1610 PRINT TAB(40);"======================================="
1620 RETURN
1630 LPRINT:LPRINT:LPRINT TAB(20);"EVALUATE OPTION SPREAD of ";TYPOP$
1640 LPRINT:LPRINT TAB(40);"Today's DATE:";DD;"-";MM;"-";YY:LPRINT TAB(40);"====
==========="
1650 LPRINT "SIGMA = ";USING"##.##";SIG
1660 LPRINT TAB(20);TYPOP$;" = ";USING"###.##";INDEX
1670 LPRINT CTHRTI$;USING"###.##";INDU;
1680 LPRINT TAB(40);CTHRTD$;DJU%
1690 LPRINT PTHRTI$;USING"###.##";INDD;
1700 LPRINT PTHRTD$;DJD%
1710 LPRINT:LPRINT TAB(20);"Market Data Date";DMKT;"-"MMKT;"-";YMKT
1720 LPRINT TAB(40);"Date of Option Execution";DEX;"-";MEX;"-";YEX
1730 LPRINT TAB(40);"======================================="
1740 LPRINT:LPRINT TAB(20);"No. of Days from Market Data to Transaction is: ";ND
MTE
1750 LPRINT:LPRINT TAB(10);"Option Expiration Date:";DOP;"-";MOP;"-";YOP
1760 LPRINT TAB(10);"No. Days Til Option Expires =";OPDA
1770 LPRINT;OPMO$;TAB(20);"No.Sprds=";NOPT%;TAB(40);"C-";CSTRK;TAB(50);"P-";PSTR
K
1780 IF MEN1=2 THEN CMKT=CMKT1 ELSE CMKT=CMKT
1790 LPRINT:LPRINT TAB(20);"Call Mkt Val=";USING"##.####";CMKT;
1800 IF MEN1=2 THEN PMKT=PMKT1 ELSE PMKT=PMKT
1810 LPRINT TAB(42);"Put Mkt Val=";USING "##.####";PMKT
1820 LPRINT:LPRINT;TAB(20);"Call Margin=";USING"##.##";CMGN;
1830 LPRINT TAB(50)"Put Margin=";USING"##.##";PMGN
1840 LPRINT:LPRINT TAB(5)"Spread Val Today";TAB(50)USING"$######..";SPRDVAL
1850 IF MEN1=2 GOTO 2500 ELSE 1860
1860 LPRINT:LPRINT TAB(5);"Proj Sprd Prft @ Expir for +/- 2 sig ";TAB(50)USING"$
######..";SPEXVAL
1870 IF SPEXVAL>0 THEN LPRINT SDOK$ ELSE  LPRINT  SDNG$
1880 RETURN
1890 REM ***SUBROUTINE for Evaluating Existing SHORT SPREADS***
1900 RESTORE 1910:GOTO 1920
1910 DATA 85,65,1,76,11235,44.4213,8,3.14,0.98,17,08,90:REM AUG MSFT C85/P65
1920 READ CSTRK,PSTRK,TYPOP,NOPT,PRFT,DJR,OPMO,SIG,SIG1,DEX,MEX,YEX
1930 CSTRK(I)=CSTRK:PSTRK(I)=PSTRK
1940 IF TYPOP=1 THEN TYPOP$= "UAL Stock, UAL"
1950 IF TYPOP=2 THEN TYPOP$= "NYSE Index, NYA"
1960 IF TYPOP=3 THEN TYPOP$= "S&P 100 Index, OEX"
1970 IF TYPOP=4 THEN TYPOP$= "AMEX Maj Mkt Index, XMI"
1980 CSTRK(I)=CSTRK:PSTRK(I)=PSTRK
1990 GOSUB 670
2000 IF MM=MOP THEN OPDA=DOP-DD
2010 IF MM<MOP OR MM>MOP THEN OPDA=30-DD+DOP
2020 PRINT "No. Days to Option Expiration = ";OPDA:PRINT
2030 SIG=SIG
2040 IF TYPOP =2 THEN TYPOP$="NYSE Index, NYA"
2050 IF TYPOP =3 THEN TYPOP$="S&P 100 Index, OEX"
2060 IF TYPOP =4 THEN TYPOP$="AMEX Maj Mkt Index, XMI"
2070 PRINT :PRINT  "The Index for your Existing Short Spread is ";TYPOP$
2080 INPUT "Enter 1 if you have today's Index value, else 2: ",LIST
2090 IF LIST=1 GOTO  2100 ELSE 2110
2100 INPUT "Enter index as nnn.nn for Today: ", INDEX:GOTO  2130:PRINT
2110 INPUT "Latest DJIA for date of Evaluation, as dddd.dd: ",DJA:PRINT
2120 INDEX=DJA/DJR
2130 IF TYPOP=1 GOTO 2170
2140 IF TYPOP=2 GOTO 2190
2150 IF TYPOP=3 GOTO 2210
```

```
2160 IF TYPOP=4 GOTO 2230
2170 GOSUB 3780
2180 GOTO 2250
2190 GOSUB 3790
2200 GOTO 2260
2210 GOSUB 3800
2220 GOTO 2250
2230 GOSUB 3810
2240 GOTO 2250
2250 GOSUB 1090
2260 IF CMGN>0 AND PMGN>0 THEN EXPRFT=PRFT
2270 IF CMGN<0 AND PMGN>0 THEN EXPRFT=PRFT+100*CMGN*NOPT
2280 IF CMGN>0 AND PMGN<0 THEN EXPRFT=PRFT+100*PMGN*NOPT
2290 IF CMGN<0 AND PMGN<0 THEN EXPRFT=MIN(PRFT+100*PMGN*NOPT,PRFT+100*CMGN*NOPT)
2300 CMKT1=CMKT:PMKT1=PMKT
2310 PRINT:PRINT:PRINT:PRINT"EVALUATION OF EXISTING SPREAD FOR: ";TYPOP$:GOTO 12
90
2320 COPRFT=PRFT-SPRDVAL-13*NOPT
2330 IF EXPRFT<0 THEN GOTO 2340 ELSE  GOTO 2390
2340 IF (CMGN+SIG)>0 AND (PMGN+SIG)>0 THEN EXPRFT1=PRFT
2350 IF (CMGN+SIG)<0 AND (PMGN+SIG)>0 THEN EXPRFT1=PRFT+100*(CMGN+SIG)*NOPT
2360 IF (CMGN+SIG)>0 AND (PMGN+SIG)<0 THEN EXPRFT1=PRFT+100*(PMGN+SIG)*NOPT
2370 IF (CMGN+SIG)<0 AND (PMGN+SIG)<0 THEN EXPRFT1=MIN(PRFT+100*(CMGN+SIG)*NOPT,
PRFT+100*(PMGN+SIG)*NOPT)
2380 PRINT TAB(5);"Proj Sprd Prft @ Expir for +/- 1 sig";TAB(50)USING"$######..
";EXPRFT1
2390 PRINT TAB(5);"Proj Sprd Prft @ Expir for +/- 2 sig";TAB(50)USING"$######..
";EXPRFT
2400 PRINT:PRINT TAB(10);"If Closed-out today Profit= $";COPRFT:PRINT:PRINT
2410 IF (CSTRK-INDEX)<-SIG1 THEN GOTO 2420 ELSE 2430
2420 PRINT TAB(10);"YOUR CALL POSITION IS THREATENED":GOSUB 3960
2430 IF (INDEX-PSTRK)<-SIG1 THEN GOTO 2440 ELSE 2450
2440 PRINT TAB(10);"YOUR PUT POSITION IS THREATENED":GOSUB 4190
2450 INPUT "Do you want a Print-out? Enter 1 for YES, else 2: ",PRT2
2460 IF PRT2=1 THEN GOTO 2470 ELSE 90
2470 REM *** PRINT-OUT ROUTINE FOR EVALUATION OF EXISTING SPREAD ***
2480 LPRINT TAB(10);"Evaluation of EXISTING ";TYPOP$;" Spread":LPRINT
2490 DMKT=DD:MMKT=MM:YMKT=YY:GOTO 1640
2500 LPRINT:LPRINT  "If Closed-out today Profit = $";COPRFT
2510 GOSUB 1090
2520 IF CMGN>0 AND PMGN>0 THEN EXPRFT=PRFT
2530 IF CMGN<0 AND PMGN>0 THEN EXPRFT=PRFT+100*CMGN*NOPT
2540 IF CMGN>0 AND PMGN<0 THEN EXPRFT=PRFT+100*PMGN*NOPT
2550 IF CMGN<0 AND PMGN<0 THEN EXPRFT=MIN(PRFT+100*PMGN*NOPT,PRFT+100*CMGN*NOPT)
2560 IF EXPRFT<0 THEN GOTO 2570 ELSE GOTO 2580
2570 LPRINT TAB(5);"Proj Sprd Prft @ Expir for +/- 1sig";TAB(50)USING"$######..
";EXPRFT1
2580 LPRINT TAB(5);"Proj Sprd Prft @ Expir for +/- 2sig"TAB(50)USING"$######.."
;EXPRFT
2590 IF (CSTRK-INDEX)<-SIG1 THEN GOTO 2600 ELSE 2610
2600 LPRINT  TAB(10);"YOUR CALL POSITION IS THREATENED":GOSUB 4860
2610 IF (INDEX-PSTRK)<-SIG1 THEN GOTO 2620 ELSE 2630
2620 LPRINT  TAB(10);"YOUR PUT POSITION IS THREATENED":GOSUB 4940
2630 END
2640 REM *** SUBROUTINE FOR COMPUTING SHORT SPREAD PARAMETERS ***
2650 PRINT:INPUT "Enter Date of Latest Market DATA as dd,mm,yy in nbrs: ",DMKT,M
MKT,YMKT
2660 REM ndmte = no. of days from latest market data to execution
2670 IF MEX-MMKT<0 THEN  MEX=MEX+12 ELSE  MEX=MEX: NDMTE=DEX-DMKT+30*(MEX-MMKT)
2680 PRINT TAB(10);"No. Days from MKT Data to EXECUTION is: ";NDMTE
2690 IF NDMTE<3 GOTO 2700 ELSE GOTO 2880
2700 PRINT:PRINT TAB(20);"MKT Data is OK to use in EVALUATION":PRINT
2710 PRINT "For ";TYPOP$:INPUT "Enter INDEX Value as nnn.nn : ",INDEX
2720 RESTORE 2730:GOTO 2740
```

```
2730 DATA 50000,0.3130:REM data for computing nopt
2740 READ CAPIT,CLTRL:REM capit = amount of capital in $, cltrl = collateral fra
ction
2750 NOPT=CAPIT/(100*INDEX*CLTRL):NOPT%=NOPT
2760 PRINT:PRINT "Sufficient Capital for ";NOPT%;" Spreads."
2770 INPUT "Enter 1 if  you want to execute this No. SPRDS else 2: ",NDES:PRINT
2780 IF NDES=1 GOTO 2800 ELSE 2790
2790 INPUT "No. of SPRDS you want to EXECUTE: ",NOPT
2800 GOSUB 2820:REM ** SUBROUTINE FOR COMPUTING SAFE STRIKE PRICES **
2810 GOSUB 2910
2820 REM: *** SUBROUTINE FOR COMPUTING SAFE 2 SIGMA STRIKE PRICES FOR SPREAD ***
2830 CSTRK=INT((INDEX+2*SIG)/5)*5:DELC=INDEX+2*SIG-CSTRK
2840 IF DELC<=DEL THEN CSTRK=CSTRK ELSE CSTRK=CSTRK+5
2850 PSTRK=INT((INDEX-2*SIG)/5)*5:DELP=INDEX-2*SIG-PSTRK
2860 IF 5-DELP<=DEL THEN PSTRK=PSTRK+5 ELSE PSTRK=PSTRK
2870 RETURN
2880 REM *** REM SUBROUTINE FOR COMPUTING MKT VALUES FOR BEST STRIKE PRICES ***
2890 PRINT:PRINT:PRINT TAB(20);"USE OPVAM MODEL to Generate Option Table for MKT
 Values"
2900 MEN1=3:GOTO  3030
2910 REM *** SUBROUTINE FOR SAFE SHORT SPREAD ***
2920 PRINT:PRINT TAB(20);"Safe CALL Strk Price = ";CSTRK
2930 INPUT "Enter MKT Price for CALL as nn.nnnn : ",CMKT
2940 PRINT:PRINT  TAB(20);"Safe PUT Strk Price = ";PSTRK
2950 INPUT "Enter MKT Price for PUT as nn.nnnn : ",PMKT
2960 GOSUB 1090:REM now we have sprdval & spexval
2970 PRINT:PRINT "The value of your Spread at open is $";SPRDVAL
2980 PRINT:PRINT  "The value of your spread at expiration is $";SPEXVAL
2990 PRINT:PRINT:PRINT:PRINT:PRINT TAB(20);"EVALUATION FOR ";TYPOP$
3000 GOTO 1290
3010 REM *** SUBROUTINE FOR COMPUTING OPTION TABLES USING OPVAM ***
3020 REM OPVAM -- PREMIUM = k0*t^(-k1*abs(index-strk)/(2*sig))
3030 GOSUB 660
3040 IF MOP=MM THEN OPDA=DOP-DD
3050 IF MM>MOP OR MM<MOP THEN OPDA=30-DD+DOP
3060 PRINT "No. days til option expires is: ";OPDA
3070 INPUT "Type of Option: UAL=1, NYA=2, OEX=3, XMI=4 Enter Number: ",TYPOP
3080 IF TYPOP=1 THEN SIG=5:SIG1=1.4:GOTO 3120:REM UAL
3090 IF TYPOP=2 THEN SIG=2.35:SIG1=1.01:GOTO 3130:REM NYA
3100 IF TYPOP=3 THEN SIG=4.36:SIG1=2.52:GOTO 3140:REM OEX
3110 IF TYPOP=4 THEN SIG=6.5:SIG1=4:GOTO 3150:REM XMI
3120 TYPOP$="UAL Stock Option, UAL":DJR=18.6578:GOTO 3160
3130 TYPOP$="NYSE Index, NYA":DJR=13.9911:GOTO 3160
3140 TYPOP$="S&P 100 Index, OEX":DJR=8.4113:GOTO 3160
3150 TYPOP$="Amex Maj Mkt Index, XMI":DJR=5.0892:GOTO 3160
3160 PRINT "Generate Table for ";TYPOP$;" for ";OPMO$;" Date: ";DD;"-";MM;"-";YY
3170 PRINT "Your index is ";TYPOP$:INPUT "Enter 1 if you have latest index else
2: ",LTST
3180 IF LTST=1 GOTO 3200
3190 IF LTST=2 GOTO 3210
3200 INPUT "Enter index as nnn.nn for today : ",INDEX:GOTO 3250
3210 INPUT "DOW JONES IA index for today as nnnn.nn : ",DJA
3220 INDEX=DJA/DJR
3230 IF LTST=2 GOTO 3240 ELSE 3250
3240 PRINT:PRINT "The latest estimated ";TYPOP$;" is = ";USING"###.##";INDEX
3250 INPUT "Number of Strike prices you want listed as nn :",K
3260 DIM PSTRK(K):DIM CSTRK(K)
3270 FOR I=1 TO K
3280 INPUT "Value of Put and Call strike price as PPP, and CCC: ",PSTRK(I),CSTRK
(I)
3290 NEXT I
3300 PRINT:PRINT:PRINT:PRINT:SIG=SIG
3310 PRINT TAB(10);"Option Index Table for ";TYPOOOP$;" for "OPMO$;" ";YY
3320 PRINT :PRINT TAB(10);"Generated by Model OPVAM";TAB(36);"Sigma = ";USING"##
.##";SIG
```

```
3330 PRINT :PRINT "Date: ";DD;"-";MM;"-";YY;TAB(30);TYPOP$;" = ";INDEX
3340 PRINT :PRINT
3350 PRINT "STRIKE PRICE";TAB(15)"CALL";TAB(35)"PUT";:PRINT
3360 IF TYPOP=1 GOTO 3490
3370 IF TYPOP=2 GOTO 3400
3380 IF TYPOP=3 GOTO 3580
3390 IF TYPOP=4 GOTO 3670
3400 FOR I=1 TO K:GOSUB 3790
3410 IF CSTRK(I)<INDEX THEN CMKT=CMKT+INT((INDEX-CSTRK(I))/O.0625)*0.0625
3420 PRINT PSTRK(I);TAB(35);USING"##.####";PMKT
3430 NEXT I
3440 FOR I=1 TO K:GOSUB 3790
3450 IF CSTRK(I)<INDEX THEN CMKT=CMKT +INT((INDEX-CSTRK(I))/.0625)*.0625
3460 PRINT CSTRK(I);TAB(15);USING"##.####";CMKT
3470 NEXT I
3480 INPUT "Do you want a Print-out? Enter 1 for Yes, 2 for No: ",PRT:IF PRT=1 G
OTO 4400 ELSE 5000
3490 FOR I=1 TO K:GOSUB 3780
3500 IF PSTRK(I)>INDEX THEN PMKT=PMKT+INT((PSTRK(I)-INDEX)/.0625)*.0625
3510 PRINT PSTRK(I);TAB(35);USING"##.####";PMKT
3520 NEXT I
3530 FOR I=1 TO K:GOSUB 3780
3540 IF CSTRK(I)<INDEX THEN CMKT=CMKT+INT((INDEX-CSTRK(I))/.0625)*.0625
3550 PRINT CSTRK(I);TAB(15);USING"##.####";CMKT
3560 NEXT I
3570 GOTO 3480
3580 FOR I=1 TO K:GOSUB 3800
3590 IF PSTRK(I)>INDEX THEN PMKT=PMKT+INT((PSTRK(I)-INDEX)/.0625)*.0625
3600 PRINT PSTRK(I);TAB(35);USING"##.#### ";PMKT
3610 NEXT I
3620 FOR I=1 TO K:GOSUB 3800
3630 IF CSTRK(I)<INDEX THEN CMKT=CMKT+INT((INDEX-CSTRK(I))/.0625)*.0625
3640 PRINT CSTRK(I);TAB(15);USING"##.####";CMKT
3650 NEXT I
3660 GOTO 3480
3670 FOR I=1 TO K:GOSUB 3810
3680 IF PSTRK(I)>INDEX THEN PMKT=PMKT+INT((PSTRK(I)-INDEX)/.0625)*.0625
3690 PRINT PSTRK(I);TAB(35);USING"##.#### ";PMKT
3700 NEXT I
3710 FOR I=1 TO K:GOSUB 3810
3720 IF CSTRK(I)<INDEX THEN CMKT=CMKT+INT((INDEX-CSTRK(I))/.0625)*.0625
3730 PRINT CSTRK(I);TAB(15);USING"##.####";CMKT
3740 NEXT I
3750 GOTO 3480
3760 REM *** SUBROUTINE FOR OPVAM Computes PMKT & CMKT ***
3770 REM *** Must Define OPDA & PSTRK/CSTRK before using ***
3780 RESTORE 3820:TYPOP$="MSFT Stock Option, MSFT":GOTO 3820
3790 RESTORE 3830:TYPOP$="NYSE Option Index, NYA":GOTO 3860
3800 RESTORE 3840:TYPOP$="S&P 100 Option Index, OEX":GOTO 3860
3810 RESTORE 3850:TYPOP$="Amex Maj Mkt Index, XMI":GOTO 3860
3820 DATA 0.1373,0.9160,0.1550,0.9036,3.14,44.4213,0.98,-.98:REM MSFT
3830 DATA 0.1523,0.7191,0.1465,0.9163,2.73,14.1484,1.00,0.20:REM NYA
3840 DATA 0.1814,0.6156,0.2123,1.1301,4.86,8.5792,1.62,-1.8:REM OEX
3850 DATA 0.3594,0.5900,0.4766,1.0904,8.8,4.9848,2.74,0.76:REM XMI
3860 READ KOP,K1P,KOC,K1C,SIG,DJR,SIG1,DEL
3870 SIG=SIG
3880 KOP=KOP*OPDA:KOC=KOC*OPDA
3890 PMKT=KOP*EXP(-K1P*ABS(INDEX-PSTRK(I))/(2*SIG))
3900 IF PMKT<2 THEN PMKT=INT(PMKT/.0625)*.0625
3910 IF PMKT>=2 THEN PMKT=INT(PMKT/.125)*.125
3920 CMKT=KOC*EXP(-K1C*ABS(INDEX-CSTRK(I))/(2*SIG))
3930 IF CMKT<2 THEN CMKT=INT(CMKT/.0625)*.0625
3940 IF CMKT>=2 THEN CMKT=INT(CMKT/.125)*.125
3950 RETURN
```

```
3960 REM *** PROTECTIVE STRATEGY FOR THREATENED CALL ***
3970 PRINT "Buy your";NOPT;"CALLs at";CSTRK;"and your";NOPT;"PUTs at";PSTRK
3980 IF TYPOP=2 THEN PROT=5
3990 IF TYPOP=3 THEN PROT=5
4000 IF TYPOP=4 THEN PROT=10
4010 IF TYPOP=1 THEN PROT=5
4020 PRINT "Sell ";NOPT;"Calls at";CSTRK+PROT:CST1=CMKT:CSTRK(I)=CSTRK+PROT
4030 PRINT "Sell ";NOPT;"PUTs  at";PSTRK+PROT:PST1=PMKT:PSTRK(I)=PSTRK+PROT
4040 IF TYPOP=2 GOTO 4100
4050 IF TYPOP=1 GOTO 4080
4060 IF TYPOP=3 GOTO 4120
4070 IF TYPOP=4 GOTO 4140
4080 GOSUB 3780
4090 GOTO 4150
4100 GOSUB 3790
4110 GOTO 4150
4120 GOSUB 3800
4130 GOTO 4150
4140 GOSUB 3810
4150 CST2=CMKT
4160 CSTPS=100*NOPT*(CST1-CST2)+NOPT*18
4170 PRINT "COST OF PROTECTIVE STRATEGY FOR THREATENED CALL = $";CSTPS
4180 RETURN
4190 REM *** PROTECTIVE STRATEGY FOR THREATENED PUT ***
4200 PRINT "Buy your";NOPT%;"PUTs at";PSTRK;"and your";NOPT%;"CALLs at";CSTRK
4210 IF TYPOP=2 THEN PROT=5:IF TYPOP=3 THEN PROT=10:IF TYPOP=4 THEN  PROT=15
4220 PRINT "Sell ";NOPT%;"PUTs at ";PSTRK-PROT:PCST1=PMKT:PSTRK(I)=PSTRK-PROT
4230 PRINT "Sell ";NOPT%;"CALLs at ";CSTRK-PROT:CST1=CMKT:CSTRK(I)=CSTRK-PROT
4240 IF TYPOP=2 GOTO 4280
4250 IF TYPOP=1 GOTO 4340
4260 IF TYPOP=3 GOTO 4300
4270 IF TYPOP=4 GOTO 4320
4280 GOSUB 3790
4290 GOTO 4360
4300 GOSUB 3800
4310 GOTO 4360
4320 GOSUB 3810
4330 GOTO 4360
4340 GOSUB 3780
4350 GOTO 4360
4360 PCST2=PMKT
4370 CSTPS=100*NOPT*(PCST1-PCST2)+NOPT*13
4380 PRINT "COST OF PROTECTIVE STRATEGY FOR THREATENED PUT = $";CSTPS
4390 RETURN
4400 REM *** SUBROUTINE FOR PRINT-OUT OF OPTION TABLE USING OPVAM MODEL ***
4410 LPRINT TAB(10);"Option Index Table for ";TYPOP$;" for ";OPMO$;" ";YY
4420 LPRINT:LPRINT TAB(10);"Generated by Model: OPVAM";TAB(36);"Sigma = ";USING"
##.##";SIG
4430 LPRINT:LPRINT "Date: "; DD;"-";MM;"-";YY;TAB(30);TYPOP$," = ";INDEX
4440 LPRINT:LPRINT
4450 LPRINT "STRIKE PRICE";TAB(15)"CALL";TAB(35)"PUT":LPRINT
4460 IF TYPOP=2 GOTO 4500
4470 IF TYPOP=1 GOTO 4590
4480 IF TYPOP=3 GOTO 4680
4490 IF TYPOP=4 GOTO 4770
4500 FOR I=1 TO K:GOSUB 3790
4510 IF PSTRK(I)>INDEX THEN PMKT=PMKT+INT((PSTRK(I)-INDEX)/.0625)*.0625
4520 LPRINT PSTRK(I);TAB(35);USING"##.####";PMKT
4530 NEXT I
4540 FOR I=1 TO K:GOSUB 3790
4550 IF CSTRK(I)<INDEX THEN CMKT=CMKT+INT((INDEX-CSTRK(I))/.0625)*.0625
4560 LPRINT CSTRK(I);TAB(15);USING"##.####";CMKT
4570 NEXT I
4580 END
```

```
4590 FOR I=1 TO K:GOSUB 3780
4600 IF PSTRK(I)>INDEX THEN PMKT=PMKT+INT((PSTRK(I)-INDEX)/.0625)*.0625
4610 LPRINT PSTRK(I);TAB(35);USING"##.####";PMKT
4620 NEXT I
4630 FOR I=1 TO K:GOSUB 3780
4640 IF CSTRK(I)<INDEX THEN CMKT=CMKT+INT((INDEX-CSTRK(I))/.0625)*.0625
4650 LPRINT CSTRK(I);TAB(15);USING"##.####";CMKT
4660 NEXT I
4670 END
4680 FOR I=1 TO K:GOSUB 3800
4690 IF PSTRK(I)>INDEX THEN PMKT=PMKT+INT((PSTRK(I)-INDEX)/.0625)*.0625
4700 LPRINT PSTRK(I);TAB(35);USING"##.####";PMKT
4710 NEXT I
4720 FOR I=1 TO K:GOSUB 3800
4730 IF CSTRK(I)<INDEX THEN CMKT=CMKT+INT((INDEX-CSTRK(I))/.0625)*.0625
4740 LPRINT CSTRK(I);TAB(15);USING" ##.####';CMKT
4750 NEXT I
4760 END
4770 FOR I=1 TO K:GOSUB 3810
4780 IF PSTRK(I)>INDEX THEN PMKT=PMKT+INT((PSTRK(I)-INDEX)/.0625)*.0625
4790 LPRINT PSTRK(I);TAB(35);USING"##.####";PMKT
4800 NEXT I
4810 FOR I=1 TO K:GOSUB 3810
4820 IF CSTRK(I)<INDEX THEN CMKT=CMKT+INT((INDEX-CSTRK(I))/.0625)*.0625
4830 LPRINT CSTRK(I);TAB(15);USING"##.####';CMKT
4840 NEXT I
4850 END
4860 REM *** SUBROUTINE FOR PRINT-OUT: PROTECTIVE STRATEGY FOR CALL ***
4870 LPRINT
4880 LPRINT "Buy Back your ";NOPT%;" CALLs at ";CSTRK;"and your PUTs at ";PSTRK
4890 LPRINT "Sell ";NOPT;" CALLs at ";CSTRK+PROT;AND PUTS AT ";PSTRK+PROT
4900 LPRINT
4910 LPRINT  TAB(10);"COST OF PROT STRATEGY FOR THREAT TO CALL = $";CSTPS
4920 LPRINT:LPRINT "You MUST update the data statement defining SPREAD"
4930 END
4940 REM *** SUBROUTINE FOR PRINT-OUT: PROTECTIVE STRATEGY FOR PUT ***
4950 LPRINT
4960 LPRINT "Buy back your ";NOPT%;" PUTs at ";PSTRK;"and your CALLs at ";CSTRK
4970 LPRINT "Sell ";NOPT%;" PUTs at ";PSTRK-PROT;"and CALLs at ";CSTRK-PROT
4980 LPRINT  TAB(10);"COST OF PROT STRATEGY FOR THREAT TO PUT = $";CSTPS
4990 LPRINT:LPRINT "You MUST update the data statement defining SPREAD"
5000 END
```

CN 00502:001

APPENDIX B

This appendix provides three sets of spreadsheet equations (SSA.1, SSA.2 and SSA.3) corresponding to three basic spreadsheets found in the text.

It is assumed you are intimately familiar with the use of one of the popular spreadsheets, like LOTUS 1-2-3 or WORKS. If not, it is worth purchasing and learning how to use a spreadsheet. But teaching you how to use a spreadsheet is beyond the scope of this book.

SSA.1 is a listing of equations for the evaluation of a new short spread position in index options, stock options, or currency options. SSA.1 corresponds to Table 7.3, What's Available and What's Best in Options for Short Spreads. If you wish to adapt this chart to those particular options you select for trading, these equations will help you adjust your spreadsheet.

SSA.2 is a spreadsheet tied to SSA.1 (Table 7.3) to permit you to print out on a handy form that option short spread you plan to execute. The print-out corresponds to the OEX evaluation form in Table 7.3.

SSA.3 is a complex spreadsheet with very long logical equations that will allow you to evaluate an existing short spread by entering the market value of the underlying financial instrument for the evaluation data. This spreadsheet will allow you to determine what protective action is required for a threatened put or call, since it provides predicted profit (loss) for ±1 sigma (1 and 30 day) and ±2 sigma (1 and 30 day) relative to the current market value. By using the graphics capability of your spreadsheet you can print out evaluation curves (such as figure 9.7) which will allow you to visualize how changes in the market may threaten your existing short spread.

```
SSA.1 OPTIONS EVALUATIONS
SHORT SPREADS                    : for +/- 2 Sigm
                                           INITIAL CA
                                                    MARGIN:
                                           EVALUATION
                                           NO. DAYS T
FILENAME: OPTEVA

                                           EXEC DTE  EXP DTE
. . . . . . . . . . .  . . . . . . . . .   . . . . . . . . . . .
STOCK INDEX OPTI
S&P 100 INDEX (O                             33077     33103
NYSE INDEX (NYA)                            33077     33103
AMEX MAJ MKT IND                            33077     33103

COMMON STOCK OPT
UAL            CBOE          NYSE           33077     33103
IBM            CBOE          NYSE           33077     33103
DISNEY         AMEX          NYSE           33077     33103
APPLE          AMEX          NADAQ          33077     33103
TIME           PHIL          NYSE           33077     33103
COMPAC         PACEX         NYSE           33077     33103
MICRSFT        PACEX         NADAQ          33077     33103
NIKE           PACEX         NADAQ          33077     33103

CURRENCY OPTIONS
AUS$           PHIL          50000          33077     33103
BRIT LB        PHIL          31250          33077     33103
CAN$           PHIL          50000          33077     33103
DM             PHIL          62500          33077     33103
YEN            PHIL          62500          33077     33103
SFRNC          PHIL          62500          33077     33103
```

```
50000
0,33
33077
=E11-F5
```

MKT VAL	NO. OPTS	2SIG
. . . .	. . . .	. . . .
345,32	=$F$3/($F$4*100*F11)	9,869115294
=-199,38*$K$3/2993,81	=$F$3/($F$4*100*F12)	4,82
=-602,45*$K$3/2993,81	=$F$3/($F$4*100*F13)	17,03969106
161,125	=$F$3/($F$4*100*F16)	10,49
117,625	=$F$3/($F$4*100*F17)	4,7
128,5	=$F$3/($F$4*100*F18)	15,6
41,5	=$F$3/($F$4*100*F19)	4,6
94,875	=$F$3/($F$4*100*F20)	8,81
60,25	=$F$3/($F$4*100*F21)	14,04
73,25	=$F$3/($F$4*100*F22)	6,29
91,5	=$F$3/($F$4*100*F23)	9,81
78,58	=$F$3/($F$4*C26*F26/2,06	
181,34	=$F$3/($F$4*C27*F27/8,58	
86,68	=$F$3/($F$4*C28*F28/1,08	
60,92	=$F$3/($F$4*C29*F29/2,07	
67,1	=$F$3/($F$4*C30*F30/2,19	
71,11	=$F$3/($F$4*C31*F31/2,27	

DJIA =   2961,14

SHRT SPRD CALL	PUT	INIT PREMIUMS CPRM
. . . .	. . . .	. . . .
=ROUND OFF((F11+H11)/5;0)*5	=ROUND OFF((F11-H11)/5;0)*5	2
=ROUND OFF((F12+H12)/5;0)*5	=ROUND OFF((F12-H12)/2,5;0)*2,5	2,75
=ROUND OFF((F13+H13)/5;0)*5	=ROUND OFF((F13-H13)/5;0)*5	4,5
=ROUND OFF((F16+H16)/5;0)*5	=ROUND OFF((F16-H16)/5;0)*5	4
=ROUND OFF((F17+H17)/5;0)*5	=ROUND OFF((F17-H17)/5;0)*5	=-2+3/16
=ROUND OFF((F18+H18)/5;0)*5	=ROUND OFF((F18-H18)/5;0)*5	=-7/16
=ROUND OFF((F19+H19)/5;0)*5	=ROUND OFF((F19-H19)/5;0)*5	0,75
=ROUND OFF((F20+H20)/5;0)*5	=ROUND OFF((F20-H20)/5;0)*5	1,25
=ROUND OFF((F21+H21)/5;0)*5	=ROUND OFF((F21-H21)/2,5;0)*2,5	1,125
=ROUND OFF((F22+H22)/5;0)*5	=ROUND OFF((F22-H22)/5;0)*5	0,5
=ROUND OFF((F23+H23)/5;0)*5	=ROUND OFF((F23-H23)/5;0)*5	1,0625
=ROUND OFF((F26+H26)/1;0)*1	=ROUND OFF((F26-H26)/1;0)*1	0
=ROUND OFF((F27+H27)/2,5;0)*2,5	=ROUND OFF((F27-H27)/2,5;0)*2,5	0,15
=ROUND OFF((F28+H28)/0,5;0)*0,5	=ROUND OFF((F28-H28)/0,5;0)*0,5	0,08
=ROUND OFF((F29+H29)/0,5;0)*0,5	=ROUND OFF((F29-H29)/0,5;0)*0,5	0,09
=ROUND OFF((F30+H30)/0,5;0)*0,5	=ROUND OFF((F30-H30)/0,5;0)*0,5	=0,21/2
=ROUND OFF((F31+H31)/1;0)*1	=ROUND OFF((F31-H31)/1;0)*1	=-0,35/2

PPRM	TPRM	INITIAL CREDIT
....	....	....
2,75	=K11+L11	=100*G11*M11*(E11–D11)/$F$6
1,5	=K12+L12	=100*G12*M12*(E12–D12)/$F$6
3,625	=K13+L13	=100*G13*M13*(E13–D13)/$F$6
3,75	=K16+L16	=100*G16*M16*(E16–D16)/$F$6
=15/16	=K17+L17	=100*G17*M17*(E17–D17)/$F$6
0,5	=K18+L18	=100*G18*M18*(E18–D18)/$F$6
0,25	=K19+L19	=100*G19*M19*(E19–D19)/$F$6
0,625	=K20+L20	=100*G20*M20*(E20–D20)/$F$6
=13/16	=K21+L21	=100*G21*M21*(E21–D21)/$F$6
1,125	=K22+L22	=100*G22*M22*(E22–D22)/$F$6
6,75	=K23+L23	=100*G23*M23*(E23–D23)/$F$6
0,49	=K26+L26	=C26*G26*M26*(E26–D26)/($F$6
=0,37/2	=K27+L27	=C27*G27*M27*(E27–D27)/($F$6
0,12	=K28+L28	=C28*G28*M28*(E28–D28)/($F$6
=(0,2+0,03)/2	=K29+L29	=C29*G29*M29*(E29–D29)/($F$6
0,05	=K30+L30	=C30*G30*M30*(E30–D30)/($F$6
=(0,37+0,09)/2	=K31+L31	=C31*G31*M31*(E31–D31)/($F$6

MKT VAL +2SIG	PROFIT +2SIG	MKT VAL –2SIG
....	....	
= IF((F11+H11–I11)>0;F11+H11–I11;(0))=$N11–S11	= IF((J11–F11+H11)>0;J11–F11+H11;0)	
= IF((F12+H12–I12)>0;F12+H12–I12;(0))=N12–S12	= IF((J12–F12+H12)>0;J12–F12+H12;0)	
= IF((F13+H13–I13)>0;F13+H13–I13;(0))=N13–S13	= IF((J13–F13+H13)>0;J13–F13+H13;0)	
= IF((F16+H16–I16)>0;F16+H16–I16;(0))=N16–S16	= IF((J16–F16+H16)>0;J16–F16+H16;0)	
= IF((F17+H17–I17)>0;F17+H17–I17;(0))=N17–S17	= IF((J17–F17+H17)>0;J17–F17+H17;0)	
= IF((F18+H18–I18)>0;F18+H18–I18;(0))=N18–S18	= IF((J18–F18+H18)>0;J18–F18+H18;0)	
= IF((F19+H19–I19)>0;F19+H19–I19;(0))=N19–S19	= IF((J19–F19+H19)>0;J19–F19+H19;0)	
= IF((F20+H20–I20)>0;F20+H20–I20;(0))=N20–S20	= IF((J20–F20+H20)>0;J20–F20+H20;0)	
= IF((F21+H21–I21)>0;F21+H21–I21;(0))=N21–S21	= IF((J21–F21+H21)>0;J21–F21+H21;0)	
= IF((F22+H22–I22)>0;F22+H22–I22;(0))=N22–S22	= IF((J22–F22+H22)>0;J22–F22+H22;0)	
= IF((F23+H23–I23)>0;F23+H23–I23;(0))=N23–S23	= IF((J23–F23+H23)>0;J23–F23+H23;0)	
= IF((F26+H26–I26)>0;F26+H26–I26;(0))=N26–S26	= IF((J26–F26+H26)>0;J26–F26+H26;0)	
= IF((F27+H27–I27)>0;F27+H27–I27;(0))=N27–S27	= IF((J27–F27+H27)>0;J27–F27+H27;0)	
= IF((F28+H28–I28)>0;F28+H28–I28;(0))=N28–S28	= IF((J28–F28+H28)>0;J28–F28+H28;0)	
= IF((F29+H29–I29)>0;F29+H29–I29;(0))=N29–S29	= IF((J29–F29+H29)>0;J29–F29+H29;0)	
= IF((F30+H30–I30)>0;F30+H30–I30;(0))=N30–S30	= IF((J30–F30+H30)>0;J30–F30+H30;0)	
= IF((F31+H31–I31)>0;F31+H31–I31;(0))=N31–S31	= IF((J31–F31+H31)>0;J31–F31+H31;0)	

PROFIT -2SIG	+2SIG SPRDVAL	-2SIG SPRDVAL	ANNUAL RETURN	PROFIT EXPIR
=$N11-T11	=100*$G11*O11	=-100*$G11*Q11	=-12*V11/$F$3	=IF(P11<R11;P11;R11)
=$N12-T12	=100*$G12*O12	=-100*$G12*Q12	=-12*V12/$F$3	=IF(P12<R12;P12;R12)
=$N13-T13	=100*$G13*O13	=-100*$G13*Q13	=-12*V13/$F$3	=IF(P13<R13;P13;R13)
=$N16-T16	=100*$G16*O16	=-100*$G16*Q16	=-12*V16/$F$3	=IF(P16<R16;P16;R16)
=$N17-T17	=100*$G17*O17	=-100*$G17*Q17	=-12*V17/$F$3	=IF(P17<R17;P17;R17)
=$N18-T18	=100*$G18*O18	=-100*$G18*Q18	=-12*V18/$F$3	=IF(P18<R18;P18;R18)
=$N19-T19	=100*$G19*O19	=-100*$G19*Q19	=-12*V19/$F$3	=IF(P19<R19;P19;R19)
=$N20-T20	=100*$G20*O20	=-100*$G20*Q20	=-12*V20/$F$3	=IF(P20<R20;P20;R20)
=$N21-T21	=100*$G21*O21	=-100*$G21*Q21	=-12*V21/$F$3	=IF(P21<R21;P21;R21)
=$N22-T22	=100*$G22*O22	=-100*$G22*Q22	=-12*V22/$F$3	=IF(P22<R22;P22;R22)
=$N23-T23	=100*$G23*O23	=-100*$G23*Q23	=-12*V23/$F$3	=IF(P23<R23;P23;R23)
=$N26-T26	=$C26*$G26*O26	=-$C26*$G26*Q26	=-12*V26/$F$3	=IF(P26<R26;P26;R26)
=$N27-T27	=$C27*$G27*O27	=-$C27*$G27*Q27	=-12*V27/$F$3	=IF(P27<R27;P27;R27)
=$N28-T28	=$C28*$G28*O28	=-$C28*$G28*Q28	=-12*V28/$F$3	=IF(P28<R28;P28;R28)
=$N29-T29	=$C29*$G29*O29	=-$C29*$G29*Q29	=-12*V29/$F$3	=IF(P29<R29;P29;R29)
=$N30-T30	=$C30*$G30*O30	=-$C30*$G30*Q30	=-12*V30/$F$3	=IF(P30<R30;P30;R30)
=$N31-T31	=$C31*$G31*O31	=-$C31*$G31*Q31	=-12*V31/$F$3	=IF(P31<R31;P31;R31)

```
SSA.2    EVALUATE
                  Today's                    =$F$5
                  ==========

2 SIG = =H11    OEX =    =F11          DJIA =  2961.14
   CALL                  =D37+B37      PUT SAF                      =D37-B37
            for          =F37+B37*F37/D37        for DJIA =         =F37-B37*F37/D
MRKT DAT         33074   EXEC DTE:     =D11      NO. DAYS:          =E40-C40

OPTION E                 =E11          NO. DAYS                     =D42-E40

        OPTION M         =D42                   NO. SPRDS:         =G11
CALL = =I11    CALL MKT                =K11     CALL MARGIN =      =B45-D38
PUT  = =J11    PUT  MKT                =L11     PUT  MARGIN =      =H38-B46
-----------

        INITIAL          =N11
        PRFT FOR         =P11
        PRFT FOR         =R11
         EXPIR           =V11


        EVALUATE
                  Today's                    =F5
                  ==========

2 SIG = =H16    UAL =    =F16          DJIA = 2961.14
   CALL                  =D60+B60      PUT SAFE                     =D60-B60
            for          =F60+B60*F60/D60        for DJIA =        =F60-B60*F60/D
MRKT DAT         33074   EXEC DTE:     =E40      NO. DAYS:          =E63-C63

OPTION E                 =E16          NO. DAYS                     =D65-E63

        OPTION M         =D65                   NO. SPRDS:         =G16
CALL = =I16    CALL MKT                =K16     CALL MARGIN =      =B68-D61
PUT  = =J16    PUT  MKT                =L16     PUT  MARGIN =      =H61-B69
-----------

        INITIAL          =N16
        PRFT FOR         =P16
        PRFT FOR         =R16
         EXPIR           =V16


        EVALUATE
                  Today's                    =F5
                  ==========

2 SIG = =H29    DM =     =F29          DJIA = 2961
   CALL                  =D81+B81      PUT SAF                      =D81-B81
            for          =F81+B81*F81/D81        for DJIA =        =F81-B81*F81/D
MRKT DAT         33074   EXEC DTE:     =D29      NO. DAYS:          =E84-C84

OPTION E                 =E29          NO. DAYS                     =D86-E84

        OPTION M         =D29                   NO. SPRDS:         =G29
CALL = =I29    CALL MKT                =K29     CALL MARGIN =      =B89-D82
PUT  = =J29    PUT  MKT                =L29     PUT  MARGIN =      =H82-B90
-----------

        INITIAL          =N29
        PRFT FOR         =P29
        PRFT FOR         =R29
         EXPIR           =V29
```

SSA.3 OPTIONS EVALUA
SHORT SPREADS

: for +/-

		INITIAL CAPITAL:		50000
			MARGIN:	0,33
		EVALUATION DATE:		33085
		EXPIRATION DATE:		33102
FILENAME: OPTEVAL.WK

NO. DAYS TIL EXP: -F126-F12

	QTY PER OPTION	NO. OPTS	1 DA 2SIG	30DA 2SIG
STOCK INDEX OPTIONS:				
OEX	100	=$F$3/($F$4*C133*I133)	3,24	9,869115
NYA	100	=$F$3/($F$4*C134*I134)	1,61	4,82
XMI	100	=$F$3/($F$4*C135*I135)	5,39	17,03969
COMMON STOCK OPTIONS				
UAL	100	=$F$3/($F$4*C138*I138)	2,24	10,49
IBM	100	=$F$3/($F$4*C139*I139)	1,15	4,7
DISNEY	100	=$F$3/($F$4*C140*I140)	1,36	15,6
APPLE	100	=$F$3/($F$4*C141*I141)	1,03	4,6
TIME	100	=$F$3/($F$4*C142*I142)	2,08	8,81
COMPAQ	100	=$F$3/($F$4*C143*I143)	2,39	14,04
MICRSFT	100	=$F$3/($F$4*C144*I144)	1,97	6,29
NIKE	100	=$F$3/($F$4*C145*I145)	1,34	9,81
CURRENCY OPTIONS:				
AUS$	50000	=$F$3/($F$4*C148*I148/100)	0,79	2,06
BRIT LB	31250	=$F$3/($F$4*C149*I149/100)	1,16	8,58
CAN$	50000	=$F$3/($F$4*C150*I150/100)	0,21	1,08
DM	62500	=$F$3/($F$4*C151*I151/100)	0,37	2,07
YEN	62500	=$F$3/($F$4*C152*I152/100)	0,56	2,19
SF	62500	=$F$3/($F$4*C153*I153/100)	0,7	2,27

SHRT SPRD CALL	PUT	MKT V EV DTE
355	335	338,68
200	193	194,59
615	580	587,26
170	150	140
120	115	111,5
145	115	117,625
45	35	42
105	85	91,375
75	45	56,875
80	65	66,5
100	80	86
81	77	79,44
190	173	186,44
88	86	86,8
63	59	63,04
70	65	68,55
73	69	74,34

```
-2SIG30
SSVAL
...........

■ IF(($I133-$F133)>$H133;0;($H133-($I133-$F133)))
■ IF(($I134-$F134)>$H134;0;($H134-($I134-$F134)))
■ IF(($I135-$F135)>$H135;0;($H135-($I135-$F135)))


■ IF(($I138-$F138)>$H138;0;($H138-($I138-$F138)))
■ IF(($I139-$F139)>$H139;0;($H139-($I139-$F139)))
■ IF(($I140-$F140)>$H140;0;($H140-($I140-$F140)))
■ IF(($I141-$F141)>$H141;0;($H141-($I141-$F141)))
■ IF(($I142-$F142)>$H142;0;($H142-($I142-$F142)))
■ IF(($I143-$F143)>$H143;0;($H143-($I143-$F143)))
■ IF(($I144-$F144)>$H144;0;($H144-($I144-$F144)))
■ IF(($I145-$F145)>$H145;0;($H145-($I145-$F145)))


■ IF(($I148-$F148)>$H148;0;($H148-($I148-$F148)))
■ IF(($I149-$F149)>$H149;0;($H149-($I149-$F149)))
■ IF(($I150-$F150)>$H150;0;($H150-($I150-$F150)))
■ IF(($I151-$F151)>$H151;0;($H151-($I151-$F151)))
■ IF(($I152-$F152)>$H152;0;($H152-($I152-$F152)))
■ IF(($I153-$F153)>$H153;0;($H153-($I153-$F153)))
```

```
-1SIG30
SSVAL
...........

■ IF ($I133-$F133/2)>$H133;0;($H133-($I133-$F133/2)))
■ IF ($I134-$F134/2)>$H134;0;($H134-($I134-$F134/2)))
■ IF ($I135-$F135/2)>$H135;0;($H135-($I135-$F135/2)))


■ IF ($I138-$F138/2)>$H138;0;($H138-($I138-$F138/2)))
■ IF ($I139-$F139/2)>$H139;0;($H139-($I139-$F139/2)))
■ IF ($I140-$F140/2)>$H140;0;($H140-($I140-$F140/2)))
■ IF ($I141-$F141/2)>$H141;0;($H141-($I141-$F141/2)))
■ IF ($I142-$F142/2)>$H142;0;($H142-($I142-$F142/2)))
■ IF ($I143-$F143/2)>$H143;0;($H143-($I143-$F143/2)))
■ IF ($I144-$F144/2)>$H144;0;($H144-($I144-$F144/2)))
■ IF ($I145-$F145/2)>$H145;0;($H145-($I145-$F145/2)))


■ IF ($I148-$F148/2)>$H148;0;($H148-($I148-$F148/2)))
■ IF ($I149-$F149/2)>$H149;0;($H149-($I149-$F149/2)))
■ IF ($I150-$F150/2)>$H150;0;($H150-($I150-$F150/2)))
■ IF ($I151-$F151/2)>$H151;0;($H151-($I151-$F151/2)))
■ IF ($I152-$F152/2)>$H152;0;($H152-($I152-$F152/2)))
■ IF ($I153-$F153/2)>$H153;0;($H153-($I153-$F153/2)))
```

```
-2SIG1
SSVAL
...........

■ IF(($I133-$E133)>$H133;0;($H133-($I133-$E133)))
■ IF(($I134-$E134)>$H134;0;($H134-($I134-$E134)))
■ IF(($I135-$E135)>$H135;0;($H135-($I135-$E135)))


■ IF(($I138-$E138)>$H138;0;($H138-($I138-$E138)))
■ IF(($I139-$E139)>$H139;0;($H139-($I139-$E139)))
■ IF(($I140-$E140)>$H140;0;($H140-($I140-$E140)))
■ IF(($I141-$E141)>$H141;0;($H141-($I141-$E141)))
■ IF(($I142-$E142)>$H142;0;($H142-($I142-$E142)))
■ IF(($I143-$E143)>$H143;0;($H143-($I143-$E143)))
■ IF(($I144-$E144)>$H144;0;($H144-($I144-$E144)))
■ IF(($I145-$E145)>$H145;0;($H145-($I145-$E145)))


■ IF(($I148-$E148)>$H148;0;($H148-($I148-$E148)))
■ IF(($I149-$E149)>$H149;0;($H149-($I149-$E149)))
■ IF(($I150-$E150)>$H150;0;($H150-($I150-$E150)))
■ IF(($I151-$E151)>$H151;0;($H151-($I151-$E151)))
■ IF(($I152-$E152)>$H152;0;($H152-($I152-$E152)))
■ IF(($I153-$E153)>$H153;0;($H153-($I153-$E153)))
```

```
-1SIG1
SSVAL
...........

■ IF(($I133-$E133/2)>$H133;0;($H133-($I133-$E133/2)))
■ IF(($I134-$E134/2)>$H134;0;($H134-($I134-$E134/2)))
■ IF(($I135-$E135/2)>$H135;0;($H135-($I135-$E135/2)))


■ IF(($I138-$E138/2)>$H138;0;($H138-($I138-$E138/2)))
■ IF(($I139-$E139/2)>$H139;0;($H139-($I139-$E139/2)))
■ IF(($I140-$E140/2)>$H140;0;($H140-($I140-$E140/2)))
■ IF(($I141-$E141/2)>$H141;0;($H141-($I141-$E141/2)))
■ IF(($I142-$E142/2)>$H142;0;($H142-($I142-$E142/2)))
■ IF(($I143-$E143/2)>$H143;0;($H143-($I143-$E143/2)))
■ IF(($I144-$E144/2)>$H144;0;($H144-($I144-$E144/2)))
■ IF(($I145-$E145/2)>$H145;0;($H145-($I145-$E145/2)))


■ IF(($I148-$E148/2)>$H148;0;($H148-($I148-$E148/2)))
■ IF(($I149-$E149/2)>$H149;0;($H149-($I149-$E149/2)))
■ IF(($I150-$E150/2)>$H150;0;($H150-($I150-$E150/2)))
■ IF(($I151-$E151/2)>$H151;0;($H151-($I151-$E151/2)))
■ IF(($I152-$E152/2)>$H152;0;($H152-($I152-$E152/2)))
■ IF(($I153-$E153/2)>$H153;0;($H153-($I153-$E153/2)))
```

```
NO CHNGE
SSVAL
. . . . . . . . . . .

■ CHOSE  (S133+T133;W133;U133;V133)
■ CHOSE  (S134+T134;W134;U134;V134)
≈ CHOSE  (S135+T135;W135;U135;V135)


■ CHOSE  (S138+T138;W138;U138;V138)
■ CHOSE  (S139+T139;W139;U139;V139)
■ CHOSE  (S140+T140;W140;U140;V140)
■ CHOSE  (S141+T141;W141;U141;V141)
■ CHOSE  (S142+T142;W142;U142;V142)
■ CHOSE  (S143+T143;W143;U143;V143)
■ CHOSE  (S144+T144;W144;U144;V144)
■ CHOSE  (S145+T145;W145;U145;V145)


■ CHOSE  (S148+T148;W148;U148;V148)
■ CHOSE  (S149+T149;W149;U149;V149)
≈. CHOSE  (S150+T150;W150;U150;V150)
■ CHOSE  (S151+T151;W151;U151;V151)
≈. CHOSE  (S152+T152;W152;U152;V152)
≈. CHOSE  (S153+T153;W153;U153;V153)
```

```
+1SIG1
SSVAL
. . . . . . . . . . .

■ IF(($I133+$E133/2)<$G133;0;(($I133+$E133/2)-$G133))
■ IF(($I134+$E134/2)<$G134;0;(($I134+$E134/2)-$G134))
■ IF(($I135+$E135/2)<$G135;0;(($I135+$E135/2)-$G135))


■ IF(($I138+$E138/2)<$G138;0;(($I138+$E138/2)-$G138))
■ IF(($I139+$E139/2)<$G139;0;(($I139+$E139/2)-$G139))
■ IF(($I140+$E140/2)<$G140;0;(($I140+$E140/2)-$G140))
■ IF(($I141+$E141/2)<$G141;0;(($I141+$E141/2)-$G141))
■ IF(($I142+$E142/2)<$G142;0;(($I142+$E142/2)-$G142))
■ IF(($I143+$E143/2)<$G143;0;(($I143+$E143/2)-$G143))
■ IF(($I144+$E144/2)<$G144;0;(($I144+$E144/2)-$G144))
■ IF(($I145+$E145/2)<$G145;0;(($I145+$E145/2)-$G145))


■ IF(($I148+$E148/2)<$G148;0;(($I148+$E148/2)-$G148))
■ IF(($I149+$E149/2)<$G149;0;(($I149+$E149/2)-$G149))
■ IF(($I150+$E150/2)<$G150;0;(($I150+$E150/2)-$G150))
■ IF(($I151+$E151/2)<$G151;0;(($I151+$E151/2)-$G151))
■ IF(($I152+$E152/2)<$G152;0;(($I152+$E152/2)-$G152))
■ IF(($I153+$E153/2)<$G153;0;(($I153+$E153/2)-$G153))
```

+2SIG1
SSVAL
. . . .

```
= IF(($I133+$E133)<$G133;0;(($I133+$E133)-$G133))
= IF(($I134+$E134)<$G134;0;(($I134+$E134)-$G134))
= IF(($I135+$E135)<$G135;0;(($I135+$E135)-$G135))

= IF(($I138+$E138)<$G138;0;(($I138+$E138)-$G138))
= IF(($I139+$E139)<$G139;0;(($I139+$E139)-$G139))
= IF(($I140+$E140)<$G140;0;(($I140+$E140)-$G140))
= IF(($I141+$E141)<$G141;0;(($I141+$E141)-$G141))
= IF(($I142+$E142)<$G142;0;(($I142+$E142)-$G142))
= IF(($I143+$E143)<$G143;0;(($I143+$E143)-$G143))
= IF(($I144+$E144)<$G144;0;(($I144+$E144)-$G144))
= IF(($I145+$E145)<$G145;0;(($I145+$E145)-$G145))

= IF(($I148+$E148)<$G148;0;(($I148+$E148)-$G148))
= IF(($I149+$E149)<$G149;0;(($I149+$E149)-$G149))
= IF(($I150+$E150)<$G150;0;(($I150+$E150)-$G150))
= IF(($I151+$E151)<$G151;0;(($I151+$E151)-$G151))
= IF(($I152+$E152)<$G152;0;(($I152+$E152)-$G152))
= IF(($I153+$E153)<$G153;0;(($I153+$E153)-$G153))
```

+1SIG30
SSVAL
. . . .

```
= IF(($I133+$F133/2)<$G133;0;(($I133+$F133/2)-$G133))
= IF(($I134+$F134/2)<$G134;0;(($I134+$F134/2)-$G134))
= IF(($I135+$F135/2)<$G135;0;(($I135+$F135/2)-$G135))

= IF(($I138+$F138/2)<$G138;0;(($I138+$F138/2)-$G138))
= IF(($I139+$F139/2)<$G139;0;(($I139+$F139/2)-$G139))
= IF(($I140+$F140/2)<$G140;0;(($I140+$F140/2)-$G140))
= IF(($I141+$F141/2)<$G141;0;(($I141+$F141/2)-$G141))
= IF(($I142+$F142/2)<$G142;0;(($I142+$F142/2)-$G142))
= IF(($I143+$F143/2)<$G143;0;(($I143+$F143/2)-$G143))
= IF(($I144+$F144/2)<$G144;0;(($I144+$F144/2)-$G144))
= IF(($I145+$F145/2)<$G145;0;(($I145+$F145/2)-$G145))

= IF(($I148+$F148/2)<$G148;0;(($I148+$F148/2)-$G148))
= IF(($I149+$F149/2)<$G149;0;(($I149+$F149/2)-$G149))
= IF(($I150+$F150/2)<$G150;0;(($I150+$F150/2)-$G150))
= IF(($I151+$F151/2)<$G151;0;(($I151+$F151/2)-$G151))
= IF(($I152+$F152/2)<$G152;0;(($I152+$F152/2)-$G152))
= IF(($I153+$F153/2)<$G153;0;(($I153+$F153/2)-$G153))
```

```
+2SIG30                                      CALL
SSVAL                                        ITM
...........                                  ...........

■ IF(($I133+$F133)<$G133;0;(($I133+$F133)-$G133))=SI(I133>G133;1;0)
▪ IF(($I134+$F134)<$G134;0;(($I134+$F134)-$G134))=SI(I134>G134;1;0)
■ IF(($I135+$F135)<$G135;0;(($I135+$F135)-$G135))=SI(I135>G135;1;0)


▪ IF(($I138+$F138)<$G138;0;(($I138+$F138)-$G138))=SI(I138>G138;1;0)
■ IF(($I139+$F139)<$G139;0;(($I139+$F139)-$G139))=SI(I139>G139;1;0)
▪ IF(($I140+$F140)<$G140;0;(($I140+$F140)-$G140))=SI(I140>G140;1;0)
■ IF(($I141+$F141)<$G141;0;(($I141+$F141)-$G141))=SI(I141>G141;1;0)
▪ IF(($I142+$F142)<$G142;0;(($I142+$F142)-$G142))=SI(I142>G142;1;0)
■ IF(($I143+$F143)<$G143;0;(($I143+$F143)-$G143))=SI(I143>G143;1;0)
▪ IF(($I144+$F144)<$G144;0;(($I144+$F144)-$G144))=SI(I144>G144;1;0)
■ IF(($I145+$F145)<$G145;0;(($I145+$F145)-$G145))=SI(I145>G145;1;0)


■ IF(($I148+$F148)<$G148;0;(($I148+$F148)-$G148))=SI(I148>G148;1;0)
■ IF(($I149+$F149)<$G149;0;(($I149+$F149)-$G149))=SI(I149>G149;1;0)
■ IF(($I150+$F150)<$G150;0;(($I150+$F150)-$G150))=SI(I150>G150;1;0)
■ IF(($I151+$F151)<$G151;0;(($I151+$F151)-$G151))=SI(I151>G151;1;0)
■ IF(($I152+$F152)<$G152;0;(($I152+$F152)-$G152))=SI(I152>G152;1;0)
■ IF(($I153+$F153)<$G153;0;(($I153+$F153)-$G153))=SI(I153>G153;1;0)
```

PUT ITM	CALL ITM VAL	PUT ITM VAL	CALL/PUT NOT ITM	PUTINIT $CRED
■ IF(I133<H133;2;0)	=I133-G133	=H133-I133	0	=N11
■ IF(I134<H134;2;0)	=I134-G134	=H134-I134	0	=N12
■ IF(I135<H135;2;0)	=I135-G135	=H135-I135	0	=N13
■ IF(I138<H138;2;0)	=I138-G138	=H138-I138	0	=N16
■ IF(I139<H139;2;0)	=I139-G139	=H139-I139	0	=N17
■ IF(I140<H140;2;0)	=I140-G140	=H140-I140	0	=N18
■ IF(I141<H141;2;0)	=I141-G141	=H141-I141	0	=N19
■ IF(I142<H142;2;0)	=I142-G142	=H142-I142	0	=N20
■ IF(I143<H143;2;0)	=I143-G143	=H143-I143	0	=N21
■ IF(I144<H144;2;0)	=I144-G144	=H144-I144	0	=N22
■ IF(I145<H145;2;0)	=I145-G145	=H145-I145	0	=N23
■ IF(I148<H148;2;0)	=I148-G148	=H148-I148	0	=N26
■ IF(I149<H149;2;0)	=I149-G149	=H149-I149	0	=N27
■ IF(I150<H150;2;0)	=I150-G150	=H150-I150	0	=N28
■ IF(I151<H151;2;0)	=I151-G151	=H151-I151	0	=N29
■ IF(I152<H152;2;0)	=I152-G152	=H152-I152	0	=N30
■ IF(I153<H153;2;0)	=I153-G153	=H153-I153	0	=N31

```
-2SG30                          -1SG30
$SSVAL                          $SSVAL
..........                      ..........

=$X133-J133*$D133*$C133        =$X133-K133*$D133*$C133
=$X134-J134*$D134*$C134        =$X134-K134*$D134*$C134
=$X135-J135*$D135*$C135        =$X135-K135*$D135*$C135


=$X138-J138*$D138*$C138        =$X138-K138*$D138*$C138
=$X139-J139*$D139*$C139        =$X139-K139*$D139*$C139
=$X140-J140*$D140*$C140        =$X140-K140*$D140*$C140
=$X141-J141*$D141*$C141        =$X141-K141*$D141*$C141
=$X142-J142*$D142*$C142        =$X142-K142*$D142*$C142
=$X143-J143*$D143*$C143        =$X143-K143*$D143*$C143
=$X144-J144*$D144*$C144        =$X144-K144*$D144*$C144
=$X145-J145*$D145*$C145        =$X145-K145*$D145*$C145


=$X148-J148*$D148*$C148/100    =$X148-K148*$D148*$C148/100
=$X149-J149*$D149*$C149/100    =$X149-K149*$D149*$C149/100
=$X150-J150*$D150*$C150/100    =$X150-K150*$D150*$C150/100
=$X151-J151*$D151*$C151/100    =$X151-K151*$D151*$C151/100
=$X152-J152*$D152*$C152/100    =$X152-K152*$D152*$C152/100
=$X153-J153*$D153*$C153/100    =$X153-K153*$D153*$C153/100
```

```
-2SIG1                          -1SIG1
$SSVAL                          $SSVAL
..........                      ..........

=$X133-L133*$D133*$C133        =$X133-M133*$D133*$C133
=$X134-L134*$D134*$C134        =$X134-M134*$D134*$C134
=$X135-L135*$D135*$C135        =$X135-M135*$D135*$C135


=$X138-L138*$D138*$C138        =$X138-M138*$D138*$C138
=$X139-L139*$D139*$C139        =$X139-M139*$D139*$C139
=$X140-L140*$D140*$C140        =$X140-M140*$D140*$C140
=$X141-L141*$D141*$C141        =$X141-M141*$D141*$C141
=$X142-L142*$D142*$C142        =$X142-M142*$D142*$C142
=$X143-L143*$D143*$C143        =$X143-M143*$D143*$C143
=$X144-L144*$D144*$C144        =$X144-M144*$D144*$C144
=$X145-L145*$D145*$C145        =$X145-M145*$D145*$C145


=$X148-L148*$D148*$C148/100    =$X148-M148*$D148*$C148/100
=$X149-L149*$D149*$C149/100    =$X149-M149*$D149*$C149/100
=$X150-L150*$D150*$C150/100    =$X150-M150*$D150*$C150/100
=$X151-L151*$D151*$C151/100    =$X151-M151*$D151*$C151/100
=$X152-L152*$D152*$C152/100    =$X152-M152*$D152*$C152/100
=$X153-L153*$D153*$C153/100    =$X153-M153*$D153*$C153/100
```

219

```
NO CHNGE                           +1SIG1
$SSVAL                             $SSVAL
..........                         ..........

=$X133-N133*$D133*$C133            =$X133-O133*$D133*$C133
=$X134-N134*$D134*$C134            =$X134-O134*$D134*$C134
=$X135-N135*$D135*$C135            =$X135-O135*$D135*$C135


=$X138-N138*$D138*$C138            =$X138-O138*$D138*$C138
=$X139-N139*$D139*$C139            =$X139-O139*$D139*$C139
=$X140-N140*$D140*$C140            =$X140-O140*$D140*$C140
=$X141-N141*$D141*$C141            =$X141-O141*$D141*$C141
=$X142-N142*$D142*$C142            =$X142-O142*$D142*$C142
=$X143-N143*$D143*$C143            =$X143-O143*$D143*$C143
=$X144-N144*$D144*$C144            =$X144-O144*$D144*$C144
=$X145-N145*$D145*$C145            =$X145-O145*$D145*$C145


=$X148-N148*$D148*$C148/100        =$X148-O148*$D148*$C148/100
=$X149-N149*$D149*$C149/100        =$X149-O149*$D149*$C149/100
=$X150-N150*$D150*$C150/100        =$X150-O150*$D150*$C150/100
=$X151-N151*$D151*$C151/100        =$X151-O151*$D151*$C151/100
=$X152-N152*$D152*$C152/100        =$X152-O152*$D152*$C152/100
=$X153-N153*$D153*$C153/100        =$X153-O153*$D153*$C153/100
```

```
+2SIG1                             +1SG30
$SSVAL                             $SSVAL
..........                         ..........

=$X133-P133*$D133*$C133            =$X133-Q133*$D133*$C133
=$X134-P134*$D134*$C134            =$X134-Q134*$D134*$C134
=$X135-P135*$D135*$C135            =$X135-Q135*$D135*$C135


=$X138-P138*$D138*$C138            =$X138-Q138*$D138*$C138
=$X139-P139*$D139*$C139            =$X139-Q139*$D139*$C139
=$X140-P140*$D140*$C140            =$X140-Q140*$D140*$C140
=$X141-P141*$D141*$C141            =$X141-Q141*$D141*$C141
=$X142-P142*$D142*$C142            =$X142-Q142*$D142*$C142
=$X143-P143*$D143*$C143            =$X143-Q143*$D143*$C143
=$X144-P144*$D144*$C144            =$X144-Q144*$D144*$C144
=$X145-P145*$D145*$C145            =$X145-Q145*$D145*$C145


=$X148-P148*$D148*$C148/100        =$X148-Q148*$D148*$C148/100
=$X149-P149*$D149*$C149/100        =$X149-Q149*$D149*$C149/100
=$X150-P150*$D150*$C150/100        =$X150-Q150*$D150*$C150/100
=$X151-P151*$D151*$C151/100        =$X151-Q151*$D151*$C151/100
=$X152-P152*$D152*$C152/100        =$X152-Q152*$D152*$C152/100
=$X153-P153*$D153*$C153/100        =$X153-Q153*$D153*$C153/100
```

```
+2SG30
$SSVAL
. . . . . . . . . . .

=$X133-R133*$D133*$C133
=$X134-R134*$D134*$C134
=$X135-R135*$D135*$C135


=$X138-R138*$D138*$C138
=$X139-R139*$D139*$C139
=$X140-R140*$D140*$C140
=$X141-R141*$D141*$C141
=$X142-R142*$D142*$C142
=$X143-R143*$D143*$C143
=$X144-R144*$D144*$C144
=$X145-R145*$D145*$C145


=$X148-R148*$D148*$C148/100
=$X149-R149*$D149*$C149/100
=$X150-R150*$D150*$C150/100
=$X151-R151*$D151*$C151/100
=$X152-R152*$D152*$C152/100
=$X153-R153*$D153*$C153/100
```